PSL LIBRARY OF OCEAN TRAVEL

MAURETANIA

LANDFALLS AND DEPARTURES OF TWENTY-FIVE YEARS

by

HUMFREY JORDAN

WITH A NEW FOREWORD BY

JOHN H. SHAUM Jr

PATRICK STEPHENS

MAURETANIA
In Cruising Trim.

MAURETANIA

LANDFALLS AND DEPARTURES OF
TWENTY-FIVE YEARS

By

HUMFREY JORDAN

WITH DRAWINGS BY
FRANK H. MASON, R.I.

PATRICK STEPHENS

British Library Cataloguing in Publication Data

Jordan, Humfrey
Mauretania.
1. Liners. Steam. Mauretania (Ship)
I. Title
623.8'2432

ISBN 1-85260-099-3

*Patrick Stephens Limited is part of the Thorsons Publishing Group,
Wellingborough, Northamptonshire, NN8 2RQ, England*

Printed in Great Britain by The Bath Press, Bath, Avon

1   3   5   7   9   10   8   6   4   2

PUBLISHER'S PREFACE

The *PSL Library of Ocean Travel* is a collection of significant books on ships and the sea, long out-of-print but now re-issued in facsimile editions.

All the books to be included in the Library — each of which has been selected by members of a 'panel' of distinguished maritime authors and collectors — have been chosen for the rarity of their original editions, for the authoritativeness of the writer, and, above all, for their readability. Autobiographies, biographies, histories of famous ships of the past and the reminiscences of eminent mariners and sea travellers are all included, and will have a wide appeal to the thousands of present-day ship enthusiasts who have a deep interest in the maritime history of the past hundred years. For the majority of such readers, these books may be unknown and would otherwise be entirely unobtainable.

Many of the original volumes used in the production of these new editions have been supplied by Mainmast Books, of Saxmundham, Suffolk, IP17 1HZ, England, from whom all volumes in the *PSL Library of Ocean Travel* may be obtained.

Mauretania by Humfrey Jordan, originally published in 1936 by Hodder and Stoughton, is the first volume in the *PSL Library of Ocean Travel*, and the publishers would like to thank John H. Shaum Jr for providing a foreword for this facsimile edition.

PSL LIBRARY OF OCEAN TRAVEL

Also available

Tramps and Ladies
by Sir James Bisset

Other titles in preparation

Romance of a Modern Liner
by Capt E. G. Diggle

A Million Ocean Miles
by Sir Edgar T. Britten

The Ocean Tramp
by Frank C. Hendry

Atlantic Ferry
by Arthur J. Maginnis

FOREWORD
to this new edition
by John H. Shaum Jr

An old book with dog-eared pages and a frayed dust-cover that obviously had seen much use — that was my first exposure to Humfrey Jordan's *Mauretania*. That was more than thirty years ago when I first began to discover the literature of the great liners. Even by then it had been long out of print. To this day, for me, it remains one of the best of the genre, and is a work that I found invaluable in my research for my own book, *Majesty at Sea*.

This is truly a classic volume for several reasons. It is a book with soul about a special ship with a soul. One has the feeling of reading the story of a living creature, rather than of the achievements of 32,000 tons of steel. There was something different about *Mauretania* that is difficult to pinpoint, even to this day. She is unquestionably one of the most famous vessels of all time, fully deserving of a full-length biography. This one is right up there with the best of them. But what was it about *Mauretania* that set her apart from the other big liners? Primarily it was her legendary speed and reliability which brought Britain the Atlantic speed record for so many years. And then there is her exceptional war career, through which she came with hardly a scratch. Beyond this, there are the many intangibles, all of which are so admirably brought out in this book.

Jordan published his work shortly after *Mauretania*'s final voyage, drawing on much primary source material which would be impossible if such a project were undertaken now for the first time. The work is supplemented by several very useful appendices, including a complete chronology — with speed data — of all the vessel's peacetime voyages. Much attention is paid to detail and atmosphere, and it only takes a few pages for you to feel transported back to the early years of this century when *Mauretania* practically owned the North Atlantic.

Reading Humfrey Jordan's book is almost akin to indulging in hero-worship. But the adulation here is genuine, for *Mauretania* earned every bit of it through many years of reliable service in peace and war. I am grateful for having come to know this extraordinary vessel through the pages of this fine book, and it is fitting that it is being re-issued at a time when interest in the great passenger liners has been re-kindled. I am pleased that present and future readers will have the opportunity to know *Mauretania* intimately through this new Patrick Stephens edition.

JOHN H. SHAUM, JR
Baltimore, Maryland, USA

CONTENTS

ILLUSTRATIONS

The drawings of the " Mauretania " by Frank H. Mason,
R.I., are taken from the copyright photographs by kind
permission of the Cunard S.S. Co., Ltd., the Topical Press,
and the Photographic News Agencies, Ltd.

PREFACE

FOR more than a quarter of a century the *Mauretania* played a chief part in the history of shipping ; during all that long period she held her place as a great figure of her times. She was designed and built as England's answer to a decade of German dominance on the North Atlantic. When she was first brought into service she was the world's largest ship. For twenty-two years she remained the world's fastest liner. When she had long ceased to be the largest ship, when after a very gallant struggle in old age she ceased to be the fastest liner, she remained during another five years of hard work the world's most famous steamship. Neither size nor speed could alone have given her her fame ; that rested on something more secure and more intangible—on her individuality. She was, first and foremost, not simply a great and successful express liner, but the *Mauretania*.

This book does not attempt to describe in elaborate and technical detail an old ship which has often been described before, which is now broken up. I have sought, by using the background of events, to show her working through twenty-five crowded years, as part of the history of those years. On the sea she, as the phrase goes, made history ; as a carrier of human freight, bringing men and women across the Atlantic to the building of those years, she was seldom divorced from, but very frequently gave assistance to, the shaping of events. Throughout that difficult period the *Mauretania* never fell short of success. That is the picture, the impression which the story of the old ship presents. Success : a marked individuality, a ship of peculiar distinction, moving successfully across twenty-five years where real success is not too easily found.

Without the assistance of the Cunard-White Star Company, this book could never have been attempted. First, therefore, I have to thank the managers of the Company for putting their records at my disposal. I am particularly grateful to Mr. R. Beynon, for all that he has done for me in turning out log-books, records and documents. The full list of voyages, here published for the first time, exemplifies their readiness to supply me with the information for which I asked. I have to thank the Editor of " Engineering " for giving me permission to quote from articles which appeared at the time when the *Mauretania* was first put into commission.

Mr. Frank C. Bowen's " A Century of Atlantic Travel," Mr. F. Reid Corson's " The Atlantic Ferry in the Twentieth Century," and Sir Archibald Hurd's " A Merchant Fleet at War " have supplied me with many facts about the marine history of the period covered.

For some stories of the *Mauretania's* life I am indebted to Sir Arthur Rostron's " Home From the Sea," Captain S. G. S. McNeil's " In Great Waters," Mr. Gerald Aylmer's " R.M.S. *Mauretania* " and Mr. Charles T. Spedding's " Reminiscences of Transatlantic Travellers."

To Captain R. V. Peel, Mr. E. Barton and Mr.

W. Sutcliffe I am very grateful for having, during busy lives at sea, written to me with information of the old ship.

Finally, I should like to acknowledge my great debt to the late Captain S. G. S. McNeil and Mr. Andrew Cockburn—the two officers chiefly responsible for the *Mauretania's* most famous voyage—for having given me so much of their time, and answered, so carefully, innumerable questions.

HUMFREY JORDAN

CHAPTER I

A PROMISE TO ENGLAND

On a June morning a little old lady, too tired to stand the strain of long ceremonial, drove to St. Paul's Cathedral and, remaining in her carriage, received the blessing of the Church, of which she was the head, on her sixty years of sovereignty. That ceremony at the steps of a cathedral marked the peak of an era. There was much official celebration and public holiday-making. England was pleased with herself, and said so, not silently. Music-hall singers—for music-halls were still a long way from their decline—sang such ditties as

> " We don't want to fight, but, by jingo, if we do,
> We've got the men, we've got the ships . . ."

and music-hall audiences received the ditties not with half-bricks but with considerable gusto.

Kipling, to celebrate Queen Victoria's Diamond Jubilee, wrote his " Recessional." The blatancy of the public's jubilee mood would seem to have affected him ; in his famous verses he preached a decent modesty. But in that jubilee year of 1897 England was not feeling modest. She despised foreigners without troubling to conceal the fact ; she recognised herself, with complete assurance, as a great nation, the head of a mighty empire, the ruler of the seas. But, with the jubilee mood still warming her citizens to a fine self-satisfaction in being Britons,

England lost, and lost most decisively, the speed
record of the Atlantic Ferry to a German ship.

Speed was becoming increasingly important in
men's lives. The year before the jubilee this fact
had been recognised in the British Isles ; men with
red flags were no longer required by law to precede
motor-cars. Naturally persons of conservative habit
condemned motor-cars as stinking abominations,
which would ruin the country-side, and the removal
of the red-flagged escort as something which would
bring death to innocent persons taking their legitimate pleasure on the Queen's highways. But the
moans of conservatives, making in certain respects
perfectly accurate forecasts, could not curb this desire
for speed. Man insisted on travelling faster on land
and on sea, though the air was still inviolate. At sea
the Atlantic Ferry had become the chief place of
international marine competition ; there the standard
was set by which the Western nations judged the
value of their mercantile navies. Speed on the Ferry
was already a matter which no nation having a
mercantile fleet could disregard.

In July, 1840, a prominent Nova Scotian merchant,
Samuel Cunard, in co-operation with Mr. George
Burns and Mr. David MacIver, had sent a small
wooden paddle steamer, Scottish built and sailing
under English colours, from Liverpool to Halifax in
twelve days ten hours. This little ship, the *Britannia*,
brought the house-flag of the Cunard, a golden lion
holding a golden globe on a field of scarlet, to the
Atlantic Ferry on the first regular mail and passenger
steamship service. International competition followed
quickly. New companies were formed to maintain
new services on the same sea crossing ; some of

them failed, some of them struggled as far as amalga-
mation with or sale to more successful rivals, some
of them survive and pay dividends to their shareholders.

The United States became the first serious com-
petitor to the English Cunard Line. A company,
officially the United States Mail Steamship Company,
but always known as the Collins Line, built a fleet
of four ships in 1847. These ships were *Arctic*,
Atlantic, *Baltic*, *Pacific*, and they first made the suffix
" ic " famous on the Ferry. Later that suffix
was to go to the White Star Company. The
Collins ships, built with government financial assistance, did what they had been designed to do ; they
put the Cunard for a time into second place. Then
luck went against the Line. The *Arctic* sank in
collision off Cape Race with the loss of over three
hundred lives. Two years later, in 1856, the *Pacific*
disappeared with her crew of 114 and 45 passengers.
The Cunard *Persia* sailed from Liverpool at about
the same time, and on arrival at New York reported
having encountered ice. It was presumed therefore
as the *Pacific* made no port and left no trace of her
end, that she had foundered after collision with an
iceberg. This second disaster hit the company badly,
but it achieved something of good : it brought effective
bulkheads, though slowly, to Atlantic liners. In 1858
Congress removed its mail subsidy policy. That killed
the Collins line. It died in the same year without
ever having paid a dividend to its shareholders.
With its death the United States flag disappeared
from the Atlantic Ferry and did not reappear until
towards the end of the century.

In its brief life the Collins Line suffered much from

Atlantic gales and fog and ice ; in its dying it proved that a new peril had to be faced, the withdrawal of any subsidy which depended upon government policy. The Cunard had faced that peril; without the assistance of a mail contract Samuel Cunard could not have launched his fleet, but he never allowed his company to be so wholly dependent upon governments and their changing policies as the Collins Line had been. So he survived where his first rival failed. But the subsidy, with all its attendant dangers of association with the scheming and manœuvring of party politics, remained, like the gales and the fogs and the ice, as one of the perils which shipowners on the Atlantic Ferry must face. None of the competing companies were to escape that danger ; sooner or later, in the struggle to own the fastest and the best ship upon the run, they all sought and obtained assistance from their governments. Taxpayers having perforce contributed to the building of the fleets, took a proprietary interest in the business ; when their ships were well placed in the race they were pleased ; when their ships failed them, in press and parliament and private conversation, they were seldom silent in their displeasure. The failure of some steamship to create an Atlantic record, or to hold what she had already created was, in the expressed opinion of many taxpayers, a sure sign that England was heading for the dogs. From the start in 1840 to the present day the Ferry to New York has never been maintained by purely private enterprise ; success upon it has so established itself as in some sort a national aim of each of the countries concerned that it is difficult to imagine that it ever will be otherwise maintained until its importance vanishes before a ferry of the air.

Gradually every maritime nation of Europe became concerned with the service to New York ; most of them, at one time or another, contributed a fine ship which left her mark upon the competition. But, after the United States had dropped out with the winding-up of the Collins Line, success in capturing or holding the record for the fastest crossing, which had become known to the public as the Blue Riband of the Atlantic, was principally, and for many years, tossed backwards and forwards between England and Germany. England, with the Cunard and the Inman lines, to which in 1870 was added the White Star, Germany, with the Hamburg-America and the North German Lloyd, between them virtually commanded the Ferry.

Wood gave way to iron, iron to steel ; paddle-wheels disappeared in favour of a single screw ; a single screw, which too frequently jibbed at the task put upon it and dropped into the Atlantic, was replaced by twin or multiple screws ; engines were improved in power and efficiency ; speed was increased from eight knots to twenty-two ; passengers were attracted by increasing comfort in accommodation. Faster and better ships succeeded each other on the North Atlantic throughout Victoria's reign. In 1892 the old Inman Line passed to United States ownership and became the American Line, but Germany and England still held fluctuating command in what had become established as an international competition. It was no longer an adventure only undertaken on account of real necessity to cross the miles of sea which divide Europe from America ; it was becoming for ordinary, unadventurous people more and more in the nature of a brief but comfortable holiday. After a period in 1888 and 1889, in which they had no effective rivals to the White Star and Inman ships, during a difficult time for shipping, the Cunard Company designed and built the *Campania* and *Lucania*, ships of just under 13,000 tons gross, designed for a speed of over 20 knots. The success of both ships was considerable ; for four years they held the record between them. According to the standards of that day, they were fitted with all possible comforts and safety devices. They had sixteen watertight bulkheads and a cellular double bottom the whole length of the ship. They had good looks ; they were built to Admiralty specifications and held the mail contract. Passengers liked their comfort and their speed, and competed to secure passages in them. They did credit to England at a time when England was pleased with herself and very certain of her credit.

More speed, more size were the chief demands of the Ferry. Human nature, urged on by advertisement and propaganda, flicked by national pride, increased the pace of the competition. In the secure and prosperous era crowned by Victoria's Diamond Jubilee, ordinary people, not pressed by urgent necessity, had already reached the stage when they felt themselves aggrieved if they had to cross the Atlantic in a smallish, slowish, but comfortable ship instead of the largest, fastest and most crowded. How much some shipowners regret the public taste for biggest and fastest ships for passenger vessels some shipowners—and their shareholders—know ; but the taste was there and had to be met. It cost money, it cost lives ; it involved continuous and anxious watching of a rival to anticipate his next move. The

Inman Line scored a point by raising the slogan of comfort for passengers, even emigrants ; the Hamburg-America improved on that by cutting fares for comfortable emigrants ; the White Star came in with its policy of plenty of space and luxury with comfort, so that ordinary people might forget about an extra knot. The Cunard and the North German Lloyd, who refused to consider any divorce from speed, had to meet and defeat these various manœuvres for attracting passengers. Competition grew more fierce. Food was improved, accommodation was improved ; the amusement of passengers became a serious consideration. The cost of maintaining ships upon the Ferry steadily mounted. Companies were eager to cut the throat of a rival, but puzzled how to accomplish the business without risking a serious gash to their own. In a business eagerly watched by the peoples of the competing nations, in a struggle so near to being cut-throat, there was bound to be bitterness. An example of this bitterness stands out, but fortunately as a rarity. The Cunard *Samaria* broke her shaft and started to sail home—not an easy or handy performance for a ship intended to steam. After nine days of sailing she was sighted and passed by the Guion liner *Manhattan*, who however took no notice of her. The commander of the *Manhattan* had at one time been in the Cunard service. It would be highly interesting to know exactly what the officers and crew of the *Samaria*, facing another nine days' sail to Queenstown, said about it. Perhaps the occasion may have led to the coining of new insults, for sailors are jealous of the traditions of the sea, and usually of the good name of the companies which they serve. The

Guion Line, after a spell of successful competition
on the Ferry, failed and her ships were sold. The
Oregon, in her day a holder of the Blue Riband and
the biggest ship on the Atlantic, was bought by the
Cunard. In March of 1886, when carrying the
mails and close on 900 passengers and crew, she was
rammed off Fire Island by a coal-laden schooner.
The watertight doors jammed ; the sinking of the
ship was certain. But the North German Lloyd
Fulda arrived in time, and by fine seamanship saved
all hands and the bulk of the mail. The Cunard
Company offered the North German Lloyd compensation for losses incurred by the rescue. The
compensation was refused, the German directors
maintaining that the *Fulda's* action was merely inci-
dental to the true tradition of the sea. One likes to
think that amongst seamen those high traditions
have ruled and will continue to rule. The *Manhattan's* conduct was an abnormality, the *Fulda's* what
was and is normal to the seas. Germany might be
rivalling England with success upon the Atlantic,
but the bitterness of international competition could
not be allowed to interfere with the sea's tradition.
Unfortunately that did not apply to public feeling.
When a German ship interfered with England's
jubilee self-satisfaction, public annoyance was stirred
by the presumption of a foreigner, and public alarm
was roused by the foreigner being German. But of
the superiority of the German ship over any which
England had yet built there could not be any, even
public, doubt.

The North German Lloyd, in the years before 1897,
had fallen somewhat behind in the competition.
The fast ships were getting old ; the Company had

nothing afloat which could attract passengers from the *Campania* and the *Lucania*.   It was a case of doing something decisive or dropping out of the race. Financially the Company was not in a good position for what was then considered huge expenditure, but the directors decided that they must gamble on a success that would again put them in a first place on the Atlantic.   They ordered two ships designed to recapture the Blue Riband and to attract passengers from the Liverpool to the Southampton route ;   and they drew German shipbuilders into the gamble.   A fine spirit either of patriotism or of self-confidence must have inspired the shipbuilders, for they accepted contracts which provided that, unless the new ships maintained their guaranteed speed both on the westward passage to New York and on the eastward passage home, the purchasers were to have the right to return them to the builders.   The designed speed was to be $22\frac{1}{2}$ knots, which in those days had never been maintained across the Atlantic.   Two German yards accepted these contracts ;   one of them lost.   The *Kaiser Friedrich* was returned to her builders.   The *Kaiser Wilhelm der Grosse* brought the Blue Riband back to the German flag, and German shipping to the first place on the Ferry.

She was a fine ship of over 14,000 tons gross ;   her four funnels, grouped in pairs, gave her a distinctive look.   She was steel built ;   two sets of four cylinder triple expansion engines, producing 28,000 horsepower, turned her twin screws.   On her maiden voyage, when as a new ship she was not being pressed, she very easily achieved a record for a single day's run.   On her third homeward voyage she obeyed the sea's tradition by standing by in mid-Atlantic to

help a burning ship. To anyone sea-minded it is
satisfactory to know that she lost nothing by her
obedience to tradition. Although delayed, she made
the crossing at the average speed of 22.35 knots.
That a ship could stand by a distressed sister and still
create a record passage put her in a place by herself,
without rivals. The Company whose house-flag she
flew gained enormous prestige. Passengers wished
to sail under that house-flag, even though they could
not find a berth in the *Kaiser Wilhelm der Grosse* herself. The following year the North German Lloyd
carried close on one quarter of the total number of
passengers landed at New York.

The *Kaiser Wilhelm der Grosse* was a very nasty blow
to English shipping ; her triumphant appearance on
the Atlantic came at a moment peculiarly unaccept-
able to the English public. It was most unpleasant
to see England so decisively beaten on the most
advertised and the most notorious of the high seas ;
it was vastly more unpalatable to discover that
nothing effective could be done to knock a foreigner,
and a German of all foreigners, from the first place
on the Atlantic Ferry. Jokes revolving about dogs
and sausages and Teuton appetites were then considered funny by quite a lot of people. German
bands played in the streets of English towns and
supplied English comic papers with expected copy.
The German Emperor had already developed the
habit of sending telegrams of which the people of
England did not approve. A thoroughly unpopular
moment for Germany to reign on the Atlantic ; but
a moment, which became a very long moment, in
which it was not possible for England to do anything
effective.

Seamen and shipowners and shipbuilders realised that it required a big and very expensive effort to fight the sea challenge which Germany had launched with such success. But the country was faced with other and more pressing jobs ; the effort could not be made.

For some years the imperial might of Britain had been preached and sung by England with a noise and vigour hardly describable as anything else than blatant. Persons not enjoying the privileges of British citizenship were by too many Englishmen loudly decried and loftily pitied. These performances did not make us popular abroad, and did lasting damage at home. There was so much noise about the Empire, so much blare and shouting and vulgarity that even moderately sensitive people grew a little ashamed. To treat little Englanders as social outcasts and national pests was inevitably to attract certain minds to the ranks of those who scorned the Empire. That attraction, after forty years of mixed vicissitudes when the blare and the shouting has vanished, still remains as an interesting survival of a racial dislike of excessive flag waving. The blatancy associated with the years between Victoria's Diamond Jubilee and death has bred a horror of national pride in many people, more particularly those who did not know those years and have only the reported vulgarity of them as a guide. To-day, for these people, any tendency towards imperialism, any belief that the Empire is not staggering with increasing speed towards inevitable disruption, any indication that people of a certain race are proud of belonging to that race are clear indications of a more than simian lowness of brow. The national vulgarity of England at the close of the last century cannot be denied, but its explanation seems to lie in human nature rather than some peculiar racial bias which must for ever fill sensitive members of that race with shame. England was getting alarmed at signs and portents which she did not want to read correctly. For so long she had been building her own considerable mansion comfortably isolated from other nations not so splendidly housed. Material security and prosperity, immunity from the social upheavals that disturbed other nations, riches and prestige had all seemed hers by right in the building. Then unpleasant things began to happen, and to happen in quick succession.

Rhodes, one of the notable builders, had dreamed of an all-red route from the Cape to Cairo. His dreams rested on working in good will with the Dutch in South Africa. The Jameson Raid dispelled those dreams. The German Emperor sent a famous telegram. England's position in South Africa was becoming difficult, Rhodes's reputation was damaged, ill-feeling towards Germany received substantial nourishment.

Kitchener, Sirdar of the Egyptian army since 1892, had for some time been busy with the reconquest of the Sudan. In the year of the Diamond Jubilee he was concerned with building a railway across the Nubian desert from Wady Halfa. Somewhat naturally the Mahdi did not approve of that; early in 1898 he moved northwards. On April 8th Kitchener defeated him at Atbara and commenced to advance on Khartoum. At Omdurman the Mahdi's army was severely defeated on September 2nd. The Dervishes fought with great courage. The 21st

Lancers charged in the grand manner of the days when war, by those not fighting, was still considered an affair of glory and romance. Kitchener marched to Khartoum. It was a successful small campaign which achieved most of its purpose. For the bulk of the public it was a heroic affair designed to avenge the death of Gordon. Gladstone, that great figure of an age then passing, popularly held responsible for Gordon's death, died while the campaign was in progress. When Kitchener, the conqueror of Khartoum, surrounded by his staff, was present at a commemorative service on the spot where Gordon had died, many people felt sincerely that a stain had been removed from England's honour. Illustrated weeklies produced battle pictures ; the Christmas numbers of that year were not behind with coloured supplements. In many nurseries and other places where they like pictorial history detailed and self-explanatory, Kitchener and his staff, stern and very martial, but visibly affected by the commemorative service, hung on the walls giving children ideas. Perhaps in some nurseries those pictures, robustly coloured, so hang to-day ; but the ideas they might inspire in children lack popularity. England in the mood of those pictures found 1898 a glorious year.

But wretched flies would get into the ointment. The Fashoda incident, butting into the successful campaign, had not improved relations between England and France. Farther afield the China seas were breeding trouble. In 1897 the Germans had annexed Kiao-Chow ; in March, 1898, the Russians demanded a lease of Port Arthur and the adjoining roadstead. Two English cruisers, lying at Port Arthur, were requested by the Russians to go. There was some war talk. But finally the English Government decided that annexation was the better and more fashionable course. A lease of Wei-Hai-Wei was demanded and obtained. China could do nothing but await the inevitable arrival of more trouble and watch England, Russia and Germany snarling at each other from their leased territories like dogs with bared teeth and hackles up. Amidst these war-like happenings England, having lost the speed record of the Atlantic, lost first place amongst the world's shipowners. The Hamburg-America Line succeeded in flying its house-flag over more tonnage, and substantially and unquestionably more tonnage, than the English P. & O., hitherto the largest owners. Two different German companies forcing themselves into top place, the one in speed, the other in size, while England and Germany snarled at each other! Two successive German blows to British maritime prestige! Inside and outside the shipping world it was not considered satisfactory. People who write letters of protest to newspapers did not miss their chance. Old Gentlemen in armchairs foresaw England's downfall. But on the eve of the South African War nothing could be done about German encroachments on the seas.

The war disorganised British shipping and damaged England's prestige among the nations ; it never went as people had hoped it would go. From the start there were black weeks and disasters. Our army in South Africa was actually defeated in battles—trivial affairs, according to modern standards of slaughter, but still battles—by ragged Boer forces. That could not be satisfactorily explained except on the basis that Boer farmers, hastily mobilised, could fight more

successfully than our professional soldiers : an intolerable explanation.   Generals in consequence became ungummed, and the armchair critic had a very
busy time.   Disasters were succeeded by a period
which, popularly, could pass for one of success.   This
period was celebrated in England by Mafeking Night,
an extraordinary example of mass hysteria, which
must have had a considerable effect on foreigners
in London on the occasion.   But the war still dragged
on ;   neither propaganda—for there was plenty of
talk of Boer atrocities—nor abandonment in public
rejoicing at small successes, nor British arms could
stop it.   It continued as a drawn-out guerilla affair ;
it became a matter of block-houses and petty skirmish-
ing.   Our troops were reduced to destroying enemy
farms and interning women and children in concentration camps.   It was not a glorious nor a well-
managed business.   Even at home it aroused protest.
Campbell-Bannerman stirred up bitter feeling by
drawing attention to the conditions of these concentration camps ;   his phrase " methods of bar-
barism " unloosed a typhoon of party feeling.   He
was accused of disloyalty and lack of patriotism, of
insulting the army severally and individually, of playing into the hands of foreigners who decried England.
Certainly there was an increasing number of foreigners
—it would hardly be an exaggeration to say that
there were a majority of foreigners—who decried
England.   They disliked her arrogance, and said so ;
they laughed at her claims to world power, and were
not polite about her trained armies who could not
subdue half-trained, irregular levies during years of
fighting, who in the end had to resort to attacking
women and children.   It is easy to understand the

bitterness which Campbell - Bannerman's attack aroused : the truth in it had a horrid taste. So the South African War petered out to a peace by negotiation in an atmosphere, at home and abroad, not pleasant for English pride.

More than a year before the War ended Queen Victoria died ; on January 1st, 1901, an age in English history came to an end. By whatever standard the Victorian age is judged—and to-day it does not seem fashionable to employ leniency in judgment of it—its importance cannot be denied. During the sixty years progress was so considerable and so great ; prosperity cannot conceivably be denied to it ; security marked it ; with all the material advances attending it there appeared, outwardly, acceptance of the ways and traditions of life and government typified by the central figure of the Queen. Ordinary people were genuinely grieved at the Queen's death. Many of them, perhaps the majority of them, realised that in the passing of that great figure, at a moment when the glory of her reign, which had been so loudly celebrated three years before, suffered a definite setback, there must be the closing of a door. The closing of that Victorian door was lamented, genuinely and deeply ; but the door was closed. In the years immediately succeeding the Queen's death insecurity began to take the place of the sixty years of increasing security to which people had become accustomed. Amongst other nations England became more and more unpopular. She had, following her loss of prestige over the South African War, to face troubles everywhere, and she did not use noticeable tact in facing them. Her press and public outcry over the Dreyfus affair,

which it is now hard to picture as other than the
unfortunate domestic business of France, is an
example.   Popularity for English citizens in European
cities could, under the circumstances, hardly be expected.   The German Emperor came in for vehement
public criticism ; the Russians were not praised.   In
politics and in popularity England was becoming
isolated.   Almost friendless in the world, the attention
of her statesmen and her people was drawn with
growing anxiety to the question of sea-power.   Germany was increasing her navy, seeking without any
attempt at disguise to rival England ; England was
anxiously replying.   The *Dreadnought* class of battleships was shortly to be launched.   But effective sea-
power has never been and never will be simply a
matter of armed navies : mercantile ships must play
an important part.   Germany was flooding the world
with cheap goods, grabbing markets, carrying passengers, too often in her own ships.   On the Atlantic
the fastest passenger-carrying ship in the world flew
the German flag and the largest shipping company
was also German.   It was an anxious moment for
England, and it became more anxious.

The Atlantic, separating the old world of Europe
from the new world of America, had long been a
species of international court in which the worth of
the mercantile fleets of the Western nations was
judged.   From the foundation of the Cunard Company and the commencement of regular services
governments had been concerned with the Atlantic
Ferry and the ships serving it.   The Cunard Company had been largely dependent on its mail contract
at the start, and from then onwards the governments
of all the nations concerned had at one time or another

assisted their shipping companies. The assistance had other ends than helping commerce ; the great ships which crossed the Atlantic were, partly with public money, designed and built so that they could, when the need arose, help the armed navies of the countries to which they belonged. Strength and position on the Atlantic were universally recognised as of the first importance to any of the great European nations ; to England, the island centre of a wide empire, it was a very vital concern. When the South African War was dragging out to its finish shipping on the Atlantic was in a depressed and difficult position, competition and rivalry were keen, com-petitors were prepared to go to great lengths to defeat a rival ; England, becoming generally isolated and unpopular among the nations, had been forced into second place by Germany and seemed a long way from the chance of regaining her old position. That was bad ; but an attack from a new quarter was infinitely worse.

Mr. J. Pierpont Morgan launched his shipping trust. Its object was to combine under one owner-ship, American, the whole of the express and first-class tonnage of the North Atlantic. Acting with Mr. Morgan was Mr. W. J. Pirrie, afterwards Lord Pirrie, the head of Messrs. Harland & Wolff. Con-trol of the Leyland Line was first acquired in 1901 ; the following year the International Mercantile Marine Company came into being with a capital of 120,000,000 dollars. Amongst other purchases it acquired the share capital of the Dominion Line, the Atlantic Transport Line, the National Line, the Shaw Savill and Albion Line, control of the Red Star and a twenty-five per cent. holding in the Holland-America

Lines—a sufficient beginning. It was, however, the sale of the White Star Line to the Morgan Combine which really excited popular alarm and outcry in England. The price was more than ten millions sterling, of which three millions were to be paid in cash before the end of the year. At the end of the nineteenth century the German companies had been concerned with the idea of some such combine, and they acted immediately when the I.M.M. became a fact. Both the Hamburg-America and the North German Lloyd Lines, with the approval of the German Emperor, entered into working arrangements, which included interchange of shares, with the new International Mercantile Marine Company. The Morgan Combine appeared a sufficiently comprehensive affair.

The excuse for the creation of the I.M.M. was that it would avert disastrous international struggles between the shipping firms on the North Atlantic. It was denied that the real object was to give America control of the Atlantic. But neither the excuses nor the denial were acceptable to English public opinion. It was shown that all the ships of the companies, purchased by the I.M.M. from England, would continue to fly their own house flags ; but that did not allay popular alarm. A formula—that lovely verbal unguent for trouble—was devised ; an attempt was made to describe the I.M.M. as " the Anglo-American Community of Interests," but the ordinary Englishman did not like it even under that resounding title. When on December 1st, 1902, three millions sterling were actually paid over in London and the White Star Company passed to the control of the International Mercantile Marine Company, average persons were seriously alarmed. Other English

companies had gone and were going, the loss of the
White Star was a final blow.   There were, of course, the
usual number of people who saw in this the downfall
of England, who found it another occasion for expressing their entire lack of knowledge as to what
the country and the world were coming to, but the
confirmed pessimists on this occasion were reinforced
by men and women of reasonable optimism.   The
name of the White Star and the names of many of
its ships were known far outside shipping circles ; in
homes where connection with the sea did not extend
beyond an annual fortnight at some seaside resort,
the company was remembered as something contributing to national pride.   That it, one of the
greatest of our shipping companies, had gone from
our control, taking lesser companies with it, caught
at popular fancy.   There was real consternation.
Wild rumours spread.   It was stated that Mr. Pirrie,
the head of a great firm of shipbuilders, had backed
the formation of the I.M.M. so as to save the money
owed to his firm by the White Star for the building
of ships.   That was proved to be pure nonsense, as
no such money was owed ; but the rumour typified
feeling.   Why was English shipping going to American
control ?   There must be some financial ramp behind
it ?   Didn't England need her shipping as much,
indeed ten times more, than she had ever needed it
before ?   Had we, perchance, ceased to be an island
people ?   The seas, apparently, no longer counted
with us.   Why not present the British Navy to
Germany for a suitable sum and be done with it ?
Call it an Anglo-German Community of Interests if
you like, but why not be thorough while you were
about it ?   Was Parliament, as usual, going to sit

and talk ? . . . Those sort of questions were asked and debated in all sorts of homes, in clubs and in public-houses. People who had no inward longing to walk the decks of a ship, who were not stirred and interested by tales of the sea, who dismissed ocean travel from their calculations on account of the sickness induced by ocean movement, were roused to a fine pitch of indignation. Explain it any way, the fact remained : the Atlantic was passing from English control.

From this distance and in view of the outcome the outcry may seem exaggerated, but it was loud and bitter. Big and little raised their voices ; the Government kept silence, although it was obvious that the Morgan combine affected the Admiralty, the Post Office and the Board of Trade. Another class of men also kept silence, in public, although they were more directly affected than anyone else : the men who worked in ships on the sea kept their opinions of the Combine largely amongst themselves, knowing that loose tongues might jeopardise their jobs. But it requires little imagination to picture their consternation. To them owners are always an anxiety and in some sort an enigma ; new owners increase the anxiety and change doubt about future intentions to wild speculation. Seamen as a race are direct ; no fancy talk about Anglo-American Community of Interests would soothe them, since communism of any sort holds small appeal to them. For sailors on the Atlantic the issue was direct. The White Star Line, for instance, together with its managers Ismay, Imrie & Company, had gone to American owners. Owners call the tune. What was the new tune going to be ? From trimmers and firemen doing their skilled jobs in grime and heat, through the galleys, along the alleyways and in the staterooms, in the offices, up to the bridge, where men not suffering from heat, peered over the dodger into the murk of a winter's night, from stem to stern of many ships being driven to schedule across northern seas there was, inevitably, alarm. Talk, explain, put it this way or that, point out that the flag was not being changed, it did not matter ; the fact remained. British ships had gone and were going to American ownership : what did that spell for the men who worked those ships ? From commanders to bell-boys a new anxiety as to the future of their jobs was bred. The big schemes of a financier had alarmed English citizens comfortably at home and had hurt their pride ; they had given the English Government new problems to solve. Out on the Atlantic in the ships that had passed and the ships that might pass they had added new troubles to the lives of thousands of English sailors.

As the outcry swelled it was said, and largely believed, that the Cunard Company must also pass to the Morgan Combine. Lord Inverclyde, who became chairman in 1902, is stated to have informed his shareholders that unless very heavy losses were to be incurred the company and its ships must be sold to the I.M.M.

It became common knowledge that Lord Inverclyde and his Board were in negotiation with the Government, seeking to come to some arrangement which would save the oldest and the most famous of the Atlantic steamship companies for England. The public talked, the press criticised and suggested, members asked questions in Parliament, but were not supplied with information. Then the *Etruria*, carrying mails, in bad weather in mid-Atlantic broke her shaft. The *William Cliff*, a Leyland cargo steamer, picked her up and took her in tow. The weather grew worse, the tower and the towed struggled for ten days to cross less than 800 miles of sea to the Azores. There the Cunard Company did what they could for the passengers and mails, chartering a Royal Mail liner. But the accident came at an unfortunate moment. The *Etruria* was close on twenty years old, a famous ship in her day, but she had a single screw ; if that went she was helpless. The history of the Atlantic shows that, in its mood, it is equal to breaking the stoutest of shafts : man has not yet been able to legislate against such an accident as that. Public opinion, however, ignored the might of the sea ; it was already considerably stirred, and it became very angry. The Cunard Company was bitterly criticised ; the reply was that the company was about to lay down two 30,000-ton ships, which, like their owners, would remain English and would be designed to restore British prestige on the Atlantic.

The announcement soothed outcry, but it did not still it. The public wanted to know more about these proposed ships and the negotiations which were going on with the Government concerning them. In Parliament members demanded a debate on the matter so that they might have an opportunity of discussing the proposals. This demand was refused ; the Government decided that there should be no discussions until the negotiations were finally concluded, accepted by the Cunard shareholders and signed by the contracting parties. On July 30th,

1903, the negotiations were finally concluded, and immediately afterwards the agreement reached was put before Parliament for ratification.

Under the agreement the Government were to advance to the Cunard Company a sum not exceeding £2,600,000 for the express purpose of building two steamships of large size and having a speed of from 24 to 25 knots to be run in the company's line between Liverpool and New York or between other ports in Great Britain and the United States of America. The company was also to receive from the Government annually the sum of £150,000. To this annual payment a condition was attached. It was provided : " If in the case of either of the two steamships, or any vessel substituted therefor, the company shall, before such steamship sails on its first voyage, fail to advance to the satisfaction of the Admiralty reasonable proofs from trials that such vessel will be capable of maintaining a minimum average ocean speed of 24½ knots in moderate weather, but shall prove to the like satisfaction that such vessel will be capable of maintaining an average ocean speed of not less than 23½ knots under such conditions as aforesaid, then such deduction shall be made from the annual payment of £150,000 as shall be agreed upon, or failing such agreement shall be determined by arbitration, by an arbitrator appointed by the Lord Chief Justice for the time being, and the decision of such arbitrator shall be final."

This proviso is interesting. Out of the formal language the fact seems to emerge very plainly that nobody concerned was too confident about the " average ocean speed of 24½ knots in moderate weather." Even to the experts, apparently, that seemed asking too much.

The Cunard Company pledged all their assets as security for the loan and agreed to an interest payment of $2\frac{3}{4}$ per cent. upon it. The agreement was to run for twenty years, and one-twentieth of the sum advanced was repayable annually. It was provided that the company should remain a purely British undertaking : no foreigner should be qualified to act as a director or as one of the principal officers of the company and no shares of the company were to be held " by or in trust for, or be in any way under the control of any foreigner or foreign corporation or any corporation under foreign control." The " principal officers " mentioned in this provision included " masters and officers and engineers in charge of a watch on board any of the company's ocean steamships."

So there was no ambiguity as to the Cunard Company remaining British. But the agreement carried matters further than that. The Government stipulated that no Cunard ship should be chartered, except to the Indian Administration, without their sanction, that all ships of the line could be taken over by Government at agreed rates, that the plans of all vessels to be built of 17 knots or upwards must be submitted for approval. That made certain of the ships ; the men who worked them must have read with relief the provision which followed. It was agreed that all the officers and three-quarters of the crew be British subjects, and that a large percentage of them must be naval reservists.

In addition to the money loaned to them and the £150,000 a year for the maintenance of the new ships, the Cunard Company were to receive £68,000 annually for carrying the mails between Liverpool or Queenstown and New York on a regular weekly service in their fastest vessels.

The Government became one of the trustees of the loan and shareholders, with certain extraordinary powers, in the company.

That, in brief, was the agreement placed before Parliament for ratification ; it was not accepted without criticism.

Mr. E. Robertson, member for Dundee, opened the attack. He pointed out that the nominal capital value of the company was £1,600,000, the market value under £1,200,000, and the value of their fleet under £2,000,000. He poured scorn on lending £2,600,000 to a " concern of this kind." He also stated that the difference between the 2¾ per cent. interest payable to the Government and 5 per cent. which the company would otherwise have had to pay must be considered as a bonus. Assuming that the object was to obtain vessels which could catch the very fastest merchantmen of other nations, then it should be shown that the Admiralty could not build vessels capable of such speed themselves, and that the British mercantile marine could not be trusted to retain its supremacy in point of speed without special inducement. The Government ought to show that a merchant ship could not be built to maintain a speed of 24½ knots unless it were of 30,000 tons and cost £1,300,000. The proposal appeared to Mr. Robertson a sudden creation due to the Morgan Combine, which did not now seem as formidable to many people as it had a year ago, and they were now able to sleep comfortably in their beds. If, however, the Admiralty were going to resort to the Merchant Navy for the sort of ships they wanted, why did they make a special selection.

The reference to unquiet sleep, although possibly rhetorical, certainly suggests a reason why the Morgan Combine was met with a sudden creation.

After some bickering, Mr. Lough, member for West Islington, proposed an amendment which covered part of the same ground. He moved " that this House regrets that an arrangement was made with the Cunard Company without first ascertaining by public competition the terms upon which the requirements might have been met by other companies."

This was followed by a word of praise for the Government, who, Sir F. Fleming (Yorkshire, Shipley) maintained, had little or no choice of action and had performed a patriotic duty, perhaps at some sacrifice, in removing the possibility of America swallowing up the Atlantic passenger and freight trade, and so had taken away the causes for a feeling of panic. The bargain was exceedingly advantageous to the country, and the effect of the policy of the Admiralty and the Board of Trade would be to restore the prestige of the British flag.

Sir W. Allan (Gateshead) believed that, financially, the Government had got the best of the bargain. But the crux of the whole question was the speed of the ships. If the Admiralty were entrusted with their designing and engineering, he could only say, " Lord help them ! " since the Admiralty had never yet built a ship which had the speed designed for her. Having congratulated the Government, he warned them—being obviously a profound thinker—that if

the ships were not properly designed and engined,
with the three screws in the proper place, they would
be failures.

One of the Liverpool members, Mr. C. McArthur,
praised the Cunard Company for having stood out
of the Morgan Combine, although sorely tempted to
do otherwise. He maintained that there had been
great danger of the control of the Atlantic passing to
America. He considered the agreement a good one
for the Government and the nation, and hoped that
it would also be a good one for the Cunard Company.

It was argued by Mr. E. Cecil (Aston Manor)
that if tenders had been invited for the ships there
would have been delay during which the Cunard
Company might have gone over to the Combine.
This member also maintained that it was more
economical to subsidise merchant ships than build
naval ones ; he informed the House that the price
paid for these new ships was less than half the cost
of a third class cruiser.

Stating the Government's case in reply to the
debate, Mr. Arnold Forster maintained that they
could build ships of equal speed to those under discussion, but that the proposed fast merchant cruisers
would be obtained at much less cost. Armed with
modern weapons and carrying an enormous supply
of coal, these ships would be able to keep the sea
for an indefinite time, eluding every vessel they
desired to escape and overtaking any vessel they
desired to engage. What would the position be if
in a naval war no vessel carrying the British flag
could cope with cruisers, such as those proposed,
which we might find employed against us ? The
Admiralty had to consider the cheapest and most

efficient method of meeting this menace. The bargain was a thoroughly sound transaction ; the Government by it were restoring the prestige of the British mercantile marine and securing supremacy on the Atlantic.

The agreement was ratified and received, generally, with approval, but as the debate in the House of Commons and the terms of the agreement itself had made clear, there were doubts and antagonisms. The future of the Cunard Company as a purely British concern had, under certain circumstances, been made safe for twenty years. That was undoubtedly satisfactory for the Company and satisfying for the public, who had been stirred to real indignation by the departure of the White Star and other famous shipping companies from British ownership. Provision, according to the Admiralty, had been made for merchant cruisers which would secure, in the event of war, our supremacy upon the Atlantic. Even then the possibility of a European war was recognised as changing into a probability, there were, indeed, many people who already regarded war as inevitable in the near future. So the talk of menace on the seas, the reference to peaceful citizens sleeping more comfortably in their beds, were not altogether out of place. The Admiralty had done something and they were confident. After the ratification of the agreement, the clamour and the outcry, in public talk and in the press, died down. Something anyhow had been promised. Two ships had been promised, the largest and fastest merchant vessels in the world, capable of acting as armed cruisers when the need arose, floating palaces of luxury and comfort when engaged upon their merchant business. All foreigners

would be shamed by these two ships and Americans,
who would be amongst the chief users of them,
would have to acknowledge that they had not succeeded in acquiring the best upon the seas.   The
public, whose money was being used, were parties
to the promise ;   the Government, who had used
the public's money, had expressed themselves as
satisfied with a sound bargain ;   critics, being critics,
cricitised an arrangement that was a national concern.
England had recognised a need and had ordered
it to be supplied.   There were many other matters
to claim her attention ;   her position amongst the
nations, changes at home.   The long reign of the
old conservatism was dying amidst all sorts of international threats ;   socialism was demanding attention,
a young Labour Party was growing vigorous ;   there
were women who maintained that they ought to
have votes and would have them.   All sorts of things
were happening to change the ways of living.   The
nation having been promised two great ships, left
the fulfilment of the promise to the builders and the
experts.

The men who in due course would man the two
ships on the seas, were, naturally, deeply interested
in all news of the building which they could obtain.
They could estimate the difficulties that separated
the promise from its fulfilment.   The proviso, that
the ships should not be condemned as failures if
they could not produce the speed which had been
so much advertised, meant more to sailors than mere
prudence.   They knew what an average ocean speed
of $24\frac{1}{2}$ knots in moderate weather on the Atlantic
actually entailed.   That it was a big demand, no
sailor of that day could doubt.   They said, of course,

in public—the officers and men of the Cunard line —that it could and would be done ; they scorned men of rival companies who said that it could not ; but amongst themselves some doubt was inevitable. Attaining 24½ knots was comparatively simple, maintaining that as an average ocean speed a vastly different affair. Failure would hit them and their jobs. When the public, content with its promise of two ships, concerned itself with other matters, there must have been many sailors, lately cheered by the fact that their Company was to remain completely English, who wondered and regretted that their directors had found it necessary to aim so high. Failure, even half success, might lead to so much trouble.

The Cunard Company and the builders had some time, four years as it turned out, in which to fulfil their promise. The history of those four years shows what they thought about it. It was a case for success or disaster. Anything less than real success, the complete fulfilment of the promise, which had been made into a national affair, would hit the Company very hard. Having with every circumstance of public advertisement undertaken to do something, excuses would be of little use if the thing were not done. Certainly the good name of the Cunard Company, probably to a large degree those of the builders, were at stake. During the years of building anxiety and doubt, for so many things besides lack of speed can cause a ship to fail, must have marched with effort. The greatest optimist in the whole undertaking could never have been completely free from the thought that he was engaged on work which might end in failure.

In 1907 the two ships, which England had been promised, were commissioned. The *Lusitania* came first, followed after a few weeks by the *Mauretania*. They were sister ships, but not twins. Neither of them ever touched half-measures ; they were both successful in full degree ; England got what she had ordered. But the *Mauretania* was always a little better than her sister. The *Lusitania* did not reach old age ; the *Mauretania* did. Her record, the story of her twenty-eight years of work, explains why her name is more famous than that of any other steamship.

CHAPTER II

CONCEPTION

SEVEN years of courage to scrap plans and start again, of refusal to be content with what might do, of boldness in adopting experiment when experiment promised justification : that, on the facts, is a true summary of the designing and building of the *Mauretania*.

From 1897, when the *Kaiser Wilhelm der Grosse* gained the Atlantic record, the Cunard Company were faced with the necessity of building something better or losing their prestige. But they had small chance of being able to estimate how much better this new something had got to be. The Germans were not standing still. The *Deutschland*, a Hamburg-American ship, appeared in 1900, the *Kronprinz Wilhelm* in 1901, the *Kaiser Wilhelm II* in 1903 ; they were all fast ships, each improving on its predecessor, and each of them in turn demanded changes of Cunard plans. Other circumstances, the Morgan Combine and uncertainty as to the Company's future, brought more changes of plan. The agreement in 1903 with the Government finally outlined the Cunard Company's task, but this outline was so formidable that it entailed still more scrapping of plans. In 1901 Messrs. Swan, Hunter, & Wigham Richardson prepared a design for a vessel 700 feet long, with a beam one-tenth her length, and a speed of 24 knots. This was not acceptable, and they tried again, this time for a ship 750 feet long with a 75 feet beam and a guaranteed speed of 25 knots. To help consideration of this design models were prepared scaled to this length, but with maximum breadths varying from 76 feet to 82 feet. After considering these models, the Cunard Company in 1902 called for tenders for a vessel 750 feet by 76 feet, but in 1903, following the agreement with Government, they amended this and called for tenders for two ships 750 feet by 75 feet, to have a speed of $24\frac{3}{4}$ knots and engines of reciprocating type driving three screws. Messrs. Swan Hunter & Wigham Richardson obtained an order for one of these two ships, which was to be engined by the Wallsend & Slipway Engineering Company, a neighbouring Tyneside firm with which the builders were connected. The preliminary work of producing and testing plans and designs was begun at once. But when, four years later, the *Mauretania* left the Tyne she was 790 feet long, had a beam of 88 feet, and was driven by turbine engines operating four screws.

In the summer of 1903 the Cunard Company knew what they had to do. The nation had been promised the largest and fastest liners in the world ; the *Kaiser Wilhelm II* had a gross tonnage of 20,000, so a tonnage of 30,000 would give the new ships sufficient margin ; the German vessel had an estimated speed of 23 to 23·5 knots, so that a designed speed of 25 should answer the matter of pace. The Admiralty had been promised merchant cruisers capable of maintaining 24.5 knots at sea for six days of continuous steaming. The company, if it were to keep abreast of interest and capital payments on its loan of public money, had to ensure that the ships should be capable of earning a profit. What had to be done was clear ; how it was to be done was not. The actual construction of the *Mauretania* was not commenced until 1905 ; for close on two years after it was known what they had to do nobody concerned with the making of the ship could be satisfied exactly even as to the matter of shape and size.

The ship had to satisfy the Admiralty, so the first data were obtained from models operated in the Government tanks at Haslar. These models were to the scale of one forty-eighth, but the company and the builders were not satisfied with that. They constructed a launch built of wood so that she could more easily be altered, 47½ feet long on a scale of one-sixteenth of the proposed new ship, and worked her in the Northumberland Dock, on the Tyne, where there was a depth of water of 24 feet and a run of roughly a quarter of a mile. That wooden launch played an enormously important part in the *Mauretania's* success ; it is fascinating to picture it running backwards and forwards up and down the dock, constantly modified and altered, loaded with new apparatus, bristling with gadgets, giving from innumerable trials and repeated experiments an accurate prophecy of what a steel ship sixteen times greater would do on the high seas. It is recorded that at first there was a great deal of trouble with the launch because, in that dock, the bottom became fouled so easily. They could not, in that Tyneside dock water, quite cure her of this habit, but they made her improve her ways and allowed in their calculations for the margin of dirtiness which they could not diminish. A small, scarcely an inspiring matter, this fouling, but it illustrates nicely the sort

of difficulties which stood between experimenting
in that dock and getting the data on which a ship,
costing more than a million and a quarter pounds,
could be designed with confidence.

The launch, as much or more than anything else,
decided the *Mauretania's* figure, not just a matter of
length and breadth and depth, but all the niceties of
curves and hollows, matters of some importance.
Hours up and down that dock, totalling weeks more
than days, went to the fixing of the ship's lines ;
weeks of calculation, produced by the weeks of running
the launch, followed. Something would be proved
not satisfactory ; there would be a change of figure
and the business of testing would begin again. The
launch was electrically driven and helping to decide
upon hull form was only one of her jobs ; she had
to experiment with propeller efficiency. Experiments
started with three screws ; when it was decided that
four would be used in the ship much alteration was
required, since a vessel driven by four screws should
not curve and hollow quite as one driven by three.
The number of screws finally decided, a whole series
of different shapes and sizes were tested, and tested
in different places until the exact form and position
of the four were finally approved. That repeated
with the rudder, which must be adapted to the requirements of the hull form and the screws. Each
depended on the other, so that a modification in
any one might entail modifications to all. Wind
resistance demanded careful attention, so the launch
went up and down the dock with deck erections in
proportion to those proposed for the ship, changing
and altering these erections until they satisfied.
A whole series of experiments was concerned with

MAURETANIA
In Dry Dock.
Lines for Speed.

the direction in which the screws should turn, inwards or outwards. Loaded with delicate recording apparatus, hanging gadgets overboard, trailing them astern, the launch helped to settle a hundred different problems on whose correct settlement the success and safety of the *Mauretania* on the Atlantic depended, problems which must be settled before the actual construction of the ship could be commenced.

Up and down the Northumberland Dock on the Tyne for close on two years, in summer when the dock would smell richly as docks do, in winter when the hands and feet of the men aboard would be numb, seldom setting out on a trip without some alteration or adjustment, often substantially changed, manned by skilled men who were giving their skill and their patience to the perfection of a ship which many of them would never see engaged upon her ocean business, that wooden launch stands as a nice example of what ship designing means.

While the launch was helping to settle her problems, another, on which the fame of the *Mauretania* ultimately depended, was settled round a conference table. The first specifications had provided for reciprocating engines, but the alternative means of propulsion by rotary engines had always, in view of the designed speed, been under consideration. Turbines were then still in the experimental stage ; they were used, but they were still a long way from being proved. There were some cross Channel steamers using turbine engines satisfactorily ; the Allan Line in 1903 were building a ship which was to have this type of machinery installed ; the Royal Navy had the *Amethyst*, whose turbines developed 12,000 horse power.

It was already obvious, even to its conservative opponents, that the turbine as a means of marine propulsion was to have a future, but it was not yet clear
how close that future might be. Yet the *Mauretania*,
if she were not to be damned by half-success, must
be capable of a sustained speed of 24·5 knots and
maintaining that speed with any form of engine was
not going to be a simple job. The magnitude of
the task demanded that nothing short of the very
best should be used in the ship.

To enable them to judge what might be the very
best the Cunard Company appointed a Commission
to investigate the question of what type of engine
should be used. The Chairman of this Commission
was the Marine Superintendent of the Company, the
members were all expert engineers or men having
considerable practical experience of ships and their
construction. There were representatives on this
committee of the builders and other firms who were
to supply the engines of both the *Mauretania* and the
Lusitania. The Engineer-in-Chief of the Navy, the Chief
Engineer Surveyor of Lloyds and Sir William White,
who, as chief constructor to the Admiralty had been
responsible for the turbine-driven *Amethyst*, were
members. The inventor of the turbine engine, the
Honourable Charles Parsons, was there to assist.
The committee was representative and its investigation was thorough ; it was composed of carefully
chosen men more capable, probably, than any other
body of men in England of deciding the issue wisely.
The problem demanded vision in its settlement
because there were no exact data available ; it went
beyond the question of whether turbine engines
were more capable than reciprocating engines of

maintaining economically and efficiently a high average of ocean speed, it concerned the matter of such engines giving the required speed, and giving it economically —for economy was vital to a commercial undertaking —on a scale more than five times greater than anything attempted until then. However carefully the committee studied the performances of turbine engines, and they investigated the performances of land installations as well as those at sea, that unknown quantity faced them : What might happen when the size of the engines was so enormously increased? Conservative marine engineers maintained that turbine engines developing that power were altogether unjustifiable. They argued that the most powerful reciprocating engines then in existence—those of the 20,000 ton *Kaiser Wilhelm II*—were only 38,000 horse power, but that to obtain that power economically and successfully half a century of evolution and gradual development had been required. It was absurd to imagine that the turbine, still in its infancy, could be expected to develop without trouble and to develop economically the enormous energy, 68,000 horse power, required for the *Mauretania*. The committee heard the arguments for and against ; they investigated data. Amongst the arguments in favour of installing turbines was that of saving space ; the engine rooms could be smaller and lower. The reduction in height was of great importance ; it rendered increased watertight sub-divisions possible and so enlarged the margin of safety in case of collision or other accident. Reciprocating engines would necessitate one of the engine rooms being well aft, which would increase the difficulty of balancing the heavy moving parts so as to lessen vibration. Turbines operating four screws would lower the power to be transmitted through each shaft and so lessen the chances of shaft failure, which has not been infrequent in high speed ships on the Atlantic. Turbines, again, did not throb and pulsate as hard driven reciprocating engines did. Cross channel passengers already knew that and travelled in the new turbine vessels when they could. Passengers' comfort is vastly important when a ship cannot pay its way without passengers' approval. The committee coming to their decision and preparing their recommendation, must have been attracted by the many advantages which a turbine-driven ship could offer, but it was their business not to let their obvious advantages over-shadow the main question whether turbines of the size required in the *Mauretania* were at that time a practical proposition. With no positive data on which to frame their decision, it is not possible that the cry of the conservative engineers, " You are trying to make turbines run before they can walk," did not cause the Committee some doubt. It was experi-ment, but the decision was unanimous. The experts having examined the problem, recommended that turbines could and should be used. The final decision remained with the directors of the Cunard Company. If the recommendation was adopted but the experiment failed, it was more than probable that the Company would be seriously, perhaps vitally, hit. The advertisement which had attended the agreement to build the *Mauretania* and the *Lusitania*, the broadcasting in the press which accompanied any item of news which might leak out about the building and the planning would not react kindly to failure. If, on the other hand, the Company played for safety, refused their experts' advice, installed reciprocating engines and found that their new ships were quickly surpassed by turbine driven vessels of some more courageous rival, the reaction was likely to be less kindly still.

Not an easy decision for any Board of Directors, a particularly hard decision for the directors of a Company which, perhaps unwillingly, had been forced into the position of pledging themselves to produce two ships which would be the means of re-establishing the nation's mercantile marine prestige. Just when this difficult decision was in the making, Lord Inverclyde, whose ability and courage had done so much to save his Company for English ownership, whose energies were so devoted to making the promised ships fulfil their promise, died. His death was a hard blow to the Cunard Company and a very great loss to his colleagues on the Board. But the difficult decision was made ; the recommendation of the Committee was adopted ; turbines, although admittedly still in the experimental stage for such vessels, were to be installed. That decision placed a milestone on the road of marine progress.

To show their faith in the decision the Company ordered that turbine engines should be installed in a new 20,000 ton passenger ship then building for their North Atlantic service. This ship, the *Carmania*, enabled them to obtain useful information ; but she had three screws only and nothing approaching the power of the *Mauretania*, so that, although useful as a guide, she could not give exact information as to the performance of the greater ship to follow her.

Besides attacking the possibility of using turbines successfully in a ship of the size and with the power of the *Mauretania*, critics had been concerned with the matter of fuel. Furnaces generating steam for engines developing 68,000 horse power would eat fuel. Daily 1,000 tons of coal would have to be transferred from bunkers to furnaces. That labour alone, it was argued, damned the ship ; it was an impossibility. The strain entailed upon trimmers and firemen was too great ; the men would not be able to endure it, and efficient steaming would be impossible. The Committee had to advise on the matter of fuel. They knew the magnitude of the task of feeding 1,000 tons of coal a day into hungry furnaces, but they believed that it could be done. They realised the advantages of liquid fuel, how it would save labour and simplify the matter of efficient steaming, but they decided against its use. The reasons given for the decision against liquid fuel were that the cost of oil was too high and its reliable supply too problematical. The second of those decisions helps to date the *Mauretania* ; it carries us back into an age when the world was still not dotted with pumps and stations and tanks supplying oil of various grades ; it shows the ship living from one era into another. About engines the Committee had been bold, they had gone for the future rather than the present ; about fuel they were prudent, but in their prudence they recognised the future and suggested provision for it. The *Mauretania* was built with bunkers and furnaces so constructed that they could be adapted, if necessary, for oil fuel more economically than in most coal burners. That was a compromise, one of the few with which the ship was concerned in her long history. With its acceptance by the Company, all the major decisions had been taken ;

the construction of the ship began. It was not until thirty years later that the ship, still steaming as efficiently as she had ever steamed, still sound, but a wonderful fulfilment instead of a promise, made her last voyage to the breakers.

While the Committee and the directors were making their decisions, and the wooden launch on the Tyneside dock was coping with changes and new demands, the builders had something definite, at least, with which to get ahead. They had to prepare their yard for the construction and the launching of a ship bigger than any ship ever launched before ; they had to prepare the berth on which she was to be built, on which her vast weight would rest with complete security, from which she would slide into the water ; they had to construct a large steel framework which should encase her enormous bulk, a complicated structure of girders and ladders, cranes and supports, in which she was to grow, plate by plate, from keel to superstructure ; they had to enlarge canteens and make various arrangements for the welfare of thousands of men and not a few women, whose work would be at high pressure and must not be unnecessarily delayed.

As there was no wharf which could accommodate her when she was afloat, they had to make other arrangements for her fitting out. Two large dolphins, small islands of heavy wooden piles, had to be placed in the river for her to go alongside ; floating cranes had to be provided ; a gangway had to be built to take the hordes of fitters from shore to ship and back again without congestion. From the time when the order for building was actually given, the builders were busy ; alterations in size and shape and

propulsive power might cause delay in the commencement of construction, but preparations for her
building and her fitting could go ahead. They
went ahead ; even while the major decisions were
pending, preparations for the finished ship were being
made not only in Liverpool offices and on the Tyne,
but, in real measure, all over the world.

Dozens of different trades were involved ; many
countries were concerned. Inevitably, the press
referred to the *Mauretania* as a " wonder ship," which
may be translated as a ship demanding only the
latest and the best. Architects and artists were busy
with plans and schemes of decoration ; woods and
marbles, silks, upholsteries, carpets, metals had to be
appraised and chosen. The woods had to be carefully selected for beauty, when they were required
for decoration, and always so seasoned and so staunch
as to remain silent in the face of sea damp and the
movements of a ship. The most skilled craftsmen
only could be entrusted with the carving, the
carpentry and the joinery. Creaking, that certain
exciter of annoyance to passengers, must be cut down
to an irreducible minimum. Decoration had to be
on a scale to excite general admiration, but since
much woodwork increases the danger of fire, elaborate
fire precautions must march with decoration. Ventilation alone was a considerable complication demanding much selection in finding the most suitable
appliances and systems ; passengers, some of them
liking fresh air and others scared of it, must be pleased ;
down in the depths of the ship the men transferring
those 1,000 tons of coal each day from bunkers to
furnaces must at all costs be assured a temperature
in which they could work. The matter of ventilation

could not be settled in a day. Plumbing and sanita-
tion—that was another not small complication in
which experts had to select, where rival firms competed eagerly to prove that each could supply the
latest and the best. Throughout the ship a mass of
pipes had to be placed so as to do the job required of
them without obtruding on passengers' notice. Little
things as well as big came in here as elsewhere ;
taps used by passengers must not hammer as taps
on badly plumbed ships are apt to do. So a search
for the valve taps which eliminated hammering.
The *Mauretania* was to carry immigrants—immigrants
in those days being a lucrative freight ; some immigrants are not too particular in matters of domestic
hygiene, so aboard the *Mauretania* sanitary devices
must be installed carefully designed to protect
pleasant immigrants from certain habits of unpleasant immigrants. Big and little things, but the
little might, if neglected, do big harm to the reputation of the ship. Electrical installation, a department by itself, under a separate staff, almost tres-
passed on the experimental thirty years ago. When
everything in this department had been tested,
selected and installed it was widely advertised that
the *Mauretania* would to a certain extent use electricity
for cooking ; that was then progressive, and a decision
not reached without much preparing. So there were
many men and women in so many places preparing
samples and arguments in favour of their wares,
demonstrating the efficiency of what they had to offer
from a ventilating system for a ship with many hundreds of rooms and compartments to be ventilated
down to a door-hook which was guaranteed not to
rattle when the ship laboured in Atlantic storms ;

and most of these men and women, representing so many businesses, were anxious to get in and complete a deal so that their goods could be advertised as to be installed in the *Mauretania* even before the shape and driving power of the ship was finally decided.   The advertisement attached to having some device installed in the *Mauretania* looked good before the ship was definitely planned; when three decades later she took many of these devices with her to the breakers it had been found rather more than good.

While the ship was planning and building, preparations had to be made beyond the Tyne and the many workshops and factories concerned with details of her fittings.   Liverpool, her port of registry, had to consider how to receive her.   The Mersey Docks and Harbour Board made ready for the new Cunarders.   The Prince's Landing Stage was then used for the big Atlantic passenger liners, but there was not a sufficient depth of water to enable a ship of the *Mauretania's* draught to go alongside.   So over twenty square miles of the river bed abreast of the Stage was dredged.   The work was not a small undertaking, as more than two hundred thousand tons of rock, clay and sand had to be removed ; but it was carried out so as to give a depth of 36 feet below low water of equinoctial spring tides which, it was hoped, would enable the *Mauretania* or her sister to use the stage under any but very exceptional conditions. Having provided for the ships coming alongside, the Mersey Board placed in position baggage conveyors and movable elevated platforms from which gangways could reach to the great height of the decks. That settled the *Mauretania's* reception so far as the

Prince's Landing Stage was concerned, and the Cunard Company must have sighed with relief. For the habit of getting completely fussed, worried and annoyed exhibited by many people, otherwise level-headed, when embarking or disembarking for or from an ocean voyage is common knowledge, and the particular trial of the staffs and owners of passenger ships. Had the Mersey Dock Board refused to move, and had the *Mauretania* been unable to berth alongside at her home terminal port, it is certain that in the consideration of a considerable body of passengers there would have been a black mark against her. But the Board did not refuse to move, or to remove, at some considerable cost, those two hundred thousand tons of rock and clay and sand ; instead, it went farther than that. It provided in the graving dock which the ship would use in Liverpool blocks of sufficient strength to withstand the increased stresses to which they would be subjected. Then, at the Company's request, the Board turned their attention to the Cunard Buoy. For fifty years, when waiting to dock or to go alongside the Stage, Cunard ships had lain in the Sloyne, a stretch of water out of the way of traffic, where the Company had two buoys, North Cunard and South Cunard. These buoys were in the tideway which, on the ebb, sometimes races at four or five knots ; the ground moorings were strong, but not strong enough to hold a 30,000 ton ship with huge deck erections exposed to the wind. A new buoy, with ground moorings of exceptional strength laid in four legs, not a small or an inexpensive undertaking, was placed in position and did its job for fourteen years. The Mersey Dock Board and the City of Liverpool made what they hoped were adequate arrangements for ensuring that these huge new ships should always use their port.

The first stage in the achievement of all this complication of planning and preparing was reached on September 20th, 1906, when the *Mauretania*, a named ship and not a number in the Cunard books, floated for the first time. The Dowager Duchess of Roxburghe named the ship and released her from the ways. The press gave much space to the launching of the ship, not forgetting to explain the name to readers as that of the Roman province of north-west Africa. The weather was favourable ; the Cunard Company marked the occasion with ceremony. It was a great occasion, but its exact significance in marine history could not then, of course, be judged. There was no hitch, no accident ; everything was successful ; the *Mauretania*, scarcely more than a vast empty shell of steel, took the water and floated upon the Tyne without having caused in her building or her launching the loss of a single human life. Congratulations, forecasts of beauty and of success were general. The country, when rivalry in armaments and competition in sea-power were bitter, when France and England, at the instigation of King Edward VII, were adjusting their differences, already making plans for each other's assistance in the European War which even then seemed inescapable, gave genuine welcome to the first appearance of the ship. But the real interest of the launch surely lies in the feelings of several hundreds of men during seventy seconds.

The designers and the workmen, the men who had planned and replanned, the men who had driven millions of rivets into thousands of carefully shaped plates, those patient people who had built and rebuilt the wooden launch, had reached a moment when, despite their care, something might occur to show that their work had not succeeded. Sailors, who in due course would have to work the ship, watched during those seventy seconds, or read of them later, with an apprehension peculiar to their kind. If something went wrong, if the *Mauretania* stuck upon the ways or became unmanageable after she had left them, the incident would be remembered throughout her career ; it would leave some small but lasting doubt in the minds of seamen as to how she might behave under more exacting circumstances when, fighting the seas, bad or unhandy behaviour might mean even great disaster. For sailors a matter of a few seconds was going to decide whether the good name of the ship was to be tarnished before she lived. The traditional bottle of champagne splintered against her stern ; a lever was moved on a beflagged platform. Hydraulic rams of 400 tons pressure were ready in case the ship should not move ; but using them, in the consideration of the anxious men who watched, would have marred the launching. They were not used. The *Mauretania* moved. In seven seconds she had travelled six feet. The time must have passed very slowly for many of the watching crowd. In fifty-five seconds, amidst the thundering of drag chains and the crashing of timbers, she had cleared the standing ways ; in seventy seconds she was at rest in the river and six tugs had her in charge. The shrieking and hooting of whistles was justified : England had successfully launched the world's largest ship. But to the men who had designed and built her body, and to the men who would man her when she was finished, relief was surely the predominant

sensation. Anything, almost, except a major accident
in the launching, could have been disguised from the
public, but even a minor failure would not be forgotten by the men whose work in life is ships. The
Mauretania sat fairly in the water, absurdly light, without funnels, masts or deck erections, as difficult to
judge for ultimate beauty as a new-born filly, but she
sat fairly, her first journey over. By travelling 951
feet, being water-borne for only 157 of them, she
had done a thing immeasurably important to her.
She had made the men who should know confident.
It was a part of her success that she never afterwards
shook that confidence.

The *Mauretania* has been described and redescribed.
Her design, her engines, her fittings and her decorations have been so often and so well detailed in print
that any lengthy redescription of them would be
absurdly out of place. A very short summary of the
main features should, now that she has gone to the
breakers and her fame is all that remains, be sufficient.
Her length over all was 790 feet, 760 between per-
pendiculars ; her breadth was 88 feet, and her
moulded depth 60 feet 6 inches. She was 5 feet
longer, $1\frac{1}{2}$ inches deeper than her sister, the *Lusitania*,
but she had the same beam. Her gross tonnage was
31,938 and her displacement 38,000 tons ; while her
displacement was the same, she exceeded her sister's
gross tonnage by nearly 1,000. Her type of engine
was the Parsons turbine, her total indicated horse-
power was 68,000, her designed highest mean speed
was 25 knots, her revolutions per minute 180 ; in
those particulars she was identical with her sister.
Generally, in shape, size, outward appearance, power
and speed the *Mauretania* was designed to be the

sister of, to bear a strong family resemblance to the *Lusitania* ; internally, in fittings and in decorations, each ship went her own way. The *Mauretania* was an English ship ; the *Lusitania* was Scottish. For years they had no rivals, except each other, on the seas. Neither of them fell short of the promise which had been given when the nation subscribed to their building, yet individuality came into the business and definitely marked the English ship as the better of the two. It was inevitable, or next-door to it, that, although the two ships were designed to be identical in power and very similar in shape and form, their performance would not be the same ; that England, in the case of the *Mauretania*, beat Scotland is, at any rate for Englishmen, worth emphasis.

As she was first commissioned, the *Mauretania* had accommodation for 2,165 passengers—563 in the first class, 464 in the second, 1,138 in the third ; she carried a crew of 938 officers and men ; so that, when full, she would carry more than three thousand persons at one time across the sea. In 1907 that was a big figure ; to-day it is not a small one. When, in middle age, the *Mauretania* was converted from a coal-burner into an oil-burner the number of the crew was considerably reduced ; from time to time during her long service her passenger accommodation was altered and improved, so that her capacity for carrying human freight was variable ; but the figure of three thousand stands as a general guide. In the days of bigger ships she was still a big ship ; but first as the biggest ship, later as a big ship, she carried these thousands of passengers over millions of miles of sea without causing a single one of them to die on her account.

Her cabin arrangement showed no originality of planning ; it followed the lines then and now generally accepted for big liners. The passengers were accommodated on six decks—boat, promenade, shelter, upper, main, lower—usually known by the letters A to F. On A deck forward there were expensive first-class staterooms, abaft them the library and writing-room, then the head of the main stairway and entrance leading to the lounge and music-room ; right aft, separated from the first-class deck and on an island, as it were, of its own was the second-class lounge. B deck provided still more expensive staterooms, the regal and other suites more frequently hired by princes of commerce and princesses of the stage than by persons of royal blood ; on its island aft on this deck there was the second-class drawing-room and smoking-room. C deck provided the third-class smoking-room and general room, the third-class galley and promenade deck ; abaft this the nursery and dining-room for children in the first class, then the galley of the first-class dining saloon and, right aft again, second-class staterooms. On D deck the third-class dining saloon was forward, then came first-class passenger rooms, the main floor of the first-class dining saloon, the galley for first and second class, the second-class dining saloon and, right aft, more second-class rooms. E deck provided rooms for passengers, third forward, first amidships, second aft. On F deck the only passengers housed were third class, paying the lowest rates, the emigrant freight for which there was at one time such keen competition. Many of the people travelling on F deck slept in portable berths, but seldom more than eight in one compartment ; there was sufficient space and privacy. It was one of the steps forward which the *Mauretania* made that her low rate third-class accommodation should be more comfortable—perhaps to-day less uncomfortable would be a more exact description—than in older ships.

The ship carried her crew here and there on those six decks. In their flat on the navigating bridge the navigating officers were above, as they undoubtedly considered themselves, the rest of the ship. The engineer officers were abaft the after funnel hatch on C deck ; the doctor, the purser and his assistants amidships adjacent to the grand entrance ; right forward the petty officers and the master-at-arms. Stewards were forward on D deck ; on E were seamen forward, greasers and firemen between the first- and second-class accommodation. F deck aft took the remainder of the ship's company. Plans of the ship show the bits of the puzzle fitted neatly together ; experience of the ship proved that the fitting was unobtrusive. Passengers were nicely segregated from the crew ; many passengers would never know that a thin bulkhead separated them from tired trimmers who had been shifting coal at high pressure, but space in a ship can never go begging, and men must be reasonably near their work. The *Mauretania* was a great ship, not an unreal series of luxurious apartments moved at high speed across the seas. The true picture of her decks is a mixture ; what the passengers saw and what they did not see were interwoven.

The woodwork of the *Mauretania's* first-class public rooms and alleyways was unusually elaborate and has become famous. Talk of the ship generally includes some mention of it and, not seldom, reference to the fact that no two panels in the dining saloon were identically carved. This woodwork was, when she was commissioned and remained until the end, part of her individuality, but to describe it or her public rooms or her private rooms would here be as out of place as to describe her engines in technical detail. As she appeared in 1907, after so many years of careful planning and building, she was an elaborately fitted and wholly modern ship. She astonished people then with her beauty and her comfort, she continued through her long life to please them, but to describe her in detail as she first crossed the Atlantic would almost amount to indelicacy. Put it this way : when she first left Liverpool for New York there were at the tables in her elaborately panelled first-class dining saloon swivel chairs ! Corpulent passengers had actually to rotate themselves past discomforted neighbours before they could settle to their food. But that was then accepted modern comfort. Go farther into detail. The young *Mauretania* had only thirty-five single-berth rooms, so a first-class passenger other than one with a long purse must be prepared for a voyage with a stable companion. Farther still. The Bibby cabin was unknown to the ship, the inside one, barred from the light of day, was not. To describe the good without the bad of thirty years ago would be unjust. The famous woodwork in the first-class remained, the interweaving of passengers and crew on her decks was substantially unaltered throughout her life ; those were features that belonged to her. Carpets, curtains, colour schemes and minor orna-mentation, swivel chairs, these and the exact arrange-ment of some of her staterooms should be considered as the clothes she wore. They were fashionable when they first appeared ; they wore out and grew noticeably unfashionable and were replaced. Although by ancient tradition a lady of the seas, the interest of the *Mauretania* does not lie in the clothes she wore, but in the work she did.

She was designed, built and fitted with extreme care. Largely experimental in the matter of propulsive power, she was made ready for her testing. Her trials were announced ; the press was informed, given due facilities for reporting upon and advertising her initial performances. The Tyneside got ready to bid farewell to the ship which had occupied the brains and the hands of so many thousands of its inhabitants for so long. The Tynesiders were proud of their work, justly confident that the ship would pass the tests required of her ; they prepared a suitable send-off. Then, without notice to the press, without any warning except to those immediately concerned, without any advertisement of her purpose or her destination, the *Mauretania* put out to sea. There was gossip on Tyneside, conflicting rumours, garbled reports. They spread, since the disappearance of the latest and largest of the world's ships cannot come about without causing talk ; but the men who knew where she had gone did not talk, so the gossip and the rumours were confined to surmise. In five days' time she returned to the Tyne, and preparations for her official trials were continued. Gossip and surmise had to die of malnutrition. But the truth about those five days is of very considerable interest ; it helps to explain why the ship achieved her wonderful work. Nothing was left to chance in the fashioning of her that could be taken away from chance. The experts were not satisfied ; even after their most elaborate calculations they had doubts ; the fear of excessive vibration, which can never be finally tested and proved until a ship is finished and fitted, troubled them. The men who had adopted experimental power made another decision requiring courage ; they put their doubts and fears to the test. The *Mauretania*, an almost completed ship, did what the wooden launch on the Northumberland dock had so often done ; she went out, but into the North Sea, to run up and down, to prove whether, although her official trials were already widely advertised and her first sailing date forecast, she would not have to be altered, and, if substantial alteration was required, to cancel her appointments and suffer the damage of gossip and rumour which the cancellation would entail. When the wooden launch ran up and down the dock there had been many occasions, heart-breaking for the men anxious for achievement, when the verdict had been " That won't do." Was the same verdict going to follow the almost finished *Mauretania's* unobtrusive expedition into the North Sea ? Imagination gets busy with the feelings of the men who ordered that expedition. If at that late stage serious trouble were proved, a slur would be cast on the ship which could not be removed. The matter could and would be hushed up, but in shipping circles and amongst sailors, at any rate, it could not be wholly hidden. That five-day expedition into the unfrequented parts of the North Sea certainly did not start without anxiety. But the men who were responsible for the ship had their policy : the best obtainable and nothing left to chance than can be taken away from chance. They held to that policy.

Secrecy, even now, is maintained about those five days in the North Sea, but there is a little tale about them worth the telling. It illustrates nicely how men faced facts directly. Speed, out on the North Sea, away from inquisitive shipping, was being worked up ; the great experimental engines were responding well, trimmers and firemen were satisfying the appetites of roaring furnaces ; on the control platform in the engine-room engineers and experts watched instruments eagerly. The dominant note of that scene in boiler and engine-rooms is obviously eagerness. The *Mauretania* was responding, she was giving the power which had been promised of her, she was working it up, from black squad to watching expert there was satisfaction, eagerness to see what more she could do. But the law of the sea that there is only one man in command of a ship applies equally to test runs as to working voyages. There was eagerness down on the bottom of the *Mauretania*, there was the final word which would excite or diminish that eagerness above her many decks. The ship was working up speed, she was really moving, she was delighting the eager men below. Then the bridge called the engine-room, the final word was spoken ; a considerable and immediate reduction in revolutions was ordered. " What in hell is the Old Man up to now ? " that might have been said—there is no record—by one or more of the disappointed men below, but it is next door to a certainty that all of them thought it. Why spoil things when everything was going well. Inquiries as to why were made, discreetly, because a commander at sea is a commander. The answer was simple and direct.

" Because," it stated, " I was being shaken off my bridge."

A sufficient answer, a comprehensive answer, an answer, in fact, which called for another, a practical one. The practical one was given, weights were re-distributed. The *Mauretania* returned to the Tyne. She did not shake, or even attempt to shake, another captain from his bridge.

On October 22nd, 1907, she left the Tyne, officially for the first, actually for the second, time. This was a public occasion for flags and whistles and crowds and noise. That night on Tyneside the pubs did a good business and men talked enthusiastically of the great ship which they had built. The *Mauretania* went north-about to Liverpool, so before she reached her home port she circled Scotland, the land which had built her sister and her rival. She commenced her trials on November 5th.

The course was between Corswall Point Light on the Wigtownshire coast to the Longships Light off the Land's End, a distance of 304 nautical miles, which should be covered in about twelve hours. The *Mauretania* was to run this course twice in each direction, steaming continuously for forty-eight hours and so getting the effects of the tides on the north and south runs balanced. On the first run south a moderate gale, of force seven, was blowing, for the first two hours four points on the port bow, for the remainder of the run dead ahead. The night was dark. That is official language which may be trans-lated into " blowing good and hearty and black as your hat." Commencing the test which was to decide whether she should actually become a Cunarder the *Mauretania* did not find pleasant conditions ; wind of force seven would set her singing, but she on that first run sang a song of speed. Humming, whining, whistling, she cut through that blackness into the moderate gale and averaged 26.28 knots. A breezy Sunday night at sea, but she seems to have enjoyed it. On Monday, steaming north, there was a calm sea with a light breeze astern, but tide and currents were adverse : she did not do so well, averaging 25.26 knots. On Monday night, going south again, there were light head winds, but the early part of the night was thick, with rain falling. Thick, that word is not used at sea unless it is meant. Picture the look-out and the men on the bridge straining their eyes to see into opaque blackness, fearful less something might appear out of the night too close to be avoided. A collision on her trials, even though it were no more than a bump, would do the *Maure-tania's* reputation no good. It could, however slight, scarcely do less than stigmatise her as an unlucky ship. But the bump in that thickness was likely to be a hearty one, for the ship averaged 27.36 knots on that run south. The weather cleared towards morning. As a horizon showed out of the murk there were men on that great new ship who knew relief. On the last run north on Tuesday the weather was favourable except for a head wind late in the afternoon and adverse tidal currents throughout ; the ship averaged exactly what she had done for the first run north, 25.26 knots. In 46 hours 44½ minutes of continuous steaming she had covered 1,216 miles of sea, maintaining an average of 26.04 knots. She had been designed for 25 knots ; it would do.

The *Mauretania* finished her long-distance trials about eight o'clock on that Tuesday evening and anchored for the night in her sister's territory near to the Skelmorlie mile, on the Clyde. Next morning at daybreak she commenced a series of progressive speed runs over the measured mile, working up from 18 to 26.03 knots. She finished her trials with two long-distance runs from Ailsa to Holy Isle and back, averaging on these 26.17 knots. That, again, would do.

The report, as printed in " Engineering," states that the turbines worked with remarkable steadiness, that there was no untoward feature, that the bearings were always cool. The steering mechanism was also proved most satisfactory. " With the rudder hard over, and all propellers running ahead, the diameter of the turning circle was but three and three-quarter lengths—a very good result." But there appears to have been a ship which might have reported otherwise on that result. The Admiralty, naturally, had representatives on board during the trials. A naval officer on her bridge wanted to be certain of what the *Mauretania* could do ; when she was running at full speed on the Clyde he requested that the wheel should be put hard over. It was put hard over, and the result was considered, in the *Mauretania*, very good. But she had just passed a tramp steamer, and the wave caused by her turning caused the tramp an unpleasant moment ; it nearly swamped her. What the company of the tramp had to say about flash liners that caused hard-working vessels to take it aboard green and solid in the Clyde is easy imagining ; if the word " good " came into the saying, the adjective which preceded is a perfectly safe bet.

Except when she encountered the Atlantic swell as she was running between the Tuskar and the Longships, her trials gave no opportunity of testing the *Mauretania's* behaviour in a seaway. It was, however, estimated from the length of the periods of the roll and the pitch in that Atlantic swell that the movement of the ship " need not be disturbing to passengers."

" A more important question "—to quote from the report of the trials published in " Engineering "— " from the point of view of the comfort of the passenger, has reference to vibration, and as so much has been said on this subject, especially by the uninformed, it may be well to consider the problem from the general standpoint before recording the results of careful observations on the *Mauretania's* trials."

That suggests that there had been and that there was talk, " especially by the uninformed," about vibration in the *Mauretania*. Something about those five days in the North Sea certainly appears to have leaked out. People were saying—as some people inevitably must—that this huge enormously expensive ship was bound to shake all comfort out of her passengers. It had become—according to the report quoted—a popular belief that the turbine, in itself a perfectly balanced engine, was the perfect cure for vibration. The report goes into detail to show that that popular belief was absurd ; it deals with impulses on each unit of propeller blade area which react on the structure of the ship ; it shows that the impulses due to one screw may synchronise with those produced by other screws and so produce vibration, however perfectly balanced engines and propellers may be. It goes on to say :

" This explanation must not be taken as apology for the two Cunard liners ; there is no need for any. The extent of the vibratory movement in the ships, considered as elastic structures, is exceptionally small . . . The high frequency of the impulses, however, tend to produce certain local movements in the lighter part of the superstructure ; but these move-ments have been overcome by local supports and stiffening. . . ."

" The lighter parts of the superstructure " ! One of those is the bridge. " These movements have been overcome " ! Henceforth the commander of the *Mauretania* is to remain unshaken at his post. Surely the authorities did not keep the secret of those five days in the North Sea as inviolate as they had hoped.

". . . in certain fittings . . . care is being taken to obviate that chatter and noise which suggest to the uninitiated abnormal vibration, when they are really due only to high frequency rather than to amplitude of motion. . . . But our analysis of the situation must not, as we have already said, be taken as apologetic . . . in many parts of the ship it was difficult to realise that she was steaming at 26 knots, and that the engines were developing about double the power hitherto exerted in the propulsion of any ship. . . . The final result is, undoubtedly, a great triumph for British shipbuilding."

And undoubtedly the writer of that report spoke the simple truth. The result was a great triumph for British shipbuilding ; but just how great the triumph was the world could not judge until the *Mauretania* had worked for twenty-seven years.

Did she vibrate ? The report of her trials quoted above answers that. Of course she did. Did she creak, and did her fittings sometimes chatter and rattle in a seaway ? Obviously. Did she, in heavy weather, cause disturbance to some of her passengers ? She did, acute disturbance, and to most of her passengers and often to many of her crew. Did she do these things excessively ? No, she did not. Consider her as an elastic structure, a delicately shaped steel shell filled with complication, which must be driven at high speed in fair weather and in foul. There must be give in her—stiffen her to the point of inelasticity and disaster follows. There must be violent movement of her if she is to sail the surface of violent seas. Cause her four 17,000 horse-power turbines to revolve each of her four screws more than one hundred and eighty times each minute, there must be vibration. She was a ship which went to sea, and these things belong, so far and certainly for some time yet to come, inescapably to ships on the sea. Her trials proclaimed her a fast ship, a staunch ship, a triumph of building. Only the years and the sea could prove her real worth. But to have written then of her that she would never be uncomfortable, that she would never exhibit the faults inseparable from ships would have been the sheerest folly. There were days and nights ahead of her—hundreds of them—when she was going to give every soul aboard her, from the most sea-sick scared passenger to the most sea-sickless sailor, acute discomfort, she was going to throw them all about and shake them, she was going to make the business of eating—for those who preserved a wish to eat—difficult, she was going to waste good liquor, smash crockery, damage fittings. She was, in fact, a ship whose business it was to face the seas's fury ; she was not an incarnation of a shipping agent's advertisement. It was to be her work to go through all weathers, fair and foul, as fast as safety would let her ; for that she was designed, and she did her designed work amazingly well and for an amazingly long time. That she did her work with no more discomfort, upon the bad occasions, to the human freight she carried than need be, that she did it with much less discomfort than many of her hard-driven kind became common knowledge. She could not perform miracles in Atlantic gales, or wholly disguise her power. But for the hundreds of men who served her and for thousands of the passengers whom she served she showed herself what she was—a good ship in a sea. There are, of course, passengers for whom no ship in any sea is good.

She was taken over by the Cunard Company, commissioned, made ready for her maiden voyage. The press was full of her ; she had come before the public to be experienced, praised and criticised. She was proclaimed a great sea beauty. Was she beautiful ? That, obviously, is a matter of individual taste. Some people of to-day, seeking only that which is newest, may find her, with her slender length and her great funnels, of the stone age ; there may still be living old marine conservatives who condemn her utterly because she had not schooner bows. Beauty follows fashions and raises controversies, so the word can be left alone. The *Mauretania* now only remains in pictures ; the pictures may not inspire. It is, however, a fact, not a statement of opinion, that to the majority of lovers of ships and the sea she stands apart from any other steamer, apart even from her sister, for fineness, for grace, for quality. To see her move was sheer joy.

On November 16th, 1907, very late in the season, when big liners on the Atlantic would normally be reaching the time for their annual refit, the *Mauretania* sailed from Liverpool for New York. She was given an adequate send-off ; she carried with her the confidence of her builders, her owners and her ship's company. It is scarcely possible that amongst all the men whose confidence she carried there was a single one who foresaw that more than a quarter of a century later she would be improving upon the records which she was setting out to create.

CHAPTER III

ROUTINE

SHIPS are inseparable from routine. Their ordinary average daily tasks are governed by it ; all action in emergency is carefully prepared for by it. In order to present any intelligible picture of the *Mauretania's* long working life, it is necessary first to give some outline of the routine aboard her, to sketch the working of her various departments, to give some description of what was done aboard her and for her between the opening of the bridge log of one voyage until the opening of the log for the next.

The *Mauretania* carried nine executive officers ; a commander, a staff-captain, a chief officer, senior and junior first, second and third officers. All of these officers, according to the agreement under which the building of the ship was subsidised by Government, had to belong to either the Royal Naval Reserve or the Royal Naval Fleet Reserve, and not less than half the crew had also to be naval reservists. All of the executive officers, naturally, held masters' certificates, and not a few of them had extra certificates. The commander had few routine duties beyond the completion of a not inconsiderable number of returns and reports ; he was, of course, entirely responsible for the ship and for everything which happened in her while she was officially in his hands. That does not mean while he was aboard her ; he might be ashore at Liverpool or New York and the ship still be officially in his hands. Opinions concerning the job of commanding great liners vary. Some passengers see the captain only as a man who appears to do very little work himself. Disgruntled members of shore staffs have been known to refer to captains as strangely limited beings, who live largely in cramped quarters and only emerge therefrom to exhibit their gold lace to admiring women or to swing their weight at the expense of their more intelligent fellows. A more average conception of them would be men carrying a more than common burden of responsibility with no more parade of the importance of their positions than is usual to most human beings who have reached high authority. But those people who like merchant captains as a race and those who dislike them will be in agreement about the heavy responsibility and the high authority of the commander of a ship like the *Mauretania*. To rule such a community wisely—and not to rule it wisely is not to rule it long—is no fool's job.

The staff-captain was the commander's understudy and second-in-command.

The other seven executive officers were watch-keepers, though the second officer kept no regular watch on the bridge while at sea. Watches at sea : even for the most land-minded sort there must surely be something for the imagination there. They are standardised for every civilised vessel which sails the seas, just divisions of time which long years of experience have shown to be convenient, but being the essence of a ship's life they demand some detailed attention. The officer of the watch, or the senior if there be more than one watch-keeper on duty at a time, is the man responsible for the ship at any given moment unless and until the commander has come upon the bridge and taken over command. Anything concerned with the ship which is not usual and routine, and many things which are normal have to be reported at once to the officer of the watch. It is his duty to record them, to deal with them or, if they merit it, to acquaint his captain with them immediately. If he should fail to let the commander know at once the things he ought to know, then the watch-keeper's life on that ship is likely to be a short one. If he should disturb his captain's sleep or amusement without real cause, his own comfort and pleasure is likely to suffer. He is a master mariner in charge, expected to know his job and do it.

To make the picture of responsibility at any time clear, the watches and the officers keeping them are tabulated :

Watch.	Time.	Officers.
First -	- 8.0 p.m. to midnight.	Junior 1st and Junior 3rd.
Middle	- Midnight to 4.0 a.m.	1st and 3rd.
Morning	- 4.0 a.m. to 8 a.m.	Chief and Junior 2nd.
Forenoon	- 8 a.m. to noon.	Junior 1st and Junior 3rd.
Afternoon	- Noon to 4 p.m.	1st and 3rd.
Dog Watches	4.0 p.m. to 6 p.m.	Chief and Junior 2nd.
	6.0 p.m. to 8 p.m.	

The cycle of watches begins not when the day changes its date but after, upon the average of the year, day has changed to night. The junior officer, if there be one watch-keeper only on duty, the junior of the seniors and the most junior of all, if there be two, keep it. The senior watch-keeper and the senior of the juniors, if there be two, keep the morning watch. Again the juniors keep the forenoon watch and the seniors the dog watches. Experience of centuries of watch-keeping has suggested the easiest and the most difficult times at sea ; the half-lights, the changes from day to night and back again, demand the men presumed to be most capable. Remembrances of " stand to " in trenches will remind many men that dawn and sundown are not on the sea alone considered troublesome periods.

In port the three senior watch-keepers, that is the chief, first and junior first officers, are on duty from nine in the morning till five in the afternoon, or " as necessary." The " as necessary " cuts both ways, it may mean shore leave or continuous duty, should the ship require it. The junior watch-keepers, when in port, keep between them the ordinary sea watches. So at any time, when the ship was not in the hands of a shore staff, refilling or undergoing overhaul, there was an executive officer in charge. Embarking and disembarking the chief officer supervised generally, the first took general charge of all seamen, the junior first was on the bridge, the second was concerned with gangways and mails, the junior second with gangways and specie, the third with gangways and after baggage, the junior third with gangways and forward luggage. Entering and leaving port and docking, the two officers who kept watch at sea together shared the same duties : chief and junior second on the forecastle head, first and third on the after bridge and after moorings, junior first and third on the navigating bridge, while the second had charge of tending the pilot, the tenders, the shell doors, and in docking, the gangways and mails.

If boat stations were ordered, the chief officer took charge of all boats on the port side, the first of all boats on the starboard side, and the other five watch-keepers of boat groups. In case of fire the chief officer took general charge at the fire, the first commanded the seamen, the junior first went to the navigating bridge, the second commanded the break-down party, the junior second the bucket and blanket men, the third controlled the fire extinguisher, the junior third went to the navigating bridge, where his special job was ventilation. If the ship were in collision the chief officer again took charge of opera-tions, the first controlled the handling of the collision mat, the junior first again went to the navigating bridge, the second was concerned with ensuring that bulkhead doors and scuttles were closed, the junior second was responsible for the bottom lines of the collision mat, the third for the fore guy, and the junior third for the after guy of the mat. At the alarm of man overboard the chief officer took charge of the lowering of the accident boat, of which one on either side is always swung outboard and ready when at sea, the first went away in charge of the boat, the second and junior second officers stood by to assist if required, the third went to look out on the after bridge, the junior first and the junior third to the navigating bridge.

Man overboard is almost certainly the commonest of emergencies in a great liner at sea. Passengers with suicidal tendencies seem to receive some peculiar stimulus from ocean wideness, and are inclined to go over the side. In bad weather when a ship is taking it aboard green, in fair weather when hands are careless and inexperienced, accidents do happen. A great ship travelling at full speed cannot be pulled up in a few lengths. At the call of man overboard the officer of the watch does not, usually, indulge

in theatrical gestures and fling the telegraph lever to
" Full astern," caring for nothing but the human
life in danger. It has been done, though not in the
Mauretania, and the watch-keeper down in the engine
room, out of sight and sound of the cause, has accepted
the emergency as great, and has obeyed the order.
But straight from full ahead to full astern demands
a very special occasion, and is a proceeding liable
to be costly. One ship indulging in the performance
at the command of an over-zealous junior, stripped
her turbine blades like cutting cheese, and thereafter,
or so the story runs, was as much concerned with
borrowing handkerchiefs and articles of underclothing
from the passengers, in order to fashion sails with
which she could make the nearest port, as with
recovering the man whom she had dropped.
Normally, when someone has gone overboard, the
ship turns and gets an accident boat away as quick
as she can get it ; she steams in a circle round the
spot where the person in the sea should be. So, to
increase the chance of rescue, the simple alarm of
man overboard is not one which any sailor would
give ; he would add to it the side of the ship from
which the man has gone, and give the officer on the
bridge a chance to turn the right way. Routine
provides for this, the commonest of alarm calls,
officers and men have their stations and defined
duties, but in practice it is the only emergency in
which set procedure is not likely to be followed. The
first available officer and the first men available for
a crew take the accident boat away. The rules for
the occasion are detailed, but the occasion does not
demand the ship's company at stations. At other
times of alarm proper stations are vitally important ;

at this the boat away and the ship turning in the right direction come before set rules.

Under ordinary circumstances at sea the second officer of the *Mauretania* did not keep a watch. He was in charge of the mails in a ship where the mail cargo was neither small nor unimportant. But in the event of any of the six men who kept watches being incapacitated he took on their duties as well as his own. He was, apart from mails, a stand by, but not an idle one.

An eight-hour day on the bridge in any weather the Atlantic chose to send did not end the watch-keeper's normal day ; they had not a few returns to keep up to date, forty of them to be exact, for the information of the managers and the marine superintendent. These covered a range from charts in the chart-room on the bridge to cargo pilferage and damaged baggage down below. There was another set of books and records to be kept by the navigating officers for the guidance of themselves ; there were twenty of these, amongst them six different logs, and they recorded from day to day, some of them from hour to hour, all the happenings in the navigation department of the ship. Occasional and quarterly returns were also required as a make-weight. A government officer would have thought nothing of it, but to the man responsible for the various returns and reports they were, after long spells of exacting work, more than sufficient. Little which happened to or in the ship was not revealed, nothing of ship's importance was omitted. Study of the paper work discloses a uniformity of style amongst the writers, facts and facts only are recorded in the fewest possible words, considerable use is made of set phrases. The

sea in all the majesty of its fury never gets superlatives ;
a full gale, or a hurricane are simply that, they are
never raging tempests.

The watch-keepers of the *Mauretania's* navigating
bridge earned their pay with a variety of duties, but
there was one which they were not called upon to
perform. The social racket was barred to them ;
they were expected to make themselves agreeable to
passengers when they met them, but they were not
expected to meet them too often, to dine with them
or to dance with them. That sort of thing was held
to be good only for ships which sail wider seas, when
the voyage is counted in weeks not days. The
Mauretania was virtually a giant ferry boat, essentially
an express carrier. She was always being driven,
and driving her was considered a whole-time job for
the drivers. So, in her first class dining saloon there
was a table for seven which, except in port, was never
occupied by seven men together. Inquisitive
passengers, and there were many such, were informed
that the watch-keeping officers sat there, that they
did not preside at tables of passengers and linger
chatting over meals, because they were busy men
and none of them ever spent a full night in bed.
That table set apart for seven symbolises the
Mauretania's job. Weeks between ports at a comfortable speed on calm tropic seas were never part of it.
The men who shared watches could eat to satisfy
their appetites ; their meals were not turned into a
social function, when they must be careful to amuse
the stranger suppliers of the Company's dividends,
who sat with them.

The Commander had social duties, but he also
had a deputy. When the weather was exacting, or

the driving of the ship more urgent than usual, or the Old Man not in a social mood, a steward would convey a polite message to the chosen few at the captain's table : " The Commander's compliments, but he regrets he cannot leave the bridge to-night." The staff-captain had to step in then ; to dine in the saloon, to make himself pleasant to and seen by passengers afterwards. But, when the business became too troublesome, he had the excuse of his duties. That left the surgeons and the purser and his assistants. The surgeons could, if necessary, murmur of desperate cases and depart, ostensibly, on their mission of healing. His assistants, anyhow, were only small beer and had their duties mostly elsewhere, so the purser himself was left as the one officer of the ship who could not, without manufacturing something in the nature of acute emergency, escape from social duties. This may suggest that the officers of the *Mauretania* should be considered men who regarded passengers as unmitigated nuisances, which is quite absurd. Very naturally they did not ; not one of them would have held to his job for long had he done so. The officers of passenger liners, as such, have to be good mixers and able to make a decent show with a constant flow of strangers, most of them ignorant of the realities of sea life. When visions of loveliness were about, and there were usually many, the watch-keepers at their table apart undoubtedly regretted that they were prevented from playing host. Being essentially human, sailor officers would enjoy feeling the weight of their authority and their position amongst passengers, not a few of them distinguished, temporarily estranged from the values of their accustomed world and ready, in most cases, to acknowledge to the full the value of ship's currency. But for the average of these hard-working men the chance of escape at the end of a full day had attractions. Bye and large, after years of it, day in, day out, facing, with rare exceptions, the same sort of crowd last voyage, this voyage and the next, an hour or so of slippers, and a pipe and a book before turning in frequently outweighed the joy of impressing with gold lace and breezy sailor tales. The purser must often have envied his brother officers their immunity from social duties or their easy escape from them. First class passengers on the Atlantic have a habit of beginning the day late and finishing it early. Officers, beginning early and finishing when they can, can be excused from really enjoying the last half of the habit.

The hotel department of the *Mauretania*—since that strangely inexact description seems inescapable—does not require detailed description. Take, broadly, the purser as the manager, the chief steward as the *maître d'hôtel* and imagination can readily supply the rest. The purser was the responsible head of the whole passenger department of the ship ; the chief steward—ranking in the Cunard Company as a junior officer—was principally concerned with the arrangements of feeding the ship's complement. The work in the steward's department approximated generally, admitting certain important exceptions, to work in hotels on shore. Food had to be stored, cooked and served, bedrooms and private sitting-rooms and public rooms had to be kept clean and their occupants attended, bars, busy bars, had to supply a prompt service of drinks. That is all hotel business to be run on accepted hotel lines ; but after that the ship steps in and makes the hotel description altogether inadequate. Everything required by the steward's department was purchased and provided by the superintendent caterer, a shore official of the Company, in consultation with the chief steward. Every man and woman in the department—and they formed a large majority of the crew—was engaged by the same shore official : to engage the staff outside an hotel is not usual. In the matter of food, stewards, drinks, stores, the *Mauretania* took what she was sent from the shore. Even the skeleton of every menu for every meal throughout the voyage was provided by the shore staff ; the chief steward and the chief chef might alter details, but they must preserve the general form. The staff of the department made suggestions about passengers' tastes and wishes ; they filled in quantities of returns and drew up numbers of reports about them, but they did not control the supply. That was the affair of the superintendent caterer in Liverpool and his assistants in New York and elsewhere.

But where the hotel description breaks down principally is over the matter of classes. The hotel which accommodates Mayfair, Bloomsbury and the Mile End Road under one roof is unknown and likely to remain so. The *Mauretania* carried within her hull the rich, the people of modest income and the very poor, and they were all important to her. The hotel description is bad enough, anyhow, but when it is mainly used to convey the impression of a floating palace of luxury it becomes purely absurd. The third-class accommodation, where there was nothing approaching luxury, was as essential to the *Mauretania* as the regal suites. Combining the services of three classes in one confined space, looking after millionaires on one floor and emigrants from Eastern Europe on another would entail drastic re-organisation in most hotels. Attempting to subject the combination to definite rules and regulations for their safety and for the well-being of the establishment would probably lead to the speedy closing of the hotel doors. The chief steward had not in his department the powers of ordering and providing which hotel managers have ; on the other hand, he had powers and duties which do not belong to the management of any hotel. The *Mauretania* was a passenger liner ; she was not a floating hotel.

When she was first commissioned the *Mauretania* carried in the steward's department one man for every four passengers ; later she altered that to one man for every three passengers carried. Every one of those men and women—for though the women were in a very small minority they were there—had a job principally concerned with food or some form or other of domestic or clerical service ; every one of them had another duty—to know the shortest way to a particular lifeboat, to guide passengers there in case of need, to be of assistance in the boat if required. Boats manned by stewards and the troglodytic oddments from the storerooms and other hidden places of the *Mauretania* took part in races in port, and were known to win them. That is getting away from hotel service.

The crew, which included all the various ratings in the several departments, signed the ship's articles before each sailing. They signed on for a particular voyage. Many of them did that for years on end, and some of them, owing to the long life of the *Mauretania*, did that in her during all their working lives at sea. Perhaps they never read the articles which they signed, but they were all acquainted with the purport of them.   They bound themselves to a ship for a certain voyage.   Physically, whatever their dissatisfaction with the service to which they had bound themselves, they could not leave the ship until they reached a port ; legally and morally, if they left her in New York they became guilty of desertion.   They might be fed up with their employment, but they had pledged themselves to a service for a period ; they could not think better of it and simply not turn up for work next day.   If they elected to desert in New York they parted with their papers and the means of finding another situation such as they had left.   At sea they might have grievances, or imagine that they had them, but the " down tools " remedy or the refusal to work was not theirs ; that became a crime, not lightly considered by any of them, called mutiny on the high seas.   For the period of the voyage they were enlisted to a service, and refusal to give the service required of them by the commander of the ship during that voyage, as they knew, would be regarded by magistrates ashore as a punishable offence and by men of their trade as a stupid folly.   Outcry, remedies, strikes were matters that must await the ending of the voyage.   Discipline at sea commanded.   The atmosphere in which work is done colours the work.   To see the work of hotel servants and of ships' stewards and cooks and pantrymen the same shade is, surely, to be colour blind.

In her galleys the *Mauretania* had to prepare a considerable variety of food.   First-class passengers expected and obtained the best.   Men and women in high places, millionaires, stars of the theatrical and, later, the film world, artists and writers in popular favour, idle people with plenty of money, others hoping to give the impression of having plenty, adventurers and staid men of business : they had all paid for good food and intended to have it. The man who produced verbal, if not documentary, evidence that certain expensive dishes could be more readily obtained on other lines was the terror of the catering department. He might be taken at his proper value, as a fellow who, having paid a first-class fare, considered it first-class behaviour to complain ; on the other hand, passengers might listen to his tales of better treatment on rival lines. He and his kind helped to maintain an unnecessary lavishness in the first-class galley. The second-class food did not suffer from that extravagance ; it was of the plain and good, value-for-money order, supplied to the least exacting of the *Mauretania's* passengers. Down in the third-class the daily menus demanded more consideration ; mixed races had to be satisfied, and unless they were given their national dishes there would be more talk of the advantages of rival lines. In the third-class galley there was a small compartment, scarcely more than a recess, with a Hebrew inscription over the entrance ; in it Kosher cooks prepared Kosher food for the ubiquitous migratory Jew. That Kosher kitchen typifies much ; it was one of the necessary adjuncts of a full passenger list. The middle-eastern Jew and the jaded, monied idler at the two extremes, but both receiving careful attention. Gastronomically the *Mauretania* was not quite an ordinary hotel.

At one time a man who had made more than a

voyage or two, before settling down ashore, as a ship's surgeon did not advance his prestige in the medical world. Doctors of passenger ships were popularly supposed to have minimum professional qualifications and maximum distaste for work. Journeys, it has been alleged, as far as the engine department to treat firemen with cramp or other complaints of their kind did not appeal to the surgeons, so they commonly supplied four large bottles of standard mixtures labelled A, B, C, D, to be kept in the far-off parts of the ship and to be administered by the engineering staff as directed. The mixtures were accordingly administered by engineers as the occasion arose, but not always as directed. A quarter dose from each of the four bottles was in some cases held to be a more likely remedy for a condition that might have been incorrectly diagnosed by a layman. The recipients of the mixed mixtures are said seldom to have suffered ill effects. Firemen in coal-burners had to have strong constitutions, and medicine with an extra kick in it had, probably, a fine moral stimulus. Those days had gone when the *Mauretania* was first commissioned. Her surgeon and his assistant did not damage themselves in their profession by taking service in her ; they were not holders of minimum qualifications. With a practice of three thousand patients and the certainty that if they shipped anyone at one of the terminal ports whose condition at the other would involve refusal of pratique for the ship, they would be faced with many explanations, they had a real job of work to do.

The *Mauretania* from the start carried two wireless operators. She was, therefore, in the van of advance.

The *Titanic* had not gone down ; big ships still carried only one operator, a man who in the course of six days at sea required food and sleep. To keep a continuous wireless watch was then progressive. The *Mauretania* kept it. But her range for sending and receiving messages was in the neighbourhood of two hundred miles, and the wireless room, as she first sailed with it, seems to-day something at which a schoolboy would raise hoots of laughter. There were changes in the ship throughout her life, important changes, but substantially the vessel which left Liverpool on November 16th, 1907, was the same as that which arrived at Southampton from her last Atlantic voyage in October, 1934. Her first wireless apparatus, however, a small collection of instruments on a table beneath the curtained porthole of a converted cabin, had not even the faintest resemblance to the chamber of complication from which she finally informed Southampton of the hour at which she would arrive.

In outlining the staff and duties of the departments of the ship the engine-room is taken last, with purpose. It was there that the *Mauretania's* reputation was made, there that her individuality proved itself. There is no getting round the fact. She was at all times very well, sometimes brilliantly, commanded ; she was never, even during the war, when there was a shortage of skilled men, anywhere, from stem to sternpost, ill served ; she deserved and she got the best that could be found for her. That does not alter the simple fact that her engine-room was the deciding factor of her success. Many things and men contributed to the result, but her engines, her engineers and the hands under them finally determined her unique place in the history of steamships. So they come last.

As first commissioned she carried 393 officers and men in the engineering department : 33 officers, 3 refrigerating engineers, 204 firemen, 120 trimmers, 33 greasers. These men had to tend furnaces which consumed 1,000 tons of coal a day and engines which developed 68,000 horse-power. They had to maintain enormous power in engines of a kind which had never been asked to produce such power before. Up on the bridge the navigating officers, directly they had got used to the feel of the great ship and had made acquaintance with her individual ways, were upon familiar ground. Before they had finished their first two-hour trick at the wheel the quarter masters would have found touch ; they had to steer a ship larger than any they had steered before, that was all. The steward's department did what they had been trained to do upon a bigger scale, and with more conveniences for doing it, than they had done before : nothing particularly exacting in that. Down below the 393 had to produce from the experimental engines a speed which many instructed men then considered impossible, and had to maintain that speed. If they failed, however beautifully she steered and rode the seas, however well she fed her passengers and however comfortably she housed them, the *Mauretania* failed. That was particularly exacting.

The chief engineer had a position different to anyone else in the ship—that, of course, applies to any chief in any steamship. He was a qualified expert in his profession in charge of a highly technical department ; he was the only man who could meet an order of his captain with " That can't be done, sir," and get away with it. Naturally he would later have to qualify any can't-be-done decision, but he could make it. He was the final authority where his engines were concerned ; his captain was a layman then. So good understanding between captain and chief was of enormous importance ; upon it rested the certainty that no order inside possibility should ever be turned down.

Under the chief there was a staff-chief. He was his senior's deputy, but, unlike the staff captain, he had other set duties. All the auxiliary machinery of the ship was in his particular charge. The same watches were kept down below as on the navigating bridge when at sea. There were three senior seconds and three junior seconds ; the remainder of the engineer officers ranked simply as juniors, although many of them had specialists' jobs. They were all fully certificated. During each watch there was one senior and one junior second engineer in charge of engine-room and boiler rooms. One or other of them was always on the starting platform, where on many dials and indicators he could read much of what was happening to his charge, where he could receive either by telegraph or telephone orders from the bridge. Two juniors, in addition, were always moving about the engine-room ; four juniors, one in each of the boiler-rooms, watched and supervised ; one electrician in the engine-room and two about the ship completed the tally of officers on watch together. By day only there were added to them one junior and two plumbers who roamed the decks looking for trouble.

The chief, like the commander up above, made his formal daily rounds. Either he or his staff chief saw to it that all was well last thing at night. Emergency brought either or both down again ; love of engines did not fetch them down, but kept them down, unless all was really well.

Each man of those 393 had his boat station high up above. As they moved about their work, always under artificial light, all sight of sea and what might be happening on it shut out from them, stooping to pass through the low, narrow doorways of bulkheads with the heavy sliding doors above, which closing cut off escape, they would have been less than human —which most certainly they were not—if they had not given occasional attention to the unlikelihood of some of them reaching the open air if emergency should call them to it.

Assume the *Mauretania* to be sailing, westward, at noon ; then her voyage, as her logs recorded it, began some time before that. She wanted, as a routine performance, eighteen hours in which to raise steam and warm up the engines. Watches commenced down below in the engineer department at six o'clock on the evening before sailing. The first watch to go on duty would have to be in the ship before that. Some of the firemen and trimmers might arrive on board more or less drunk. If on the great occasion of her first sailing some of them did not do so it was greatly to their credit. They were, nearly to a man, Liverpool Irish, men who could and did justify the dreadful demands of feeding the furnaces of a hard-driven coal-burning liner better than any other race, or mixture of races, in the world. Brutish men often, because their skilled work made brutal demands, but workers and loyal to the right kind of handling, loyal also to their ship.

At sea, always assuming them to be properly handled, they worked in four hour spells, two of those for each man during the twenty-four hours, lifting and placing individually five tons of coal each day. For the trimmers, shovelling the coal from the bunkers, wheeling it to piles handy for the men who fed the fires, in a ship rolling and pitching, seemingly anxious to make a jest of muscle-saving, balanced swing of pick and shovel in an atmosphere choking with coal dust, in a tropic temperature, it was not weaklings' work. For the firemen, the men who put the coal from the handy piles into the hungry fires, it was something that often gave pause to the men who drove them at it. The thing in those hard-driven ships was reduced to an affair of intensive minutes. Seven for feeding coal into the apertures whose breath scorched the feeders, seven for wielding the long slicers cutting and clearing clinkers, seven for raking over, and the man who was behind his job on any seven minutes a weakly, incompetent fool amongst his fellows. A pause, a short one, then a gong announced the beginning of another of the seven-minute bursts. That for four hours on end in coal dust that no ventilation could remove, scorched by furnaces, half choked with the gases produced by watering white-hot clinkers and ashes. When they had finished their watches they often took the air with chests bared to the Atlantic cold; that astonished some people who had not seen them working. They could not get drink aboard, so they toiled and ate, good food and plenty of it, roughly served, and slept exhausted and, when they got ashore, often got drunk and kept drunk. That disgusted some people—possibly the sort of people who purport

to regret the day when oil superseded coal as fuel
on hard-driven ships. The Liverpool Irish did their
work better, according to the men who know, than
any others in the world. Next to them, in the
opinion of many experts, were the Hungarians.
But—and here all the engineers, who kept those
efficient and very tough men to their deadly spells
of seven minutes, agree—it was work the passing of
which calls for no regret.

The work of that first watch at sea in the evening
would be difficult because the drunks would be in-
efficient, and the not-so-drunks hard put to it to
bear the extra strain. But, with proper handling,
the work went on. Topsides the *Mauretania* was
smoother running.

During the night before raising steam the ship was
in the hands of a navigating watch-keeper, a boat-
swain and his mate, six seamen, three boys, two
carpenters and two masters-at-arms. These were
her official guardians, but there would be other
people in her, sleeping and attending to rush jobs
which were not included in routine. The routine
work for the official guardians during that night
when the ship lay alongside, curiously dead and
inert, like all ships resting from the sea, dimly lit,
largely silent, was not exacting. The bridge log
would record merely that lights, moorings and gangways had been duly inspected and that the officer
of the watch had gone his rounds. At eight in the
morning the loading of cargo was resumed and the
Mauretania took on some appearance of activity. At
ten a buisness began which in British ships is no
formality. The Board of Trade Inspectors came
aboard and became inquisitive. A boat here and a

boat there was picked out and examined ; it was manned, swung outboard, rigged, lowered, and cast off when in the water. All fire appliances were inspected and tested. Down below in the engine and boiler-rooms there was more inspecting and testing and passing. At about five in the afternoon loading cargo ceased, to be resumed later, if necessary. The ship was then nearer to her sailing and becoming more herself. That night was more active.

Before six o'clock the first of the firemen and trimmers were aboard ; at intervals throughout the night, so as to be there for duty when their watches began, the remainder arrived. They did not observe strict silence in arriving ; faults might be found with their deportment and conversation ; the masters-at-arms were called upon to mix tact with firmness ; but the men rolled up for duty through the night, though some of them could not immediately perform it and were qualifying for an appearance later before the chief and a verdict of " logged for five shillings."

All the officers, except perhaps the commander, would come aboard that night. Many of them would dine in the ship, so would some of the shore staff and representatives of the management. In the early hours of the morning, round about three o'clock, the second officer was busy with the arrival, checking and stowing of mails. The hour at which the mails began to come aboard and the time when loading cargo was resumed were usually on that night the only entries in the bridge log, other than reports of rounds, lights, moorings and gangways.

At seven in the morning all members of the crew not already on board joined the ship. Some of them in those far-off days of individual liberty might have taken advantage of the early opening of dockside public-houses, but the number would be small. Stewards, anyhow, had immediately important business in front of them. They had to get their lists of the passengers allotted to them and to judge as best they could from the names and descriptions the type of passengers they were to serve. Familiar names would be welcomed or regretted, unknown ones would be optimistically but shrewdly considered. At eight o'clock the crew were mustered for the Board of Trade inspection, and were afterwards put through boat drill. At nine the main engines, steering gear, whistles, telegraphs, telephones, watertight doors and many other details were reported and entered in the bridge log as correct. The *Mauretania* was then ready for her passengers.

Below the watch-keeping engineers were at their stations ; the pressure of steam was rising and the engines warmed. The watch-keeping navigating officers took on their embarkation duties. Each gangway had an officer in charge of it, and not far from the ship's officer an unobtrusive person from Scotland Yard who practised observance. But as the trains arrived and their loads came aboard it was not the police only who practised observance. The group at the head of the gangway, officer, leading steward, master-at-arms would be as keen to recognise ship's nuisances as old acquaintances or friends. Being warned of the arrival of someone given to making trouble is a help in suppressing the nuisance.

When specie was being taken aboard the junior second officer met it and accompanied it to the strong-room, where the commander and the purser

locked it up, each retaining his own key. A
curiously unspectacular performance : wooden boxes
of gold, totalling perhaps some vast fortune, carried
by drab porters, accompanied by impassive clerk-
like persons in bowler hats, being shown the way
by a junior officer. One feels that the commander
ought to have saluted the precious burden while
multiple forms of receipt were formally signed and
sealed. But the fortune was locked away with all
the appearance of a wholly dull proceeding.

Passengers immediately after embarking were the
particular trial of the purser and his staff. The scene
has been too often described to require any further
description.

While the passengers were still crowding the gangways the pilot came aboard and passed the time of
day and the latest marine gossip with any officers
on the bridge. " All friends " having been warned,
rewarned, and finally shepherded ashore, all gangways but one in charge of the second officer were
landed. The bugle sounded, the watch-keeping
navigating officers went to their stations and the
commander appeared on the bridge. A few men,
shore staff and officials left the ship at the last moment
and the second officer stood at the head of the gangway, cocking his head at an awkward angle to watch
the bridge, waiting for his captain's signal, a nod or
a raising of the hand, never by any conceivable
chance a bawled order. On nine occasions out of
ten, with the punctuality of a mail train, the last
gangway would be landed at the exact moment
advertised for sailing and the orders to let go all
would have been given within the next few minutes.
Directly the tugs cast off the bugle sounded another

call and the navigating officers and seamen took on watch duties. A search for stowaways was made ; the passengers, assuming the ship to have sailed at noon, were fed, and then, after a reasonable period for digestion, were mustered at their boat stations. That done, the *Mauretania* reverted to sea routine. She called at Queenstown, later in her career at Cherbourg, for more mails and possibly a few passengers, then headed westward for America.

The entries in the bridge log during the days at sea were, normally, prosaic records of the fact that the senior officer of each watch had gone his rounds, that various set duties had been performed, compasses checked, lookouts, lights, wells, ventilation reported ; quite a comprehensive but, normally, scarcely interesting record of things examined and found correct. The correctness of other entries in the log would have been disputed by many of the passengers, especially those conveniently situated in the second class, nicely adjacent to the propellers. But when the ship was being driven, which was at all times on her ordinary business, there were even persons in the first-class paying high rates for their staterooms who would have found, had they happened to read it, immoderation in an estimate by the officer of the watch that there was a fresh breeze and a moderate sea.

Those estimates of weather conditions entered in the bridge log were continuous, but the period of entry varied considerably ; so did the entries concerned with the revolutions of the turbines. Sometimes the engines would be full ahead for a whole watch or for the whole of many watches ; sometimes the weather would be entered hourly, but no more.

Against those comfortable happenings there might
be set entries at intervals of a few minutes : revolutions went up and down, keeping pace with the terse
statements about wind and sea and visibility.   When
the log had much to say, one deduction is safe : the
commander was not in his bed or showing his gold
lace to passengers.   He was quite close to the chart-
table where the watch-keeper was making close
entries.

The officers of the watch, or one of them, whenever
he could get a horizon and the sun or the stars took
a sight to make sure of the position.   He did not
wait for a fixed hour to fix his ship, because with
northern weather the precious horizon might take
it into its head to vanish.   The noon formality, with
officers checking each other's observations, was a
formality and dependent on the weather.   Assurance
as to where on the Atlantic Ocean the *Mauretania*
might happen to be did not wait for that.   Whenever possible the position was fixed, pencilled with
a mark on the chart, and recorded in due course in
the log.   The bridge log dealt with routine, weather,
the ship's movement, but all news of the ship came
up to the bridge.   Conditions might be bad, the
watch-keepers uncertain about calling the commander, when one of them might be called from
strained watching to the telephone to be informed
of the terrific news that the hot water for certain
bathrooms on lower C deck was running cold.   He
would pass that valuable information on to the engineering department, record it in the proper place,
and turn back to the difficult mood of the sea ; but
he would not feel surprised or annoyed at the nature
of the message, because the officer of the watch on

the bridge is in sole charge of the ship and must be informed of all the troubles and quite a lot of things which are not troubles.

A ship being a small space and highly organised, little goes on in her which is not known to her officials, who, like doctors and solicitors, are largely silent about their knowledge. Night watchmen see things and report them to the proper quarter because it is the ship's business to know.

Passenger routine in the *Mauretania* varied considerably with the class of passenger. Few first-class passengers breakfasted in their saloon ; all third-class passengers who had appetites did in theirs. There is a story of young English athletes returning in the second class from a considerable defeat by American universities who liked to lie abed. The staff captain on his rounds did not disturb their slumber on the first day eastward. Later that day he made their acquaintance and yarned pleasantly about all sorts of things, including ships. Next day the cabins of the youthful athletes were unoccupied and ready for the morning inspection, the defeated English runners strolling contentedly about the decks. The first-class passengers in the *Mauretania* had, in reason, no daily routine except that of their own making, which was generally not to smell the sea air until afternoon, but to make lengthy acquaintance with the conditioned air of the public rooms at night ; the third class were ruled by a time-table of meals and lights out. For some tastes the third class had the best of the morning.

During the voyage the second officer inspected the mail daily, and before the *Mauretania* had made her landfall he had it, in most cases, stacked under shelter on the promenade of C deck. When the mail was a heavy one it was stacked and placed under guard several hours in advance. The guards were not always silent, a habit which annoyed the engineer officers, whose cabin windows faced the pile of mail-bags ; so the zeal of a navigator would come in for criticism. But the second officer could doubtless meet his critics fairly ; the time given him to unload the mails was not lavish.

The ship stopped and picked up the pilot off the Ambrose Light, proceeding immediately he was aboard. In roughly another hour she arrived at quarantine and anchored. The port doctor came aboard. The mail tenders arrived and made fast on either side. Having granted pratique, the doctor left and the immigration authorities came aboard. The mails were unloaded into the tenders alongside ; immigrants were dealt with and transferred to their tenders. In approximately four hours' time from the moment of stopping after the ocean passage the *Mauretania* proceeded ; and she berthed to disembark the remainder of her passengers about two hours later. Having disembarked them—occasionally one or two were returned to her as unfit for entry into the United States and had to be taken home again—she reverted to port watches and conditions, but not to idleness.

She would have, the number varying according to the conditions of Atlantic trade, some days at New York. She was bunkered, she took in such luxury stores as she required, she was cleaned inside and out. There was quite a lot of " spit and polish " to be done before she could be passed as ready for her return. During these days in New York all ranks got shore leave according to their importance and merit and

according to their responsibilities and duties. That
shore leave made those who served the ship for long
almost as familiar with New York as they were with
Liverpool, or later, with Southampton ; it robbed
them effectively of any insularity. Occasionally some
of the crew did not return from shore leave, though
most of these men, probably, the burst over, shipped
again under less pleasant conditions, the sea being
their only calling. Others returned from shore leave
with a scramble, caught their ship by a small margin
and suffered for their temporary inability to perform
their duties by contributing a portion of their pay.
Having completed her turn round, the *Mauretania*
went through the same embarkation routine, except
that there was no inquisitive Board of Trade to inspect
her, and, with a new crowd of passengers aboard,
untied for the eastward passage. On this passage
she followed a different lane of sea in a slightly
different mood. Eastward, although she was a ferry-
boat making short voyages, when judged by the
standard of ships which cross the world, there would
be the homeward-bound feel throughout her crew.
She called at Queenstown, dropping mails ; she disembarked passengers and cargo at Liverpool some
three weeks after she had left the port. The voyage
was ended ; she paid off.

The voyage was ended, but not the *Mauretania's*
routine. The shore staff fell upon her for their spell
of routine. " Spit and polish," more intensive and
more comprehensive than in New York, was carried
out. She had a minor refit each time that she
finished a voyage. She bunkered again, since owing
to the prodigious appetite for coal she could not
carry much more fuel than was required to see her,

with a decent margin for the chances of the sea, once across the Atlantic. That bunkering deserves a little attention. It was a filthy business, anyhow. Those strange persons who speak of coal burning with regret must be either coal-owners or ignorant of the mess and discomfort of coal dust everywhere. Sometimes it was more than mess and extra labour.

The *Mauretania* and her sister, although arrangements had been made for their accommodation, were, when they were commissioned, at times a little too much for the Port of Liverpool. On certain neap tides she could not coal alongside, but had to lie at the Cunard Buoy in the Sloyne and fill her bunkers there. The anchorage in the Sloyne was open, exposed to weather and tides, under bad conditions there was plenty of movement on the water. The coaling of the *Mauretania* at the Cunard Buoy was, during the years when it took place, one of the discussed events of Merseyside life. The men who did the job were carefully selected—they had need to be—and specially trained. Pride went to the work as well as skilled performance, for the men selected could show themselves amongst other riverside workers and riverside women certainly as no weaklings. The lighters made fast alongside and the coal was man-handled into the ship. Platforms were rigged and manned ; men below filled baskets, not small ones, and these were hove up by hand to the first platform, and so on up, to be emptied into the coal ports and passed down again to be refilled. The business is primitive and immemorial ; it still goes on in many ports of the world where coal burners call and must lie at anchor when bunkering. But now, except in outlying places, the method is obsolete ; these days the men who do it are usually lithe natives. The work is always hard ; when there is a lop on the water and the lighters are uneasy it is difficult ; when conditions are bad it is very dangerous. A man can injure himself or kill himself by a little carelessness or lack of knowledge of his job. Those Merseyside coal-heavers, being specially selected and proud of their selection, made a point of scorning bad conditions. It took a lot to stop them from letting the riverside have a laugh at them " Giving the *Mary* 'er coal." There were times, not a few, when the officers of the *Mauretania*, trained in driving, had with lighters grinding and plunging alongside to settle the matter summarily. They cast off the hawsers and ordered the tug to tow the lighter to safety. The *Mary* had to wait for her coal.

The secret of the *Mauretania's* success is variously given. But this was surely part of it : from the time when she was no more than a rapidly changing conception, from the days when the wooden launch was busy with alterations in the Northumberland Dock, through all the years when she was in commission, living her routined life backwards and forwards across the Atlantic, this inanimate steel ship commanded a singular and loving pride from almost every soul who served her.

CHAPTER IV

MAKING REPUTATION

THE *Mauretania* did not jump into immediate fame. She acquired it comparatively slowly. When the *Lusitania* made her maiden voyage in September, 1907, and crossed the Atlantic westward without being in any way hurried at an average speed of 23.01 knots and followed this on her next westward crossing by taking the record with an average of 23.993 knots—how her owners must have wished that they could have made it a round 24.00, which would have looked so much better—even pessimists had to admit that the chances were good that the two Cunarders, about which there had been so much talk and feeling, might do what the nation's money had backed them to do. November is not an ideal month in which to make Atlantic records, but the *Mauretania* was ready and she had to go. Her sister had already proved that she was not a failure and, to the experts, that in time she was likely to give the full performance promised of her. The *Mauretania* was expected to prove herself, too, although it was winter weather. On November 16th she began her working life from Liverpool with what may be described as the usual company of "first-nighters" aboard. The management, the builders, the Admiralty, experts and critics were all represented ; those people who get a peculiar thrill out of any first occasion were there, having in many cases booked their passages directly the booking opened. These first-occasion enthusiasts got full value for their money.

The maiden voyage is kindly to the historian ; it illustrates, excellently and fully, a good number of the difficulties which ships and shipping companies have to face and overcome. It deserves some close attention.

The special boat train was fifty minutes late in arriving at the Prince's Landing Stage at Liverpool. Passengers on it had plenty of time to digest the news in the daily papers and to discuss the prospects of the voyage. They certainly read, almost certainly with interest, that the *Mauretania* was taking across £2,750,000 in gold. The German Emperor was staying at Windsor Castle and had, with King Edward VII, shot over the royal coverts the day before. The papers were full of his visit and how he and the Emperor were pleased with the enthusiasm of their public reception. The Motor Exhibition was open in London and there was considerable description, illustration and advertisement of the latest wonders of a mechanical age—including a valveless marvel—high, small-tyred, perky and draughty vehicles which could be purchased at very much the same sort of prices as their successors of to-day.

Mr. Balfour had made a speech at Birmingham. He had denied that the Unionist Party was in any way entangled in class obligations ; he had stated that the opponents of the Unionist Party were, in effect, singularly inept. He dealt with the fallacious doctrines of the Socialists and declared that, upon the whole, the House of Lords had faithfully discharged its duties. He criticised the Chief Secretary for Ireland with dignified but not flattering words.

Mr. Birrell, in his view, was not making a good show about cattle raiding ; in fact, Mr. Birrell could not be considered a practical statesman at all. There was a good deal in the papers about cattle raiding in Ireland, and several gentlemen in their clubs, including Sir Edward Carson, had sat down to writing tales about it. The Prime Minister, Mr. Campbell-Bannerman, had been seized with sudden illness while visiting in the country, but was going on satisfactorily. Mr. Lloyd George was about to talk to a feminine deputation about women's votes. He told them that he was, and always had been, in favour of giving votes to women, and that the Prime Minister shared that view ; at the same time he explained to the deputation that there was not the very slightest possibility of the Government bringing in legislation to provide women with something which he and the Prime Minister believed they ought to have. That was not at all practicable. Still, he gave them good advice : he told them that it was very wicked and deplorable that they should upset Liberal meetings when the Liberals were so sympathetic to them. Mr. Winston Churchill was reported to be in Uganda, making speeches. The politicians were shown in the Press to be in good voice.

While the boat train was losing time, Prince Charles of Bourbon was married in England to Princess Louise of France. The Third Duma, opened in Russia two days before, was not getting on at all well. The magistrate at Marylebone was hearing the Druce case, and friction amongst officers in a battalion of the Guards was being made public. The money market was flat ; the American market being particularly depressed. Consols stood at 81$\frac{6}{8}$ and War

Loan—for the benefit of those children of to-day who think that a product of 1914 and after—at 97⅞.

Oscar Ashe was running a Shakespearean season at His Majesty's Theatre ; "The Merry Widow" was being played at Daly's and "The Gay Gordons" at the Aldwych. People of less frivolous taste in amusement could go to listen to a Shaw play at the Savoy and a Maugham play at the Court. But that night in London they could not see and hear "The Mollusc" because Charles Wyndham and Mary Moore had been commanded to Windsor. At Drúry Lane "The Sins of Society" was making money and stirring simple souls. On station bookstalls and in lending libraries assistants were offering as well worth reading to hesitant buyers "John Bull's Other Island," "Bunkum," "Eternal Feminine" and "Running Water."

In spite of books and newspapers and a longer opportunity of discussing what they had been doing in London and how the day's news revealed the world in a remarkable condition, many passengers must certainly have wondered and asked why, on an occasion like the first sailing of the world's largest steamship, the train could not be run to time. A little thing, but irritating. Irritated passengers require handling. Aboard the waiting *Mauretania* the men who had to keep passengers in a good temper and those who had to run the ship to time had also questions to ask about railway staff work. But the fact that the train was late did not lessen the enthusiasm of a considerable number of the inhabitants of Liverpool, nor did the English climate. A crowd of somewhere around fifty thousand persons waited in the wet and cold to see the ship off.

MAURETANIA

" Berthing " in Ocean Dock,
Southampton.

On that November evening the *Mauretania* untied
from the Prince's Landing Stage just after 7.30. The
weather outside promised well, but whatever it might
develop she could, at least, feed her passengers in
comfort before they smelled the Irish Sea. Part of
the trouble, of course, was that many of the people
aboard honestly believed that man in this large vessel
had contrived something which could defy the discomfort of the seas. All down the Irish Sea that
belief persisted ; it was an extremely smooth passage,
a very comfortable night. Queenstown was reached
at nine on Sunday morning, and after embarking
passengers and mails the *Mauretania* left for her first
experience of ocean at eleven o'clock. The newspaper correspondents aboard sent off telegrams saying
how well the ship had behaved and how everybody
was looking forward to a good passage. The weather
was then hazy with a smooth sea ; and in the hour
from leaving Queenstown until noon on Sunday the
Mauretania showed her pace. After that she began
to catch it, and the pious believers in man's mastery
of the seas found their faith shaken. The ship was
being pushed along, not driven, but kept at it ; she
bowed to her first acquaintance with the winter
Atlantic, and quite a lot of people were annoyed at
the nature of her obeisance. She did not linger long
in bowing ; up to noon on Monday she covered
571 miles of sea. By then it was blowing close on
a full westerly gale with a high sea, and even hard
pushing was out of the question. She was putting
her nose into it, feeling for the first time the touch
of great seas, taking tons of them aboard. Those
seas tested the ship. A spare anchor on the foredeck broke adrift and the seas started playing with

it—a good game when played with a weight of ten tons on a thin steel eggshell of a vessel. When she met the weather the *Mauretania* could lift her stem sixty feet and more, then bury it in the next comber, cleaving a way through the water, thrusting it to either side, but not all of it. The water which was not thrust aside could deal with men as a swatter deals with flies ; the forecastle head, when she was being pushed into the weather, was often a place where men could be squashed out of existence. The ship was slowed down and turned to give her fore deck some shelter. For something over two hours she lurched and rolled and wrestled with the Atlantic, making enough speed to steer her, perhaps three knots, not more, while officers and seamen dealt with the anchor that had taken charge. Not a nice job when the shelter from heavy seas coming aboard was only comparative, and a mistake with the capering mass of metal meant certain injury and probable death for the man who made it. Add to the violent movement of ship, water and escaped anchor, cold and rattling wind, and all niceness is removed from the undertaking. Passengers were not admitted to view the proceedings. The anchor was secured. The *Mauretania* turned back to her course and proceeded. Her run to noon on Tuesday was 464 nautical miles, which made the chances of a record passage very slender. The weather then began to improve ; the second-class passengers in the stern, getting the full effect of the lift, thrust and dive, certainly appreciated the change. The run to noon on Wednesday was 563 miles, with the ship rolling, a slow roll, and the weather still improving, though not good. At noon on Thursday 624 miles were logged, six more than the *Lusitania* had ever done ; that strange, inspiring thing, a record, had been achieved. When the ship's position and that run were posted, a good many drinks were lowered to celebrate the occasion, and the men below whose feeding of the furnaces had made the run possible, although the liquid they consumed did not in their view qualify as drink, felt justifiably pleased with the occasion. The *Mauretania* in spite of adverse weather had managed to cross more of the Atlantic than any other ship had ever done in a single day.

The next day, Friday, she passed Sandy Hook and anchored at 11.13 a.m., having run into the worst enemy of ships on a crowded sea—fog. The United States of America was suffering a financial depression ; there was anxiety on Wall Street. Most of the men, travelling for business, on board were particularly anxious to get ashore and cope with their own aspect of the depression. They saw, most of them with indignation, a notice posted at 1.0 p.m. saying that the *Mauretania* would lie where she was until the fog lifted, and that might not be until Saturday morning. They put their indignant heads together and formed a deputation, which waited on the Commander to inform him how extremely important it was for men having urgent affairs to settle that the ship should proceed to dock at once. Captain Pritchard, who certainly had not slept much since the *Mauretania* left Liverpool, heard the deputation politely ; he was sympathetic but firm. His ship would not proceed until the weather cleared. There was disappointment aboard ; hanging about at anchor almost within shouting distance of the landing stage is never an amusing business. Someone, almost certainly, put forth the opinion that the captain ought to be made to go on, and found something of a following. The ship's staff called out their tact, and cursed the fog as heartily, though not so openly, as any passenger. Captain Pritchard's own views are an easy guess. He had got to the summit of his career. He commanded the world's largest and fastest liner. Did they really imagine that, on her maiden voyage when any accident would be trumpeted about the seven seas and extremely badly received by the owners, he was going to risk a crash in the New York river? While the deputation's reception by the Commander was being discussed, and the staff were pouring tact on the discussion, the weather played another joke. The fog rolled rapidly away and the *Mauretania* docked at 6.15 in the evening. She had crossed from Liverpool to New York in five days eighteen hours, seventeen minutes, at an average speed of 22.21 knots.

She bore small scars of her first fight with the Atlantic. A window or two on the promenade deck was smashed, there was damage on the foredeck, rails were twisted, sea-water had come in and left its stains where sea-water should not have been. She had not—the newspaper correspondents reported, and the report is indicative of what their lay minds thought of the weather—loosened any rivets! She had—and that was general report—not been steady; but then the sea had not been smooth.

At 1.35 p.m. on Saturday, November 30th, she left New York for Liverpool. The following day she ran into fog, which she carried with her for thirty hours. Most of that time she saw nothing of the sky and very little of the surrounding sea. She had, of course, to slow down, but whenever visibility improved she would stride out again. Those thirty hours of slowing down, increasing speed, then slowing down again, were the sort of thing which was to be expected at that season of the year off the Banks. But they were not on that account any the less wearing for the men on the bridge and up in the crow's nest, who must strain their watching of the opacity ahead until their tired eyes manufactured dancing spots on the fog. They were not easy for Captain Pritchard, who had to make the nice distinction between a safe speed and the best speed which could be made, given the conditions. His job, his anxious job was neither to linger nor to jeopardise, not either but both. The runs to noon on Sunday and on Monday, 490 and 548 miles respectively, were governed by the circumstances but cannot be called poor. The *Mauretania* left the fog on Monday, but found a moderate westerly gale with big seas. The next day she spoke to the *Lusitania*, and learned that her sister, westward bound, was having a roughish time of it and was behind her time. To noon of Wednesday with a sixty-miles-an-hour wind behind her, the *Mauretania* logged 556, two better than the *Lusitania's* best, and giving her for the twenty-three hour day of the eastward passage an average of just over 24 knots. That was a run which pleased the men who served her, though the movement of the ship, steaming fast before wind and sea, made some of the passengers critical. On the last day of the passage, about one in the afternoon, the *Baltic* was passed. She had left New York two days before the *Mauretania*, and it had not been expected that she would be passed before Queenstown. She had a reputation as a very steady ship, but was seen to be making heavy weather of it. Passing her then, and seeing her a long way from being steady, must have pleased the *Mauretania's* staff and instructed the critical passengers, proving to them that ships will be ships. The eastward passage was completed in five days ten hours and fifty minutes, at an average speed of 23·69 knots. The *Mauretania* had taken the eastward record from the *Lusitania* by twenty-one minutes. Not a wide margin but good enough for rivalry. Taking into consideration those thirty hours of fog and the subsequent labouring of the ship in a following sea which would mean increased propeller slip, the performance proved that this new ship, with her sister, stood in a class apart. The general public and the press, however, seemed a trifle lukewarm.

Outward bound, especially on that day when the spare anchor took charge, it had been noticed that the *Mauretania* was given to pitching in a sea-way, but her roll had been described as big, slow and not disturbing. Homeward, some of the correspondents aboard amended that verdict ; they found the same bigness of roll, but not the slowness or, apparently, the absence of disturbance. The pitch, also, as she steamed before that westerly weather, attracted more attention. In one case the inevitable passenger of wide experience, on this occasion one with a record of forty crossings, was quoted as saying that he had never seen a ship " plunge " as the *Mauretania* did. Up on the bridge they were recording that the ship was pitching and spraying forward, sometimes amending that to pitching heavily and spraying over all. If some passenger did not ask some member of the ship's company whether he had ever known worse weather at sea, some marvel was performed. The fact was that the weather was bad. If there were any persons aboard who enjoyed it, wind, big seas, rain, cold and violent movement, they were strange creatures. If anybody said that he enjoyed it, he was probably a liar. Those of the crew who were housed right forward and right aft certainly neither did enjoy it nor pretended to do so, although stomach trouble did not concern most of them. When the bed on which you are lying happens to be rising and falling forty or fifty feet and oscillating into the bargain, sleep is difficult ; and to be robbed of sleep after a hard day's work is not pleasant. Uncomfortable nights and days at sea are not the perquisite of those who suffer from sickness. The *Mauretania* in bad weather was undoubtedly like every other ship which has yet been launched—far from comfortable.

She arrived at Queenstown and discharged mails and some of her passengers ; she steamed up the Irish Sea to Liverpool, sheltered water after the ocean passage, to discharge the rest. There was some little trouble with the boat trains again, and some criticism of the arrangements. On her maiden voyage the *Mauretania* did not get a really eulogistic " press." A correspondent of *The Times* had several things to say. He admitted the merits of the ship, but he did not fail to criticise. He found that there was vibration when she was travelling at speed ; he considered it difficult to read and impossible to write anywhere on her upper decks. He emphasised the " plunging " and the roll. Generally, there seems to have been astonishment, almost resentment, outside shipping circles, that this huge ship should behave as other ships when the ocean got hold of her. It seems hard on the *Mauretania* to blame her for that ;

it must have been disappointing, though hardly un-
expected, for the owners. The floating hotel and
luxury palace on the sea business are excellent for
advertisement, if only the sea and the floating part are
properly emphasised. Speed is undoubtedly a lure,
but the implications of steaming fast in a sea-way
should not be forgotten. A few more thousand tons
does not intimidate the ocean. It seems a pity that
passengers should so persistently expect them to do
so, and show annoyance when they do not. Her
maiden voyage proved to sailors and to the shipping
world that the *Mauretania* was a very fine vessel. It
is human that many people were astonished when,
in that winter weather, she also proved herself a ship
upon the sea. Yet even those people who complained
or were astonished at the fact that she behaved like
a ship could not go the length of saying that she
behaved like a bad ship. There was vibration when
she was being driven fast, but the vibration that
knowledgeable people had expected. She was lively
in a sea-way—the dive and swoop of her pitch and
the way she had of throwing water unexpectedly at
men on her bridge, became famous—but nobody with
any sense of justice could ever have called her anything but a good sea boat.

The publicity and advertisement which had
attended the *Mauretania* since her conception made
much of her size and luxury and her speed. Photographs illustrating her wonderful lines, her bows and
her stern had been published in the papers ; they
suggested speed and movement. In the shipping
columns of the daily newspapers, actually before she
sailed on her maiden voyage, she and her sister were
advertised as the world's largest and fastest liners.

There was just one word about speed ; there were several about luxury. Orchestras—lounges—daily newspapers—*à la carte* dinners no extra charge—stress in a short advertisement was laid on those. It certainly seems that some simple souls had allowed the several words to obscure the meaning of the one. Yet some of the public were obviously disappointed when 30,000 tons, driven by engines of 68,000 horsepower, were thrown about uncomfortably by the Atlantic. Some of the public will undoubtedly be disappointed when, in the future, 100,000 tons are treated as contemptuously. Shipping companies setting the luxury lure have their troubles.

One happening of the *Mauretania's* maiden voyage undoubtedly gave real satisfaction to men of different positions connected with the ship : Cunard directors thinking of profits, and Liverpool-Irish trimmers and firemen thinking of tired bodies. Her appetite for coal proved reasonable. Bunker space for sufficient coal to take her from Liverpool to Liverpool was obviously impossible in a ship of her consumption. Coaling at New York had always been recognised as a necessity. How much she should carry at the start of each passage and how much she was likely to burn on each, was carefully calculated. A round figure of 1,000 tons a day had been given as a likely consumption ; and that round figure had been used as an argument against the possibility of her success. Not even a Liverpool-Irish black squad was considered capable of feeding fires with appetites of that size. The calculated consumption was checked and rechecked. Actually the *Mauretania* left Liverpool for New York with 6,770 tons of coal in her bunkers. She steamed on that occasion 3,040 nautical miles, and took five days eighteen hours and seventeen minutes about it. She encountered bad weather for the whole of the open sea passage from Queenstown to Sandy Hook, and reached New York with 1,350 tons of coal left in her bunkers. There she took in 5,061 tons of American coal, and returned to Liverpool in five days two hours and fifty minutes, finding worse weather homeward bound than she had on the outward passage. Home at Liverpool she had 1,020 tons of coal left in her bunkers. For the westward passage she had consumed 856·5 tons per full twenty-four hours to drive her main engines, and on the eastward run 917.13 tons. She had not reached the 1,000 tons a day mark or anywhere near it. That was encouraging, for although she had not been driven she had met with consistently bad weather, which would increase the percentage of propeller slip. Later, when she was really driven, the consumption sometimes went over 1,000 tons a day, but rarely. One thing that first voyage made certain— whatever the conditions, her bunkers were sufficiently large to carry all the coal she needed. Even so, she was a good customer to the coal merchants.

Another thing emerged from that maiden voyage, something which cannot, like the coal, be reduced to figures, something which some people, not sailors, may consider of slight importance. She showed herself a happy ship. Captain John Pritchard commanded her, Mr. J. Currie was her chief engineer. How much those heads of departments made the atmosphere, how much they were forced by the ship herself to make it, is conjecture, but it is not fanciful. The *Mauretania* started happy and she remained happy ; and nobody but the grossest, land-minded materialist will find in that anything but one of the real causes of her success.

On her seventh voyage, in May, 1908, westward bound, about two hundred and fifty miles from Daunt's, the *Mauretania* made her first acquaintance with propeller trouble. Like most ships, she was to know more of this very common mishap, but that was her first experience of it, and it put record-making out of the question for the time, though it did not put the ship out of commission. The trouble occurred on a Sunday evening in May ; the ship was slowed down for three-quarters of an hour or so while the extent of the damage was estimated ; then she proceeded. One of her propellers had, it was assumed, struck some submerged object and shaved off a blade. That entailed extra work for the other three propellers, and some extra fuel consumption. She had not so far been pressed for records, so she was able with her three propellers to maintain much the same speed as she had shown before. While a new set of propellers was being designed and made, she made eight voyages running on three and a bit. Her times for those eight voyages were by no means bad, but she could not do much during that period towards teaching the *Lusitania* how to cross the Atlantic. In January, 1909, she made her first voyage with her new propellers. Originally she was fitted with propellers which had their blades bolted on to a boss, but this boss had been found unsatisfactory. The new design was a four-bladed propeller cut in one piece. Its use was immediately satisfactory.

After that the fight between the two sister ships settled down into a stern affair, actually more important to many dwellers on the Mersey than cup-ties and league football. The *Mauretania* was English built, the *Lusitania* came from the Clyde, so there was an international contest flavour about it. The competition concerned world records, a certain means of maintaining interest. Whoever won, since the two competitors stood apart from all other ships, the winner was bound to be British. It was a glorious business, and played with much of the customary heat attendant on international contests. In Mersey riverside public-houses arguments about the merits and speed of the two ships were animated if not dialectically distinguished ; some of them led to trial by battle and to the champions of either side being run through swing-doors into a rainy street. Officers strained friendships on the matter, and their wives were expected to feel as they did. Of course the two ships did not race against each other ; that would have been contrary to Cunard policy and the rules of the Atlantic. Passenger ships at sea never race ; the practice might lead to all sorts of dangers. It just happened that there was a good deal of feeling, and effort, about one of them making a faster passage than the other. Sailing in January with her new propellers, the *Mauretania* began to build up averages of well over 25·0 knots and to maintain them. After a year of work she was giving all that it had been hoped and promised that she might give. But the *Lusitania* was always close to her tail.

The *Mauretania* no longer exists, the *Lusitania* has been for more than twenty years below in the sea, yet it is still necessary to walk warily in conversation concerning their respective speeds with men who served in either of them or both. The whole rivalry of two ships very much faster than any other ships of their kind was pre-War, and therefore, for many people of to-day, belonging to an almost unrealisable age ; records of that age appear paltry, the heat of competition slightly amusing ; but it is unwise to exhibit such a spirit to the men who served these ships. It is most unwise to venture an opinion as to which ship was actually the faster. Goaded by argument, or mere seeming disbelief, the champions of the " *Lucy* " will tell a hard luck story. It concerns a westward passage, and the decimal figures of the average speed are apt to vary with the teller and the depth of his indignation. Anyhow, they are not essential. The point is this : the " *Lucy* " had made a passage to the Nantucket Light-vessel which was very clearly fast enough to give the " Geordie " plenty upon which to chew. From the Nantucket to the Ambrose Channel Light-vessel is only one hundred and ninety-three miles, and the " *Lucy* " was moving between them at a speed of more than 27 knots over the ground. Everything, up to that point, was very lovely. The whole ship, even the trimmers and firemen when they had a spare second, was on the grin. Then fog came down, and not only fog, but confounded fishermen bobbing about the fairway in their miserable little boats. The grins disappeared with the visibility, coal became heavier to lift, the *Lusitania* docked in New York to a fast passage, but not to one which was going to make the *Mauretania* do much chewing. So you see—when the *Mauretania* hailed from Newcastle and was a " Geordie," and the *Lusitania* from the Clyde could be any sort of Scot fancy dictated, there was bound to be feeling.

There is another tale about the rivalry which is not told so often. The *Lusitania* was trying to build

up averages of over 25 knots and was having some
trouble about it—propeller trouble. Her propellers
were of quite different design to those of the *Mauretania*. The blades were long and narrow, they have
been described in many ways, but a botanical simile
used about them serves well. The *Lusitania* had propeller blades after the fashion of a long leaf, say
verbena ; the *Mauretania* had more squat and stubby
affairs, say the petals of a pansy. The long blades,
besides not giving the speed expected of them, were
not infrequently in trouble ; they touched things,
particularly going in and out of port, and got smashed.
On one occasion, in those early days, the *Lusitania*
came home with very little left of the blades of both
propellers on the same side. It made her awkward
to steer, and disposed of any likelihood of an average
of 25 knots. She was docked for repairs ; but there
was not a set of new propellers for her, and she was
urgently needed for service. There was, however,
a complete set of the *Mauretania's* pansy affairs. So
they fitted those and sent the ship to sea. The Scot
with the " Geordie's " pansies had not the least difficulty in maintaining an average of over 25 knots.
Almost certainly the designers of the long leaf-like
blades were annoyed when they heard about it, but
not nearly—and here " certainty " cannot possibly
be qualified—as much as the men who served and
loved the *Lusitania*.

Records give the final word in speed to the
Mauretania. While the two ships competed, she was
always able to register the fastest passages. The
Lusitania put something up ; the *Mauretania* knocked
it down. That does not, necessarily, mean that she
was the faster ship. In 1907 the Boat Race was in

England an amazingly popular event ; it has not yet become unpopular. The times for the full course trials are duly published in the papers and discussed. Yet nobody who has ever rowed in a race would regard those as more than a very general indication of the comparative pace of the crews. A horse in training at Newmarket gallops a mile faster than a rival in training at Epsom ; the man who backs the Newmarket horse on the strength of that is quite likely to enrich the bookmakers. Since the *Mauretania* and the *Lusitania* never raced against each other, in the only real sense that they tore side by side across the Atlantic together, the winner cannot be named. No decision without a race. The *Mauretania* was a happy ship and a lucky ship. Perhaps her luck generally followed her in the matter of Atlantic conditions, when she had to knock down something which her sister had set up. Luck, that should satisfy the " *Lucy's* " most sensitive admirer. Anyhow, the *Lusitania* had gone from making passages fourteen years before the *Mauretania* knocked down all that she had set up before.

Speed gave the *Mauretania* fame, but it did not give her her particular place in the history of ships. For a much longer period than any other vessel ever has, she held her position as the fastest liner in the world. That is inspiring for those people who cannot think beyond records. It is in itself a wonderful performance. But had the old ship rested on speed and speed alone, it is certain that she would have gone to the breakers many years before she did. Speed, up to a point, is a necessity for all first class express liners on the Atlantic ; after that point it becomes a necessity for one or two ships only and, at that, as propaganda for their owners. The cases in which any passenger gains any real advantage from a record passage across the Atlantic are rare. The odds against obtaining any material benefit from arrival in England or America four or five hours before the advertised time must be very large indeed. On the other hand, the advantage of knowing that the odds are considerably in favour of a vessel arriving punctually at her destination is immense. It was because she offered that advantage more certainly, perhaps, than any other ship which has sailed the seas that the *Mauretania* gained her unique reputation. Look at her early records when she was making reputation.

After she had had her propellers changed she settled down to show what she could do. At the end of October, 1908, she was taken out of commission for annual refit, when she was supplied with new propellers. She came into commission again towards the middle of January, 1909, and remained continuously in commission until the end of November, 1911. During that period of three years less one month she had no major refit at all. What had to be done to keep her in trim was done in the few days between her regular sailings. The period between her leaving Liverpool on one voyage and leaving Liverpool on the next one was throughout those three years, upon the average, less than three and a half weeks. That is sustained work. From January, 1909, to the end of November, 1911, she made forty-four full voyages, that is to say she crossed the Atlantic eighty-eight times. On seventy occasions her average speed was over 25 knots and on forty-six of these seventy crossings the average was over 25·5 knots, while on two it was over 26 knots. On fifteen of those eighty-eight passages her average speed was over 24 knots ; on three occasions only, in three years, she failed to reach an average speed of 24 knots. That is sustained fast work.

The *Mauretania* followed lanes from the time when she was first commissioned. They were not the internationally statutised lanes of her later years, but they were lanes. She crossed the Atlantic on courses which varied with the direction and the season of the year. There were two lanes westward, long and short, and two different lanes eastward, long and short. Both westward courses were well apart from both eastward courses, so that the danger of collision between ships going in opposite directions in fog on the crowded Atlantic should be minimised. There were two lanes in each direction for use at different seasons, because ice is one of the terrors of that northern sea. The main southward set of the ice from the Arctic regions is from the middle of January until the end of July, so during that season ships take a long course to the south to avoid it as far as possible. From August to the middle of January the ice is more locked up, so ships from England to New York and from New York to England can with reasonable safety take a shorter, more direct course. When the *Mauretania* started making her reputation, the *Titanic* disaster was yet to come ; there were no ice patrols, but the lanes were marked on the charts and usually followed. Cunard ships followed them. The *Mauretania* followed them. During those three busy years of gaining fame, her following of them is remarkable. In 1909 on her fifteen westward passages, she made nine long lanes and six short ones ; there was a difference of four nautical miles between the maximum and minimum mileage in the long lane crossings and of two miles on the short ; eastward, with the same proportion of long and short, her variation in mileage was three miles for each. In 1910 she had a variation of one mile for the long lanes and none for the short going west, five for the long and three for the short going east. On fourteen voyages in 1911 she covered exactly the same distance on ten long westward passages, but showed a difference of four miles between the longest and the shortest of the short ones. Eastward that year her variation in miles covered was one for long, two for short. Eighty-eight crossings of the Atlantic without ever going more than five miles in somewhere near three thousand out of the shortest way any particular lane would let her go. Six consecutive crossings on one lane and ten consecutive crossings on another when she did not vary the distance covered by a single mile. That was sustained good seamanship and singular obedience to her helm.

Backwards and forwards for three years without rest. Three times in each of those years, in the spring, at midsummer and in the autumn, she was allowed four weeks between one sailing and the next, on the others she was only allowed three. Out of Liverpool on a Saturday, out of Liverpool on a Saturday for New York again twenty-one days later ; that was the *Mauretania's* ordinary programme. She was driven across through any weather she might meet, maintaining those amazing average speeds. Children born while her new propellers were being fitted were running about and talking long before she got a rest. Fog and ice, roaring gales and huge seas delayed her often ; she had to slow down for them. Slowing down entailed speeding up when the chance came. Very often she would be changing her speed every few minutes, seizing her chance, jumping again into her stride as visibility improved, as wind and sea moderated, slowing down again within perhaps a quarter of an hour at a return of bad conditions, driving ahead again the moment the opportunity came. Because she was a ship and the seas always her master, she could not defy them and be driven recklessly through them ; because she was the *Mauretania* she must live up to the standard which she had set. At times, at very many times, her logs show her accelerating and slowing like a prudently driven car in a hurry on a slow road, taking the dangerous places sanely, jumping ahead instantly as the moment to move arrived. Only rarely did she find the weather which would allow her an unvarying " full ahead " from departure to landfall. It is not surprising that the Cunard Company considered relief captains a necessity. The ship had no time to rest, but the man alone responsible for her was from time to time made to do so.

At New York damage, for naturally the sea was constantly doing her and her contents minor harm, which urgently demanded it was repaired, but over there she only had time and opportunity to, as it were, wash her hands and face. When she had rushed back to Liverpool and tied up at the landing stage, a somewhat bedraggled vessel externally, with grimed funnels, rust and salt stained sides, perhaps with visible scars such as missing ventilators, smashed boats or twisted rails and stanchions, it was then that they fell upon her. The invasion took her before the last of her passengers were ashore ; the army of workers did not leave her until, four days later, another set of passengers were about to come aboard. The Commander often got ashore on the tails of the passengers, the privilege of responsibility, the rest of the officers when they could. If much wanted doing or explaining in their own particular job, they might be on or about the ship during most of her few days at home. The Chief, particularly if anything of importance had to be done to his engines, would be there to see that it was done to his liking. When the *Mauretania* made her home port at Southampton, to carry on and to improve the standard she had set during those three years, there was quite a considerable migration of modest households from north to south. Men, none of them, not even the Commander, earning what business would consider big money, had to be near their work during their shore leave.

The army of shore workers made a horrible mess of the ship before they cleaned up. They were men and women who knew their jobs, but not the trim ways of the sea. Within a very short space of time dinner baskets and tea cans, bottles of stout and cigarette ends were lying about where, at sea, the sight of such things would have induced an apoplectic atmosphere. The decks were littered and dirty, the alleyways untidy. Painters were everywhere, in bosun's chairs up the funnels and the masts, on stages over the side, in the staterooms and in the public rooms. Carpenters, joiners, plumbers, filled the ship with noise ; upholstresses were busy stitching, char-women scrubbed and polished, filling even that sanctuary of men, the chart house, with feminine gossip. The *Mauretania* inert, with no pulse beating, was refuelled, revictualled, re-stored, repaired and cleaned from truck to keelson ; the work went on day and night. It was efficient, because the workers were selected for their efficiency ; it was done at high pressure ; but it had not the sea's discipline about it. There was a great deal of chatter, whistling, singing of the latest popular ditty, plenty of unnecessary noise.

A rush job had to be done by ordinary human beings. When the job could be done while the *Mauretania* was docked and inert, the ship and the human beings were lucky. Often they were not. Having discharged passengers, conditions in the port of Liverpool might not permit the ship to dock ; she would have to move out to the Cunard Buoy in the Sloyne and attempt to tie up there. She would unbend an anchor and pass the cable down to the men on the buoy, hoping for the best. Sometimes her hopes were vain ; more than sufficiently frequently for those concerned with the business, conditions in that exposed anchorage were too bad to allow the men on the buoy to get the cable shackled. When an attempt to tie up had been proved impossible, or when, as sometimes happened, the danger of some or even all of the men on the buoy being swept off it was too great, the *Mauretania* proceeded to anchor, bending on at express speed the anchor that she had unbent. With both anchors down forward she would often drag, carrying both chains and both hooks along the Mersey mud down river. When she had reached the limit of the ground where she could drag in safety, she picked up her anchors, steamed up river and dropped them again. Perhaps, if the conditions held, she had to repeat the performance throughout the night. She would have

been safe and more comfortable spending the night
at sea on those occasions, but she had to be handy
for tying up to the buoy or docking directly weather
and tides would let her ; also, on the ebb, she could
not get to sea without real danger. The big ships
had a sufficiently anxious time getting to sea with the
flow of water against them, attempting it when
steaming with the stream was seeking trouble. When
the *Mauretania* made Southampton her home port
instead of Liverpool, nobody practically concerned
with the handling or the working of the ship had any
real regrets.

But whatever the conditions in the Port of Liverpool,
the work had, somehow or other, to be done in the
time. Coaling was under any circumstances a foully
dirty business ; if it had to be delayed owing to bad
conditions it made cleaning up afterwards a hectic
rush. Every conceivable precaution was, very naturally, taken, since the cleaners were no more fond of
extra work than other people. While coal was being
loaded down the fifty chutes, the interior of the ship
was closed and, so far as men of experience could
make it, sealed. Every crack received attention, the
mouths of ventilator cowls were covered with canvas,
and the man who opened up anything unnecessarily
did not make himself popular. But since coal dust
has a fine knack of entry through minute spaces, it
found its way in. The ventilation system, supplying
conditioned air to the rooms, was its principal front
door. That door was carefully watched, the rooms
were blanked off from the air supply before coaling
began, but, coaling finished, it was too often found
that somehow the door had got ajar. When the
ventilating system was turned on again a fine grey

cloud would be puffed from the louvres with a fine effect on paintwork or clean linen. In the circumstances of bad conditions, coaling necessarily delayed, a rush throughout those precious few days, cleaning up held over to the last moment, it might happen that the louvres in some particular cabin were forgotten and not tested for their puff. If a passenger, say a lady in a frock which gave her pleasure, found the cabin stuffy and switching on the ventilation made contact with the grey cloud, there might be, and assuming the frock to be giving real pleasure there certainly would be trouble. That sort of trouble had to be rare. Little things, but they helped to prevent idleness in port.

Three years without resting. Eighty-eight crossings of the Atlantic, seventy of them at an average speed of over 25 knots. Forty-four voyages, thirty-five of them each completed, from Liverpool to Liverpool, in seventeen days with an allowance of four days in port to get ready for the next. That was what made the *Mauretania's* reputation.

From 1908, when she took the Blue Riband of the Atlantic from the *Lusitania*, she remained for more than two decades the fastest liner in the world. She was, during those years of establishing her reputation, continually improving upon her own former runs, constantly achieving new records, with which only the *Lusitania* could hope to compete. In September of 1909 she averaged 26.06 knots for the westward passage, and did precisely the same thing again in the following September. In March, 1910, she attained for a short period a speed of 27·48 knots. In May, 1911, she averaged 27.04 knots for a whole day's run. These speeds were then wonderful—

they are not slow to-day ; they were much beyond anything for which she had been designed. They undoubtedly brought her fame and then more fame. But no records for voyages or single passages, day runs, or isolated bursts, however brilliant they might be, could be responsible for her reputation. Records of speed must be associated with luck and good conditions ; by their nature they cannot be everyday events. The *Mauretania* had much to do with records of speed ; but she had much more to do with reliable performance. Three years with all their varied weather unable to vary her time table. By the end of 1911, when she got her rest, men and women who were anxious to arrive punctually at their destinations travelled in the one ship in the world which seemed incapable of causing them to miss appointments.

She was then, when she had proved herself and certainly earned a spell of rest, the fastest passenger ship in the world, but she was no longer the largest. The White Star *Olympic*, with a gross tonnage of 45,324, nearly half as much again as the *Mauretania*, made her maiden voyage in 1911. She was a fine ship, but she was never designed to compete with the *Mauretania* in speed. Her size and her comfort were intended to be her lure ; they lured successfully those passengers who had the largest and latest complex highly developed, but they could not rob the *Mauretania* of her reputation. After a three-months' rest and refit she came into commission again at the beginning of March, 1912, as the world's second largest liner. A month later she had, but for a few days only, to take third place on the list of size ; then, in circumstances of peculiar tragedy, she went back to second place again.

In April the *Titanic*, a little larger than her sister ship the *Olympic*, and so actually the world's largest vessel, sailed from Southampton for New York with something over two thousand persons aboard. She was not engined or intended for speed records ; the slogan, as it were, under which she sailed was " Great comfort, great space, reasonable speed." By some strange irony she set out upon her maiden voyage labelled and advertised in the public mind as a ship which could not sink. On the night of April 14th, in Lat. 41° 45′ N., Long. 50° 14′ W., being on her proper seasonal course, she struck ice, a glancing blow which opened up most of her compartments on the starboard side. Within approximately two hours, in calm sea with little wind, she sank with the loss of nearly three-quarters of her complement ; 815 passengers, and 688 of her crew died in a disaster which is infinitely the worst suffered by any ship flying the Red Ensign.

Every circumstance of tragedy seemed to attend the ending of the *Titanic's* only voyage. The quantity of ice about in the spring of that year was most unusual. The *Titanic*, of course, carried wireless and sent out her urgent S O S call at once. At that moment there was actually a ship equipped with wireless within twenty miles or so of her, but, keeping no continuous wireless watch, she did not hear the call for help. There was another ship, without wireless, hove to amongst the ice almost within sight of her. Help was close at hand, but it could not be summoned. The Cunard *Carpathia*, then commanded by Captain Rostron, did pick up the call ; she came to the call as fast as she could. Only designed for fourteen knots, she made seventeen on that dash ;

but she was several hours steaming away, and the *Titanic* had sunk long before she arrived. The *Carpathia* rescued from the boats 706 persons, many of whom would, in all likelihood, have died of cold and exposure without her aid. About that aspect of the disaster there was a horrid absence of the small amount of luck which might, had it been there, have made so much difference. The *Carpathia* did not keep a continuous wireless watch, the operator just happened not to have turned in ; but the *Carpathia* was too far away to arrive before the *Titanic* had sunk. The S O S was sent out about half an hour after midnight ; if the operator in that ship, not twenty miles away, had just happened to be listening-in, so many of the dead might have lived. Luck in that was against the *Titanic*.

Another aspect of the tragedy is pure ugliness. It was advertised throughout the world, arousing bitterness and shame ; it was fully exposed, and uglier things were said than even the ugly truth. Details of that ugliness need not be recorded here, but the bare facts require mention since they reacted so importantly upon the *Mauretania* and all other ships on the Atlantic. The *Titanic* did not carry sufficient boats to accommodate all of the persons aboard her. After she had struck the ice it was approximately two hours before she sank—a long time. The weather, calm sea and absence of wind were ideal—if that word is not out of place in such connection—for getting the boats away. It is generally admitted that a major sea disaster has seldom occurred when boats could leave a wrecked ship with less difficulty or danger. Yet, with that known shortage, boats left the ship half empty. Worse, the high tradition of the sea was not obeyed ; men left the ship in boats when there were women and children left behind. Something, very terribly and very badly, went wrong.

The *Mauretania* on that night was a day out from Queenstown. She took a course to the southward, after receiving news of the disaster, to avoid the unusual amount of ice. The *Olympic* was homeward bound from New York ; she picked up her sister's calls and answered them, but hundreds of miles of sea divided them, and she could give no help. Very shortly afterwards she was taken out of service for alterations designed to restore public confidence in a ship of her design. The civilised world—the sterotyped phrase is really applicable—was appalled and alarmed.

Inevitably the disaster brought many new regulations and some international agreement concerning safety at sea. That there should be boats for all became a loud, popular cry. There are still people who argue that it is a stupid and useless cry, since however many boats a ship may carry, it is indisputable fact that in the majority of major accidents at sea, circumstances, the list of the ship or the weather make launching all or even most of them impossible. It is also argued that too many boats are a definite danger, since the weight of them will cause a heavily listing ship to capsize more readily, so rafts are advocated instead of boats. But such arguments did not and do not please the majority of passengers. They wish to be assured, and it seems a very reasonable wish, that the chances of their meeting, in emergency, that cry " There is no more room " may be as far as possible removed. The

Titanic brought them that assurance at a great cost of human life.

The less ugly aspect of this disaster led to a much surer approach to safety on the Atlantic. It brought forward the full importance of wireless communication between ships. The lesson of the chance that the operator of the *Carpathia* just happened to have his head-phones on as he was getting ready for bed went home. It became compulsory for ships of a certain size to carry wireless and to keep a continuous wireless watch. To-day that has been reduced to a definite standardised procedure internationally observed. Twice in each hour of every twenty-four, from fifteen to eighteen minutes past and from fifteen to twelve minutes to, the wireless operator on duty is obliged to break off the sending or receiving of all messages, however urgent, and to listen-in on a 600 metre wave for distress calls only. Six minutes in each hour solely devoted by every ship carrying wireless to listening for calls for help is a long way from the *Carpathia's* operator unlacing his boots before he removed his head-phones, or that other operator sleeping when twenty miles away the world's largest ship was asking desperately for help ; but the *Titanic*, not getting the help which was so near, opened the movement on that long way.

Together with increased attention to wireless communications there marched, as another outcome of this disaster, the Ice Patrol.

This patrol started, as a result of the Board of Trade conferring with the Atlantic shipping companies, with the *Scotia*, an auxiliary whaler of 357 tons launched in 1872, sailing from Dundee in March, 1913. She was too small a ship for the purpose.

The United States then took over the patrol with their Coastguard Force, and have maintained it since. The cost is shared by the countries concerned, who make contribution on the basis of the tonnage of their Atlantic shipping. During the months of April, May and June—the ice season—the path of the ice-drift in the vicinity of the steamship lane is patrolled. News respecting movements of ice is broadcast from the patrol vessels and individual messages are also sent to all ships in the area. The ships, in turn, inform the patrol vessels of all details, place, time, direction of drift of any ice sighted by them. The system was introduced immediately after the loss of the *Titanic* and remains in force.

The *Mauretania*, together with all other passenger ships, increased the number of boats carried. She increased the efficiency of her wireless service. It had always been common knowledge that she had been specially designed with an unusual number of watertight compartments in order to reduce the chances of her being sunk by enemy fire when, in the event of war, she might be serving as an auxiliary cruiser. That, when the *Titanic* had so terribly exploded the myth of an unsinkable ship, was not forgotten. It was also remembered by a public grown a little alarmed that the Cunard Company could substantiate their claim that no ship flying their flag had ever caused the death of a passenger. So the *Mauretania* continued her work, putting up a new record here and there to keep the *Lusitania* in her place, without any damage to her reputation or any loss of popularity. But the loss of the *Titanic* and the feeling that it had aroused had given a very real shock to the shipping world. British owners and

British seamen were determined that some of the things which had been said should never be said again about ships flying their ensign. The Cunard directors had an idea ; they put an additional officer first into the *Mauretania* and afterwards into the other big ships. The idea was generally followed by most other companies ; but, like many innovations, it was not entirely approved by many of the men whom it affected. The additional officer was called the staff captain ; he ranked next to the commander, was not a watch-keeper and was, in every case, a man who had already commanded a ship of his own. He had nothing at all to do with the navigation of the ship except in the event of the commander becoming incapacitated, when he took command. He relieved the captain of certain social duties, and generally he filled the sort of job the commander in a ship of the Royal Navy fills ; but he was really appointed for a specific purpose arising out of the *Titanic* disaster. That specific purpose was emergency organisation. He had to co-ordinate the action of each department so that, if the need arose, the work of saving would move smoothly in rough moments. It is purely idle to pretend that the crew of a great liner are not ordinary human beings influenced by the ordinary human emotions, that because they serve a ship at sea they do not show the weaknesses which are apparent in an office, or a factory, or a regiment, or a cathedral close. The various departments have views about their own importance and a critical eye upon the others. The bridge officers believe, with reason, that without them and their seamen the ship would founder. The engineers and the men under them know that without them and their skilled labour the ship could not even begin to cross the seas in order to be in a position to founder. The purser and his men realise that without success in their department a passenger ship would either not be ordered to go to sea or would soon be taken out of commission as a non-paying proposition. When none would exist without the others a certain jealousy, some carefulness about departmental dignity is quite inevitable. Coming down from the general to the particular, the *Mauretania*, like all other great liners at that moment, had suffered a hurt in pride because in one of her kind disaster had discovered faults. This co-ordinating staff captain person looked like a nuisance if he were not, since he came from the navigating branch, an insult to the other two departments and a definite slur on the tradition of the ship. Men of irreverent habit called these master mariners who had commanded ships of their own sanitary inspectors. It is hard to imagine that, at the beginning, these staff captains had anything but an anxious and difficult time. To do their job without damage to good feeling in the ship required tact and a nice touch in handling men.

Before the *Titanic* went down the *Mauretania* had made reputation. In the difficult moments which followed, when the Mercantile Marine was devising remedies, some of which stung the sore of its hurt pride, she went on adding to her reputation. But she did not cease to be a happy ship.

CHAPTER V

UNRIVALLED

AN American journalist, meaning to be complimentary, once wrote of the *Mauretania* that she was a " shippy " ship. Precisely what he wished to convey, with his manufactured word, is not clear ; it can, however, be presumed that he wished to emphasise that what impressed him most about her was neither her size, her luxury, nor her speed, but her quality as a ship. If that were his meaning, he had certainly hit upon the reason which made her for so long a period the most popular of all the carriers of human freight in service on the Atlantic. She was as men say of a horse, all quality. Beauty is a different thing ; there are some people, though they are rare, who deny that she was beautiful ; there are none who can deny symmetry, proportion, the fineness of line which distinguish quality from commonness. To her quality she added individuality ; even her movements were her own. To continue the horse simile, she might be hot at times, but she was always a beautiful ride. She did not wallow in a seaway, although she might be wet in one ; in good weather and in bad she had a grace of action which made most other ships look like labouring tugs. That was her primary distinction : even the sea-timid and sea-careless recognised it at once. To that she added speed, comfort, reliability and her own atmosphere. She was very much a ship, to get back to the American journalist, but always very definitely herself. When the Cunard Company, with close on eighty years of experience of ships behind them, recognised those two essentials of greatness, quality and individuality, on her first voyage, they set about making sure that the public, a little disappointed that she had not done more spectacular things, should recognise them too. Because the *Mauretania* had those qualities—for all the Cunard mastery of the difficult business of passenger pleasing could not have simulated them—they succeeded.

They played up to her individuality. Her human freight in all three classes was always cosmopolitan ; upon the average she carried more passengers of foreign birth than of British. Wherever the trouble centre of the world might be at any given moment, it was probable that she would be carrying citizens of the country where the trouble centred. To whatever the daily newspapers of the world happened to be devoting headlines she could almost certainly produce some temporary inmate who was more than generally concerned. If a government fell, or a minor war were started, no matter where, there would be somebody aboard her who could claim the event as of domestic importance to himself. The success of an explorer, bringing man's footsteps to some place hitherto untrodden by human feet, of a new opera, of a book, the winning of a game played with a ball, the fact that somebody had jumped higher than somebody else or that one horse had beaten another horse in a race, a marriage or a divorce, the conviction of some criminal, any of these coming into the news found generally in the *Mauretania* some passenger who could say with truth " That is not far off my own particular patch of country." Her human freight was mixed, very mixed, but her owners saw to it that she should keep her individuality while pleasing the mixture. Take a very small example. The roast beef of England was given considerable prominence in her bill of fare. In the third-class, of course, the patrons of the Kosher kitchen would not eat it, in the first saloon less simple dishes might be in much greater demand, but in both the beef was there and duly advertised until it became a tradition of the ship. It was deliberately made institutional because of its Englishness. The rivalry which had been there in her building exhibited itself as part of her individuality. She was a cosmopolitan carrier better known, perhaps, to foreigners because she carried more of them than to her own people, but in herself she was and she remained essentially English. Her first-class dining saloon was panelled and decorated in the French style of the middle sixteenth century ; in it was served food prepared after the fashion of all nations, yet many of her passengers found in the room much of the atmosphere of an English country house. That, naturally, when it became apparent, was carefully encouraged ; but if the suggestion had not been there in the ship it could not have been entirely manufactured. The beef and the first-class dining saloon are examples ; the thing itself, the impress of personality, went throughout the ship. It supplies probably the reason why the *Mauretania* had so large a list of regular customers, men and women whose business took them frequently across the Atlantic, who insisted on making their crossings in her unless sheer necessity forced them into some other ship. She sailed with full lists of passengers long after she had parted with the glamour of newness and the lure of size ; she still filled her accommodation when she had lost her first place for speed. She was never without rivals, for at first, when she stood so far ahead of most other express liners, she had her sister to compete with ; yet she was never deserted by popular favour because she was never just one of several large, fast, comfortable ships, but always very much herself.

The Atlantic Ferry demands a special form of passenger pleasing, because it is a ferrying of passengers in short, hurried passages across a none too genial ocean. Its predominant merit from the standpoint of those who serve the ships on it is that passengers have not the time to get really bored. The ferry ship is only at sea for a few days ; the dreaded last weeks of a long voyage are unknown, those last weeks when so many of the passengers have exhausted the attractions of available amusements, grown tired of each other's company and fall back on petty squabbling amongst themselves and stern criticism of the ship, its servants and its food, of which they have been consistently eating too largely. The Atlantic Ferry ship never has to contend with real heat, but against that she never has the long spells of calm, warm days and nights when even the most fractious of mortals are lulled by the magic of waters into a mood of contemplative well-being. Much of her sea-time is put in under conditions when her decks are largely deserted ; she makes complete voyages when she sees nothing but grey skies and grey, uncomfortable seas. She has not to face long-voyage boredom, but the promise of certain fine

weather ahead is one she cannot offer. Each passage
is a hurried performance, a dash between terminal
ports ; everything has to be concentrated. One
crowd of passengers has to be shipped, housed, fed,
amused, pleased, unshipped, and preparations have
to be completed for the arrival of the next crowd
all in the space of a week or ten days. The *Mauretania*
did that concentrated ferry work for longer than any
of her kind. Amongst the crowds of mixed nation-
ality which boarded her on sailing day she carried
at one time or another a large number of the men
and women whose names were familiar in the world
of their day. Legions of the very rich knew her
private suites, thousands of the very poor made westward passages in her third-class hoping for a new
chance in life and some of them made eastward
passages in her again, having found their chance
and changed their travel class. Men and women
travelled in her on their way to shape history, to be
acclaimed as geniuses or to be exposed as charlatans.
Frequently, at one period, she was the last that many
young, active males knew of comfort before meeting
violent death. The bulk of her passengers, of course,
were ordinary people about the business of ordinary
lives ; but they shared with the great or the extraordinary amongst their fellow passengers a moment
of interlude in planned living. The few days on the
Atlantic were a break in routine for the large majority
of passengers, even if the routine was only that of
seeking pleasure. A little bad weather, provided of
course it was not too bad, would be welcomed by
many. It was an experience for subsequent allusion,
and this increased the interest of the short respite
from their everyday affairs. Directly the ship had

sunk the land below the horizon they would surrender
themselves to a temporary metamorphosis until the
land grew from the sea again. Individuals would
react individually, some of them would become more
genial than their land habit, others more unapproach-
able, some would consume a great deal more alcohol
than they usually allowed themselves, and others
would affect rationing and physical culture. Scarcely
one of all those land-folk would not make some
small acknowledgment of the alchemistic power of
the sea, or fail to expect that this ship, which had
got them for a moment into a queer confined life
with a background of command and discipline,
should not also provide them with the means of
enjoyment.

That long procession of mixed crowds bringing
the corners of the earth into one hull, presenting
themselves to each other in a strange environment,
jostling each other more closely than on the pave-
ment of a crowded city, isolated by leagues of water
from all the other habitats of men, presents fancy
with a picture of much fascination. The immense
and varied interest of the human freight the *Mauretania*
carried can never conceivably be detailed. Strangely,
there is now no longer any complete record of the
people she carried ; the passenger lists have gone the
way of the ship. Anyhow, a list of names, even a list of
the names of those selected by the management for
special attention, would make queer reading, since many
that claimed attention thirty years ago would now pass
without recognition. By showing the ship making
voyages against a background of events, some picture,
not wholly formless and confused, should emerge ; the
long procession should take on some coherent shape.

When the *Mauretania* began her working life, the broad trend of events in the countries of the customers with whom she was chiefly concerned was marked. America, believing in the Monroe doctrine, and that it was possible for a great nation, largely dependent on trade with other nations to keep apart from international disputes, was greatly occupied with trusts, mergers, big business and the making of money or losing of money on a big scale. The peoples of the Continent of Europe were vigorously rattling swords, indulging in minor wars and military operations, which all pointed inevitably to war on a major scale. England was bitterly occupied with party politics and domestic disputes. She was wrangling around the death-bed of an old conservatism, and making tentative advances to the new political party of Labour which was destined to annihilate the Liberalism which made the advances. In the background of the public mind, too occupied with calling its political opponents names to think much of outside affairs, but never far away from the foreground of the minds of politicians was the threat of European war. When the parties had breath to spare from the abusing of each other, which was not often, they paid attention to the growing German menace ; but that started them blackguarding each other again over the question of what were or were not adequate safeguards against the menace. For those who get a thrill from party bickering and like plenty of meat in political vituperation, it was a glorious period.

On her second voyage the *Mauretania* carried as one of her passengers Mr. Whitelaw Reid, then American Ambassador to the Court of St. James. It is to be presumed that on arrival he had much to say to his government about party feeling in England and sword-rattling in Europe in relation to big business. But on that December voyage, which brought passengers at an average speed of 23·00 knots to New York a few days before Christmas, big business on the Continent of North America was very definitely represented. A Mr. J. W. de Kay, of Mexico, had engaged not one but both of the regal suites. Whether Mr. de Kay achieved the ambition of a lifetime in securing for himself the entire regal accommodation in the world's newest and most expensive liner is mere idle speculation ; but his expensive crossing is worth a momentary glance. Plutocrats in those days were not so given to proclaiming that they were being ruined by taxation as they are now ; like Mr. de Kay, they preferred to advertise their wealth. One instance of that kind should be sufficient ; it can be taken that until August, 1914, the *Mauretania* never made a crossing without big business occupying some of her more expensive suites. As against that, attention was being given to other passengers than those who had money and liked splashing it about ; at this time second-class fares were reduced from £10 to £8 10s., and fifteen shillings was taken off the third-class rates, so that a passage could be had for £6. The *Mauretania* did not live by millionaires alone.

She celebrated the homeward passage of her third voyage, in January, 1908, with her first rescue of lives at sea. The record in the log gives the time and place, and states : " Picked up three men in a dory, crew of barge *Fall River* which had foundered. Proceeded full speed." The time was three o'clock in the afternoon, when even the latest risers would have begun their day, so the spectacle, a form of passenger pleasing not quite usual, was watched by a large crowd. The weather was bad : " Strong wind, high seas and snow squalls." Picking up the three men was not easy ; sighting the dory in snow squalls with a big sea running is a solid tribute to the watch kept by the ship. Captain Pritchard received from the President of the United States the usual pair of binoculars for meeting the occasion in a manner which is, fortunately, usual to such men and such ships.

When in February the King of Portugal and his heir were assassinated in Lisbon, the *Mauretania* was in dock having minor adjustments and alterations carried out, which included the replacing of certain deck plates with thicker ones so as to reduce vibration She was back again in service on the twenty-second of the month, while consideration of that murder was still shocking decent men. In her mixed crowd she carried Portuguese. Homeward on that voyage she put up a new record for the eastward passage. On April 2nd, when Campbell-Bannerman resigned his office of Prime Minister, she was one day out from New York, and before reaching Queenstown some of her passengers, rigid adherents of precedent, were certainly finding food for conversation in the fact that Asquith had gone to Biarritz to kiss the hands of his King in a foreign town. Lloyd George's promotion from the Board of Trade to the Exchequer was hardly being passed in silence.

The English Budget of that year introduced Old-Age Pensions and considerable protest from certain people because the State was asked to provide five shillings a week for old persons of seventy not having otherwise more than £21 per annum on which to

live. While this consideration for the aged poor
was being made into a nice party issue, the *Mauretania*, taking her millionaires, and her seconds and
thirds at their new cheaper rates, made a voyage
not without interest. She left Liverpool on May 27th
and arrived back again there within thirteen days
twelve hours. On the westward passage she averaged
24·86 knots ; in New York she loaded 6,000 tons of
coal in twenty hours. She also loaded quite a
number of bishops and delegates for a Pan-Anglican
Conference in London—one of those jolly eccle-
siastical gatherings which combine uplifting discussion with tea-fights and getting together, as well as
a good deal of talk, proper and earnest talk naturally,
about sex. She also shipped a Mr. Byrne, of
Shanghai, who was making people talk about Jules
Verne and his book, " Around the World in Eighty
Days." Mr. Byrne travelled from Shanghai to Liverpool, pausing for four days in New York, in forty days.
It was then considered good going, and the *Mauretania*
helped him. She made the eastward passage at
24·10 knots, which was well below her fastest ; but
the bishops and the delegates and the Americans,
who were then talking about what effect Taft succeeding Roosevelt would have on big business, and Mr.
Byrne, were all very pleased. They passed a resolu-
tion saying that they were, and that the *Mauretania*
was a fine ship. They seem to have been very sane
people.

In August, King Edward VII went over to
Germany to pay a visit to the Kaiser, taking with
him Sir Charles Hardinge, the permanent secretary
to the Foreign Office. Sir Charles Hardinge made
tentative proposals concerning the curtailment of

naval building, and was rebuffed by the Emperor. The *Mauretania* during that month made two voyages to New York. In October the swords rattled more loudly in Europe, and some of the smaller ones came out of their scabbards. The Sultan Abdul, who was popularised by an English poet by the title of " The Damned," was deposed, and the Young Turk party came into power. On the fifth of the month Bulgarian independence was proclaimed, and the next day Austria annexed Bosnia-Herzegovina. The *Mauretania* sailed from Liverpool on October 10th just after Asquith had informed Balfour that he had never known a general European War to be so imminent. Yet, of course, the passengers took aboard with them newspapers which scouted the idea that England could be dragged into war, and gave solid attention to party differences. While that crisis passed, while the *Daily Telegraph* published a famous interview with the German Emperor representing him as representing himself as struggling for the goodwill of England, while France and Germany grew heated over an incident at Casablanca and the shadow of war grew deeper, while the year passed without the passing of that shadow, the *Mauretania* was empty of her mixed crowds—in dock having her new propellers fitted. Whether she would come into commission again under the Cunard flag or the White Ensign must have seemed, to some of the people who served her, a question not easy to decide.

When the *Mauretania* got back to service, and under her own house flag, in January, 1909, to show what she could do with her new propellers, Brigadier-General Sir H. G. Rawlinson, who within a few years was to be commanding in the field a body of men

at times about the size of the entire British regular
army in which he then served, but still only one of
several such bodies, travelled in her. If American
pressmen in New York hoped to obtain from him
some statement which could be converted into head-
lines about the European military situation, it is
very certain that they went away disappointed. The
situation was quite suitable for head-lines, but the
journalists had met a type of man who did not talk.
French and English soldiers were already preparing
detailed plans for the landing of a British Expedi-
tionary Force in France in case of need. The size of
the naval estimates which the House of Commons
was being asked to pass was giving the Government
considerable embarrassment, and its opponents the
occasion to utter loud party cries. " We want six "
was one of those cries. The Government wanted to
keep the popular mind on social reforms and to
appease the large number of its supporters who would
hear nothing of war ; at the same time the growth
of the German Navy was a danger which could not
be ignored. The Admiralty maintained that they
needed six new battleships, and the Opposition fell
upon that with their loud supporting cries. The
Radical wing of the Government held that four would
do, and pressed for full explanations as to the exact
situation which was said to call for six. A Liberal
Government could not give those explanations ; it
dare not say openly that the situation was getting
out of hand, that Europe was staggering from one
crisis to another, that what Asquith had confided to
Balfour a few weeks before might be applied to
almost any moment until the inevitable one arrived
which changed imminence into actuality. So, being

politicians, they had recourse to a smoke-screen of verbiage, in which the bitterness of party attacks flashed, and, being Englishmen, they found a typically English solution. Without any full explanations, instead of the six battleships demanded by the Admiralty, eight were ordered. Before the noise over the naval estimates was anywhere near full development the *Mauretania* made her first crossing of the Atlantic at an average speed of more than $25\frac{1}{2}$ knots. That, like the battleships, was more than had been asked, for the Government had only required $24\frac{1}{2}$ of her and her designers 25.

The political noise let loose in April, 1909, made the naval estimates row seem like feeble squeaking. Lloyd George introduced his famous Budget which, according to its vociferous opponents, was destined to tax landowners and their class, the people responsible for English freedom and English greatness, out of existence. Popular fancy and popular feeling went all out over that Budget ; controversy about it, and arising from the Lords' rejection of it, contrived to obscure other and vastly more important issues. For more than two years that Budget and the struggle between the Lords and Commons, and the general elections that resulted, turned the minds of many Englishmen and Englishwomen from anything but party politics. It is hard now to recapture any of the spirit of that controversy, or not to wonder where all the heat of it was bred. By the standards of to-day the taxation proposed in that Budget looks simply trivial, and the idea that in a democracy a non-elected upper chamber could be allowed to veto without restriction the acts passed by the lower elected chamber, seems simply absurd. Now that ordinary men and women seem, perhaps happily, incapable of putting the same spleen into domestic politics, when very many voters regard the casting of their votes not as the expressing of high faith but a matter in which they hope to pick the man who will do least harm, it is almost a relief to turn from the political bitterness of those years to something like the *Mauretania*, where solid achievement can be found. From the introduction of Lloyd George's Budget in April, 1909, until the passing of the Parliament Act in August, 1911, there was not a single month in which the *Mauretania* was not about her business on the seas, carrying her mixed crowds and pleasing them.

At the end of 1909 Captain John Pritchard retired from the sea after serving it for fifty-one years. His place in the *Mauretania* was taken by Captain W. T. Turner, who was transferred to the command of the *Lusitania* shortly before the beginning of the War, who went down with her in 1915 but was rescued after being in the water for three hours. By the end of 1909 the *Mauretania* had already established with American big business the " and party " habit. The principle, of course, is the same as that well-established ritual which begins : " What about a little lunch and we'll talk it over." The " party " is fed and suitably wined, talk flits pleasantly from winning racehorses to winning women, golf to politics, bridge to taxation ; at the suitable moment, but not indecently early in the proceedings, when the " party " is judged to have been mellowed and aware of its host's nice touch in hospitality, the purpose is introduced, which begins : " What about fixing things now ? " The business lunch is within the orbit of

almost any ordinary man ;   the " What about a little
trip to England in the *Mauretania* ? " required a
certain largeness in affairs.   But the ship was a fine
ship, a famous ship ; it became quite early in her
career the habit to make clear the largeness of an
affair by offering that invitation.   The business
of feeding and wining the " party " was then pro-
tracted over several days ; and there were many
other diversions.   But the principle was the same ;
in the *Mauretania*, carrying it into practice merely
cost a vastly greater sum.   The few records of the
passengers which she carried during these years all
include several examples of a name associated with
big money followed by the word " and party."   But
any estimate of how much actual business was done
between drinks and amusements is purely speculative.
The drinks and the amusements are not.

On May 6th, 1910, King Edward VII died.   As he
lay dying the *Mauretania* was arriving in New York.
She sailed eastward on May 11th, so that none of her
passengers watched the pageant of his burial.   But
for a short moment England's domestic quarrelling
was stilled.   The personality of the dead king had
made a real impress on the minds of his people.
It was felt that his influence in both home and
foreign affairs had been considerable and wise.   His
humanity had made him a living figure to thousands
of persons who had never seen him.   Only a few
months before, a throne had disappeared in revolution in Portugal.   Many men were saying that
the days of kingship were ending.   The death of
Edward VII of England gave pause to that saying.
Citizens of republics scorning the power and influence
of kings, people in the British Empire agitating

against these hereditary heads of states, were brought
to thinking. No reasonable person could claim that
monarchy in England was just an empty survival ;
it was shown as something not only old and dignified,
but vital and adaptable, nationally valued. As a
crown passed from one man to another, people, even
the declared antagonists of kings, realised that the
man whose body lay in state in Westminster Hall
had filled with benefit to his subjects a high office
for which there was no exact substitute ; and many
of them hoped anxiously that his successor might not
let that office fall. In the *Mauretania*, playing a real
and not a very inconsiderable part in the life of her
times, there was talk of the dead king and what effect
his death might have. The ship had a full list of
passengers. Rich people were travelling eastward to
enjoy a London season ; poorer people in the second,
and even in the third, to spend a carefully calculated
summer holiday in England and in Europe. There
was talk of how this death of a man whom so few
of the talkers knew would affect their enjoyment and
their holidays. There was talk of clothes, and many
republicans were most careful, in a little piece of
England in mid-Atlantic, to show conventional
respect.

On July 2nd, 1910, the *Mauretania* sailed from
Liverpool and made a good westward passage at an
average of 25·31 knots, but her passengers had something else to think and talk about than the speed of
the ship. A negro, Johnson, had been seeking to
box a white man, Jeffries, for the heavyweight
championship of the world ; there had been many
difficulties in the way. New York had refused to
allow the fight within her jurisdiction ; San Francisco,

with a long-standing reputation for toughness, had first consented and then refused ; finally Reno in Nevada—now better known as a resort of film stars with marriage difficulties—consented. On July 4th, a national celebration of freedom and independence, Johnson, in the intervals of laughing and talking to his seconds, the crowd and his opponent, soundly defeated Jeffries and proved that he was the best heavyweight boxer of his age. It was his hour and he made the best of it with considerable facetiousness. Wireless communication with ships was then an infantile affair, but the *Mauretania* got the result of the fight before she had reached mid-ocean. She learned the results of the result of a fight between a white man and a black when she got to New York. In England there seems at first to have been a certain amount of surprise that the contest was decided on the merits of the boxers, a verdict in favour of Jeffries had been anticipated. More violent emotions than surprise were aroused in the United States by Johnson's victory. Because a negro had out-boxed a white man in a fashion which could not be ignored by any referee, and because other negroes were pleased at the result, quite a large number of republican citizens with white skins indulged in the agreeable pastime of beating up coloured men. White mobs, including a company of United States Marines who marched out of their barracks and obtained a splendid victory over a single black man, killed and injured negroes in numbers which must have been highly satisfying to the eager champions of the dominance of white races. When the negroes fought back before being killed or injured or tried to anticipate annihilation by getting in first with attack, there was

much outcry. A casualty list of somewhere around
a score of dead and many hundreds of severely
injured resulted and was advertised in the newspapers
of the world. The American Press broke into head-
lines about colour riots and naïvely deplored the fact
that negroes had been given the chance of celebrating
—the method of celebrating being, of course, ill-
treatment at the hands of large, homicidal white
crowds. Horror at Johnson's victory travelled in
the *Mauretania* and other ships, engendering violent
discussions, across the Atlantic, spreading over Europe
and almost over the world. The firm, which had
photographed the fight for what was then known as
the bioscope and had paid $100,000 for the exhibition
rights, had the greatest difficulty in finding any hall
or theatre where they could show their pictures.
Ordinary people wanted to see those pictures, but
mass sentiment deemed the spectacle degrading for
white eyes. The following summer Johnson came to
England and arranged to box another white man,
Bombardier Wells. That turned a glow into flames
again. A Nonconformist minister, the Reverend
Mr. Meyer, stepped into the limelight and remained
there for months ; he invoked all sorts of people,
local authorities, bishops, Members of Parliament,
innumerable writers of letters to the press ; he
dragged in Mr. Winston Churchill at the Home
Office. The fight was banned in England. An
attempt was made to hold it in Paris, but France had
been stirred by the outcry and would not have it ;
so the contest was abandoned. There were people
who said it was hard luck on Bombardier Wells ;
perhaps they believed it. For a year and a half,
under the growing shadow of war, in the midst of

all manner of domestic difficulties, millions of people on both sides of the Atlantic were much concerned with the harm which might result from an athletic contest between a white man and a black, when it was a practical certainty that the black man would win. That was a very serious business a quarter of a century ago.

When the second general election of the year 1910 was warming to its work, the *Mauretania* got away from the noise to do a job of work which helped her reputation. She sailed from Liverpool on December 10th under orders to bring home a cargo of passengers for Christmas. The weather was not kindly on the westward passage and she made the poor average, for her, of 23·94 knots. At New York a larger and more hurried army of workers than usual took her in hand as she tied up ; she was bunkered with 6,600 tons of coal, took in fresh water and stores, shipped her new passengers, and was off again on December 17th. There were many of her mixed crowd who wished on Christmas Day to get their legs beneath tables as far away as Russia and Germany and Spain. The agents ashore had told them that they would easily be able to do that ; Mr. A. A. Booth, the chairman of the Cunard Company, who was in the ship on that passage, was almost certainly asked by some passenger or other, possibly Melba, who was there, whether the *Mauretania* could do it to time. She could, although the weather would only let her steam at a steady 25 knots. She called at Fishguard, to disembark the passengers who were in a hurry, and arrived at Liverpool in a few hours over twelve days from leaving it. More than six thousand miles of sea covered in winter weather, with a turn round at New York included, in a very little over three hundred hours, was decent going. No record of fast steaming, the Atlantic had seen to that, but a fine, solid success of organisation and efficiency and seaworthiness. While, perhaps, Melba sang to her fellow passengers, while, certainly, people in all three classes talked about how they were going to spend Christmas, if the ship did not let them down, there were men up topsides and others down below doing concentrated and continuous work. It was because she so seldom allowed the sea to make her let her passengers down that the *Mauretania* was creating her own reputation.

In the following June, when England was enjoying an extraordinary and not a seasonal respite from domestic quarrels, she was again ordered to meet the occasion. All ships eastward bound were being well filled with people anxious to have a look at the sights and celebrations attending King George's coronation on June 22nd, some few of them to take part in the ceremonies. A lure was held out to republican big business : the *Mauretania* would take the makers of big money over, give them five days in England to see the Coronation sights, and have them back again in New York in just over a fortnight. She did what she was advertised to do ; but again the weather was not in her favour, on both passages eastwards and westwards there was fog about and on neither could she average as much as 25 knots. She left New York on June 14th, the last of the big ships to leave with Coronation visitors, carrying two thousand and thirty-nine passengers, amongst them an English polo team. She landed the majority of her passengers at Fishguard on the 19th and the rest at Liverpool early on the 20th. While many of the slower ships, delayed by the hazy weather, had a hard job of it to get their human cargoes over in time, the *Mauretania*, starting last, was punctual. She sailed again from Liverpool on the 24th with several of the passengers whom she had brought from New York ten days before, and she disembarked them, as it had been advertised that she would do, a little more than a fortnight after she had embarked them.

That Coronation voyage stands as a milestone in the *Mauretania's* history. During the westward passage with more than two thousand of her mixed freight, more than one thousand of them in the third class, and so people who, if they saw the Coronation processions, were likely to see them from the pavements after a long, tiring wait and not from the stands of the privileged, she ceased to be the world's largest passenger liner in commission. The *Olympic*, the new White Star ship built by direction of the Morgan Combine to answer the challenge of the *Mauretania*, had sailed from England just about the time that the *Mauretania* was leaving New York. The two ships passed each other, far apart of course, on their eastward and westward tracks somewhere about mid-Atlantic. The *Olympic* made a faster passage than had been expected ; she averaged over $21\frac{1}{2}$ knots. That was good, since she had not been designed for speed records. She was undoubtedly comfortable and, by the standard of 1911 with her 45,000 tons, she was enormous. The *Mauretania* had been forced from her high position as unrivalled for those who think in terms of size. It was definitely a milestone, but by then she had already established herself and not merely her size and speed.

That Coronation voyage helped to settle another matter : one more injustice to Ireland. It pushed home the fact, which was becoming more and more obvious, that Queenstown was a poor sort of port of call for passengers in a hurry. Fishguard was better, but not good ; it necessitated a long train journey for London passengers ; Liverpool was, and had long been, an uncomfortable necessity. The *Mauretania* had to begin and end her voyages there because it was her home port and the headquarters of her owners ; but it was and always had been a difficult port for ships of her size. That winter was to drive home once again the difficulty. She had changed from the largest to the next large ; there were other changes in the air. But Ireland, looking out for injustice, fought strenuously and for some time successfully the change from Queenstown.

After the brief interlude when the crowning of King George V had concentrated public attention on high ceremony and ordered dignity, domestic politics, industrial relationships and international affairs broke into alarms and excursions. As a make-weight to other troubles the Reverend Mr. Meyer got busy with the negro boxer, Johnson. France, early in the year, had had trouble in Morocco and had advanced to occupy Fez. Germany maintained that this advance entitled her to a good portion of the French Congo by way of keeping the balance true. Bargaining about the partition of parts of Africa was going forward when Germany suddenly sent the *Panther* to Agadir. Agadir, a small port on the coast of Morocco, at that time had no German inhabitants in or near it nor any trade with Germany, so that the appearance of a German warship there had a not less startling effect than, say, the introduction of a lady of easy virtue to a Victorian vicarage tea. General European war ousted even the Reverend Mr. Meyer from the limelight. Lloyd George, not then popularly considered as a supporter of wars, made a speech at the Mansion House on July 21st, and informed his audience that, if we were to be treated as of no account in the Cabinet of Nations, " peace at that price would be a humiliation intolerable for a great country like ours to endure." That was plain speech, and it had the approval of the Prime Minister and the Foreign Secretary. When English men and women spending August holidays in Germany received hints that it might be well to curtail them and get home while the going was good, they realised that the position was not just talking. War was very near.

But even the figure of war with limelight full upon it, could not keep Englishmen from enjoying party disputes. The Parliament Bill, designed to destroy their power of veto, was before the Lords. Suggestions for the reform of their House had been put forward by certain of the Lords themselves, and turned down. Nobody wanted reform except as an eternal proposal for the future. The way of solving the problem without reform was thoroughly English, either the Lords should pass the Parliament Bill, which allowed them to delay legislation but not to prevent it, or they should be turned, by the creation of a considerable cohort of new peers, into the world's most comic legislative chamber. It looked a good thing for the Government and the Parliament Bill, but the press and the party leaders and agents worked hard to keep the game going. Cartoonists had an easy time

drawing pictures of aged noblemen as " diehards "
and " backwoods-men," Lord Halsbury's features
were in much demand.   Political writers still declare
the issue to have been in doubt and make drama out
of the debate on August 11th, when the questions of
Parliament Bill or comic opera upper chamber was
decided.   The Bill won, by a decided though not a
great majority, and the diehards turned round on
the bishops and said it was all their fault.   But, with
war so close, the fine spirit of party bitterness had
been given a nourishing meal.

   To the international and political struggles England
was able to add some serious industrial disputes :
employers and employed got down to it vigorously.
The *Mauretania* was involved there.   The railway
workers had gone on strike.   The unions declared
that dockers and stevedores, firemen, trimmers, seamen and stewards should keep the party spirit strong
and come out in sympathy.   The *Mauretania* was due
to sail from Liverpool on August 12th ; she just got
away with the newspapers starring the Lords' debate
but giving some notice to war and strikers.   The
Lusitania, to follow her a week later, was held up ;
she had to cancel her sailing and finally to sail on a
Sunday after being kept idle for eight days.   By
then the *Mauretania* was home again, and the Liverpool
shipowners, led by the Cunard chairman, had
managed to compromise the dispute so far as they
were concerned.   She made her regular sailings
throughout that autumn and with very full passenger
lists ; the luck, for it was obviously only the luck
of dates, that she had not been held up when other
liners had been did her good.   Even strikers, people
said, could not stop the ship from doing her job to

time ; and more people than ever booked passages
in her. It had, however, become necessary for her
to give more attention to something which she had
never ignored : crew pleasing. Quite busy times for
the pre-war fashion.

The acuteness of the war crisis commenced by the
arrival of the *Panther* at Agadir passed in November.
The situation was judged so uncritical that King
George was able early in December to sail for India
and the gorgeousness of the Coronation Durbar at
Delhi. But there was still something doing at home.
Lloyd George introduced his National Insurance Bill
and party politics jumped on it gladly with loud
shouts about stamp licking. The *Mauretania* was to
have repeated her Christmas voyage, leaving Liverpool on December 9th and getting her passengers
from New York spread over Europe comfortably in
time for the annual festival of peace and goodwill,
but the Port of Liverpool stepped in there and
made her do what strikes had failed to make her do,
miss a sailing. On December 7th she was lying at
the Cunard Buoy in the Sloyne when during a
strong southerly gale she broke from her moorings
and went aground. She had done that before and
she was to do it again ; under certain conditions of
wind and tide the Mersey was a bad place for a big
ship offering a huge area of wind resistance. The
first time she grounded in the Mersey was on the
evening of the day preceding her second voyage ;
she then did herself no damage and was able to keep
her sailing appointment. On this second occasion
she had to be dry-docked, and the *Lusitania*, which
had only arrived from New York on December 6th,
had to turn round in a hurry and do the Christmas

carrying. Those little tricks of the Mersey, as well as the fact that it was situated in a corner of England well off the direct continental route were making owners more inclined to listen to what master mariners had to say, that Liverpool in some respects had its disadvantages for very big ships.

As the *Mauretania* had to go into dry dock she was given a thorough overhaul and did not come into commission again until March 2nd, 1912. While she was in the hands of shore-workers, two sailors placed their names amongst those which history will not forget : Amundsen, by leading men for the first time to the South Pole on December 14th, 1911, Scott, who reached the same Pole a month later, by the tragic and gallant end of himself and of the party whom he led.

That year started with the war being brought a little nearer, for in January Haldane went on a mission to Germany, which failed. At home a Bill to give votes to women was withdrawn from Parliament, and the wild women became more wild. Strikes gave considerable trouble ; during March and the first half of April the coal-owners and the miners held up the work of the country with their disputes. King George, who had returned from India in February, was not present at Aintree for the Grand National, which Jerry M. won, as he had intended to be, because he considered that with the country so disturbed and industrial distress so prevalent his presence at public amusements was not fitting. The coal-owners resented interference between themselves and their employees ; the Government, who had intervened the year before in the railway strike, ignored that resentment and introduced and passed a

Minimum Wages Bill. The principle that the Government should step in and attempt settlement of industrial disputes, which affected the welfare of the community, was established. That was an event which, developing, was to penetrate into every corner of English living. The Home Rule Bill was introduced, bringing Irish affairs once more to the foreground of party politics, starting preparations for civil war, making its contribution to the certainty of European war. The Turks, for minor wars were in being, were defeated by the Balkan League. The Marconi case, in which British ministers were accused of using their official positions for their own financial advantage, left an unpleasant taste behind. Woodrow Wilson became President of the United States, a happening not without serious consequences for his country and for the world. It was not an uneventful year.

For ships and those whose business is the sea it was dominated by the sailing of the *Titanic*. Passenger carrying and passenger pleasing had suddenly to face great difficulties. There was alarm and fear amongst travellers not usually unduly sensitive to either ; there was a temporary refusal to go to sea for pleasure amongst the timid. Any shipping disaster, however small, will affect passenger lists. As the long inquiry progressed and the press savoured each unhappy detail, dwelling upon the evidence of men whom Roosevelt had described as " better dead," the Atlantic shipping companies had a hard job of it to re-establish confidence. The *Mauretania* left Liverpool the day before the disaster ; from the moment when, a few hours out from Queenstown, she received news of it and altered her course so as to give the ice a wide berth, all ranks and ratings of her crew had to start playing parts with passengers. Before the full extent of the loss of life was known, and it was a source of bitter complaint that the first official report published was that the passengers had been saved, decency forbade the crew of the *Mauretania* from saying what was, humanly, in their minds, " Thank God it was not one of ours." After that, as the facts became known, the last thing that any of them wished, but the thing which so few of them who came in contact with passengers could escape, was to talk about the affair except with others of their kind. The *Titanic*, belonging to the International Mercantile Marine, had been American owned, but she had been almost entirely British manned : that necessitated much careful treading. Amongst the large mixed crowds which the *Mauretania* carried there were many people who recognised that there was one subject not popular with her crew and avoided it, but there were more people who did not avoid it. The same question in many different forms : " Has the *Mauretania* been made safe ? " had to be answered patiently and as far as possible convincingly. The obvious reply, that there is no absolute safety anywhere on sea or land, was not going to be popular with the sort of people who could not prevent themselves asking those questions. The assurances given by badgered stewards to nervous passengers have not been recorded. That is unfortunate, because some of the reasons supplied for the *Mauretania* being a safe ship must have been original and diverting. For a time her passenger lists were affected, like those of every other liner but much less than many. She went on carrying her millionaires, statesmen, diplomats, stage stars and her larger proportion of ordinary people. On December 7th of that year the Mersey did not prevent her from sailing for New York to bring back a large crowd in time for Christmas.

Legislation in England was having a definite effect upon one class of her passengers. There were fewer English emigrants in the third cabin. The idea, supported by legislation, was spreading that a better time lay ahead for the poorer workers. That led to many young people deciding to hang on for the better times at home instead of going off to seek them elsewhere amongst strange surroundings and strange people. On the lower decks of the *Mauretania* the falling off of the numbers of British-born emigrants was not very marked, as the crowd there had always been mixed and very far from mainly English, but it was noticeable. It was significant ; a growing preference for hanging about in the hope of being looked after instead of setting out to take a chance at doing something new can scarcely be ignored.

In mid-January of 1913 the Commons passed the Home Rule Bill, and shortly afterwards the Lords, as had been expected, threw it out. That merely entailed delay before the Bill could become law, but a use was made of the delay which must have surprised foreigners unacquainted with the habit of Anglo-Irish affairs. Ireland began to drill and arm in two camps ; eminent lawyers prepared themselves to become combatants in a civil war, and the party spirit was not allowed to sleep. In May King George and Queen Mary went to Berlin, and it was hoped that better relations between Germany and England might result from the visit. In June Aboyeur won the Derby on an objection to Craganour's running, but before Craganour led Aboyeur past the post a woman had thrown herself into the race, brought down the King's horse, injured the jockey and killed herself. There were other women doing queer things like that at the time, and some people proclaiming them martyrs. That same month the report on the Marconi case was published ; the two ministers involved had to admit indiscretion, and the party spirit had another jamboree. At Ghent Bombardier Wells, having failed to get into a ring with Johnson, got into one with the Frenchman, Carpentier, and did not thereby improve his reputation as a fighter. During August the London Conference of Ambassadors which had been sitting for months attempting to find some means of removing the menace of war, gave up the attempt. In October the German Emperor informed Austria that he would back her in any action which she might take against Serbia. Early in July the Royal Standard was for the first time broken from the *Mauretania's* main mast. Liverpool was making a big effort to maintain her position as a port for important shipping. King George and Queen Mary opened the Gladstone Dock and afterwards inspected England's most famous liner.

The *Mauretania* was in continuous service throughout that year ; she made fifteen voyages to New York and back. Carrying a larger number of lifeboats, and with her precautions in case of emergency reorganised, she went steadily on with her job of restoring confidence. She did not during the whole of 1913 make anything in the nature of an exceptionally fast passage, she just kept time and brought her mixed crowd to their destinations as it had been

advertised that she would do.   Speed on the Atlantic
was for the moment less in popular favour than
reliability.   On December 7th she sailed again on a
Christmas voyage.   That was the last occasion on
which she used Queenstown as a regular port of call.
With the ending of the year the first phase
of her life was over.   In six years she had made
eighty-six voyages, and had only once failed to sail
on the day on which she was advertised to do so.
By then there were a large number of people, not
only in the first saloon but in the second cabin as well,
who used her regularly to get about their business ;
the same names recurred again and again in her lists.
She finished with her Liverpool-Queenstown-New
York—New York-Queenstown-Liverpool phase firmly
established as not only the fastest liner afloat but as
a ship of character.

On January 3rd, 1914, Lloyd George informed
representatives of the Press that the prospects of the
world had never been more peaceful.   A comforting
statement, but not one that convinced.   Even people
wholly ignorant of, or wholly unconcerned with
foreign affairs had known prospects in Ireland to be
more peaceful.   Although none of the parties liked
the proposal or would take it seriously, the fact that
Lord Roberts was advocating conscription as an
immediate necessity gave many ordinary persons
pause.   The comfortable theory that the old man
had reached his dotage was a great deal too easy for
universal acceptance.   He was an old retired soldier,
not without experience ;   he had given his working
life to the regular army.   Conscription for the
majority of regular officers of that day was an
extremely unpopular, almost a revolting idea.   It

meant that the army as they knew it would pass.
Lord Roberts was running against his kind. Unwillingly, some men saw in that not a senile whim
but a conviction based on knowledge. There was a
feeling growing in ordinary minds which forbade
belief in peaceful prospects.

After an eight-week overhaul the *Mauretania* came
back into service at the beginning of March, but
using Fishguard instead of Queenstown. It had
been intended that she should go back again into
service on February 14th, but an accident, the only
one involving the death of men working in her, had
occurred. There was an explosion of a gas cylinder
in use for brazing. Four workmen were killed, six
injured, and the starboard high-pressure turbine was
damaged. The incident is mentioned because it is
unique in the ship's history. It was not her habit
to demand the lives of those who worked for her.
She was three days out from New York, with a cargo
of passengers, several of whom were travelling over
to see the Grand National run, when the Curragh
incident occurred. English officers were asked by
their general to say whether, under certain circumstances, they would obey their orders. Their decision
was that they would not, and they were told to
consider themselves dismissed from the army. A
bewildered public, both English and foreign,
wondered what this sort of behaviour could be
called. Nobody could give them an exact
answer. The Government and the Army Council
were much embarrassed, but with the assistance
of dialectics the incident was covered over and
the officers concerned retained their commissions.
Ireland once more had supplied the world with

news, but news that could not be very clearly interpreted.

Then events began to move more swiftly. While Germany and Austria were discussing the details of the Schlieffen plan of invading France through Belgium, there occurred another sea disaster which at other times would have held first place in men's attention. The Canadian Pacific liner *Empress of Ireland*, eastward bound, was feeling her way in a thick fog down the St. Lawrence when she collided with the *Storstad*, a Norwegian tramp, and sank off Father Point in a few minutes. One thousand and twenty-three men, women and children lost their lives in those few minutes. The civilised world had still a little time to wait before deaths on that scale in that short time were to become common ; it was shocked. But, somehow, it was too pre-occupied with a shadow hanging over it to be stirred as it might have been. The *Mauretania* was three days out from New York when the *Empress of Ireland* went down on May 29th ; once again, as she did her job on the sea, she received the news that another ship had failed in doing hers. She carried westward on her next voyage the members of the Commission who were to inquire into the disaster, and to exonerate the English ship and her officers from all blame.

Less than a month later, one day out, westward bound, she received more news of sudden death— that the Archduke Franz Ferdinand and his wife had been murdered at Serajevo. The cry of " Wolf " had been raised very often, children had been born and grown to adolescence, almost to manhood, listening to it. Yet when the wolf did really approach, mass instinct recognised it without hesitation. Statesmen and politicians struggled desperately to avert the change from anticipation to realisation. Recollection of those weeks of July shapes a picture of most ordinary men and women going about their affairs with terrible though formless imagination in their hearts, but convinced beyond any argument that war, for which they could find no real reason, must involve them. When on August 1st the *Mauretania* sailed from Liverpool for New York, but not to arrive at New York, men aboard her and throughout the country were saying that, if England were kept out of the War by her Government, she would be for ever disgraced.

CHAPTER VI

WAR SERVICE

IT was one of the specific purposes for which the *Mauretania* was designed that, in the event of war, she should serve as an auxiliary cruiser. Much had been made of that when the agreement under which she came into existence was made public. She was built with this purpose prominently in view. Armour-plating on a liner primarily designed for speed was clearly impossible ; the engine and boiler rooms were located below the water-line, as were the rudder and the steering gear. The subdivision of the ship into compartments was arranged to meet her requirements as an auxiliary cruiser. Her bunkers were placed so as to give the maximum protection possible to the most vulnerable parts. She was provided with strengthened platforms where six-inch guns could be mounted, four on the fore-castle, two on either side ; eight, four to starboard, four to port, on the shelter deck abaft the beam. Directly war should be declared she, with the rest of the Cunard fleet, came mechanically under Admiralty disposal, to be employed as the Navy ordered. The *Mauretania's* employment in war-time had been proclaimed and advertised from the moment when the nation was informed that it was providing the money for her building ; long before that, when the subsidy and the agreement attaching to it were under discussion, her place and work in war had received attention from the authorities in Whitehall. Her speed and her cruising range had been mentioned by the Admiralty spokesman in the House of Commons, as rendering her particularly qualified to act as an auxiliary cruiser ; her qualification for so acting had been given as justification for the expense to which the country was being put to build her. Her war-time job was considered, presumably with due care, long years ahead. It is curious to find that she never did it—was, indeed, never asked to do it.

The use of liners as auxiliary cruisers had been considered by all the powers for many years. The idea had its opponents, but it was generally accepted. Germany alone of the belligerent nations appears to have carried the idea well beyond the stage of theorising, and to have formed something like detailed plans for using her liners. The largest and fastest liners used the Atlantic, so it was there that most of the prospective auxiliary cruisers would be found. On July 29th, Germany instructed her merchantmen in the Atlantic by wireless ; before war had actually come these ships had received their orders. The *Kronprinzessin Cecilie*, carrying specie worth £2,000,000 and so a prize immensely worth the having, was nearing Europe. When she got her orders, she turned and beat her own record for the westward run, finding safety in Bar Harbour, Maine. Other big German ships at sea got safely to neutral ports or, being in them, remained where they were. War came, and the big English ships, which had been earmarked as auxiliary cruisers, were unwarned.

The *Lusitania* was due to sail from New York. Although there was no information concerning the position of certain German ships, she sailed on

August 5th, trusting to her speed to give her the
heels of any enemy she might meet. Rumours that
she had been destroyed reached England before her,
but she made her home port without incident. The
Mauretania, when war was declared, was westward
bound ; she received wireless orders to go to Halifax,
and went there. Nobody of her ship's company
could answer passengers' questions, nor forecast the
ship's future or their own. A very large percentage
of the navigation officers of the Cunard Company
were in the Royal Naval Reserve, as were a considerable proportion of the crews. These men had a
defined programme ahead : they had to report at
once for duty on arrival in a British port. What
would happen to the ships from which they might be
taken, who would serve the ships if they were taken,
were matters of pure speculation. There were no
known plans. If the *Mauretania* became what she
had been designed to become in war-time, who would
serve her ? As she hurried for Halifax, the whole
of her crew, from her commander downwards,
—as men all over the world were doing—wondered what was going to happen to them and the
jobs into which they had put their pride. The confusion and the uncertainty continued. The *Mauretania* made three more voyages, exciting voyages so
far as rumours and the chance of meeting an enemy
were concerned, carrying passengers across the Atlantic.
    Meanwhile events rather than plans enabled the
authorities to come to some decision about the
employment of the world's fastest merchant ships.
On the outbreak of war the Admiralty had immediately taken over the *Aquitania*, then at Liverpool,
together with the *Carmania* and the *Caronia*, and had

started stripping them of their fittings and converting them for use as auxiliary cruisers. It was an expensive business carried out at high speed and with the usual prodigality of war-waste. The *Aquitania* was completed and sailed as an armed cruiser on August 8th, but was unfortunately damaged in collision. She returned to port, where at the end of September she was dismantled and laid up. Before she was dismantled for the second time within a matter of weeks, the *Carmania* and the *Caronia* had sailed, with captains of the Royal Navy in command, but with some of their own officers and other ratings retained aboard as having special knowledge of the ship.

So the *Mauretania*, doing her ordinary job under extraordinary circumstances, had at least some data to use in speculating on her probable fate. On the analogy of the *Aquitania* she would certainly be mauled about, but after mauling and remauling might be left idle ; on the analogy of the other two, if used, she would certainly be commanded by strangers from another service. Captain J. C. Barr, lately commanding the *Carmania*, was now, with temporary rank of Commander R.N.R. and wearing a uniform clearly distinguishable from a Commander R.N., navigator and adviser on what had been his own bridge. The prospects, whatever they might be, called for and received much comment.

Before the *Aquitania* was dismantled for the second time, the *Kaiser Wilhelm der Grosse*, the ship which in 1897 had taken the Blue Riband of the Atlantic from England and had so started the events which led to the building of the *Mauretania*, was sunk. She had had plans long prepared, and she carried them out. She was fitted and armed and sailed as an

auxiliary cruiser, getting through by way of the
Norwegian coast and a turn westward in northern
latitudes without difficulty and without interference
from the English Navy. She sank a trawler off
Iceland. She stopped two liners with women
passengers aboard, but allowed them to proceed.
On August 24th, off Rio de Oro, on the west coast
of Africa, in Spanish territorial waters, she was found,
with colliers alongside her, by H.M.S. *Highflyer*, an
obsolete cruiser. The *Highflyer*, as the phrase goes,
could not have seen the way the *Kaiser Wilhelm der
Grosse* went. But, having heard of the enemy's
movements, by panting and gasping and straining
her ancient engines, had managed to catch her coaling. One of the world's fast liners captured, and
sunk by a poor old totterer. It was a bad business
for those people who had banked on the great liners
doing great work as auxiliary cruisers. So bad a
business that the whole idea of using such ships for
the purpose for which they had been subsidised,
collapsed. The biggest ships could not put into
the smaller ports to coal ; coaling at sea, they were
exposed to considerable damage, which was bad ;
tied to the slow business of bunkering from colliers
alongside, they were the easy victims of much slower
ships, which was fatal. The idea of these large
auxiliary cruisers had been proved, somewhat late
in the day, the biggest sort of mistake.

So the authorities who had made the mistake had
to decide what to do with the *Mauretania*. They
requisitioned her, took her off the Atlantic, dismantled
her, and did nothing. What could they do ? She
was an enormously expensive ship to run ; the world
was struggling in a time when passenger comfort in

crossing the Atlantic was not the important thing it had been ; the passengers must do with fewer and smaller liners. But what other use was there for her ? She was too big and she burned too much coal, which was daily becoming more precious. England was not fighting a distant colonial war. There was then no need of the largest troopships. Dominions troops could be brought to England as fast as the country could accommodate them in smaller, less expensive vessels. Through that first winter and early spring, when the second battle of Ypres was being fought and gas was being introduced into war, it seemed that the *Mauretania* had failed completely. She had been designed for peace and war purposes, and in the latter capacity seemed impossible. She was too precious to risk unnecessarily on the Atlantic, where German submarines would covet her as a most delectable plum. One of her huge kind would do there, and the choice had fallen on her sister, which after all was not the world's fastest merchantman. So she lay, with the bigger and slower *Aquitania*, doing nothing, not wanted.

The tragic muddle of the Dardanelles gave the *Mauretania* her chance. That which was commenced as a purely naval operation was changed, the sea operation having failed, to a landing, but only after the Turks, fully aware of what was proposed, had been given ample time to prepare their defences. There were changes of plan, compromises, jealousies and misunderstandings throughout, but one thing was plain and uncompromising from the start : since there was going to be fighting on a considerable scale some distance away from England, troops from home would need ships of adequate size to transport them to the new slaughtering ground. Here, then, was a chance to use the big ships. The dismantled *Mauretania* was prepared as a transport. The first attack of April 25th had been launched, and had already shown itself abortive before she made her first voyage to Lemnos. She sailed in May from Southampton, carrying 3,182 troops. Captain Daniel Dow commanded her ; a few weeks before he had been brought ashore from his own ship, the *Lusitania*, for a period of leave after months of strain on the Atlantic. So he took the *Mauretania* on her first war service, while her sister passed out of service.

Here is not the place for any description of the *Lusitania's* end. An unarmed passenger ship, she was torpedoed by the German Submarine U 20, commanded by one Schweiger, off the Old Head of Kinsale on May 7th, 1915. She sank within twenty minutes with the loss of 1,198 children, women and men. That deed of war has been appraised by humanity ; it remains as a reminder of what may happen when nations fight. Historians find in it a tragedy which yet served the Allies' cause. That sinking and that slaughter of defenceless noncombatant people needs no discussion here, but it must have a place. The two ships were sisters, much in outward appearance alike, rivals in speed very much beyond the achievements of all other ships of their kind. It is surely not false sentimentality, it is certainly not false to sailors and ship-lovers, to feel glad that when the *Lusitania* sank her greater sister's idleness was over ; that the *Mauretania*, left without any rival, should be doing something to hasten the time when such sinkings should cease.

It was not a cheerful moment in which to enter the war ; it may well be argued that there were no cheerful moments to enter it ; but May, of 1915 was already past the dawning ; it was in the growing daylight of reality. The first frenzy of war excitement was over ; it had taken with it to death, in many cases, the sort of men who said : " This business knocks everything else endways. There is only one thing for me to do." That the other sort of man would be needed but might take some fetching, that the fetching would certainly be unpopular was already plain. An autumn, a winter and a spring had divorced any association between war and romance and glory ; it was even then established as a stationary business of killing, chiefly distinguished by mud and sordidness. The first stage was over ; enemies faced each other in long lines of trenches, and the question whether they would ever do anything else was already being asked. Criticism was everywhere ; leaders who had been popular idols had fallen. Ammunition and guns and all sorts of equipment were known to be short. Neuve Chapelle, Hill 60 and Festubert had been fought in quick succession, and had demonstrated even to the optimistic that attacks on that scale were worse than futile. Sir John French had begun to quarrel with the politicians. Amongst certain commanders in the field the idea had already germinated, possibly to the exclusion of all other positive ideas, that to maintain the fighting spirit of the troops, small attacks, although nothing of value could proceed from them, must be constant. The troops were becoming fatalistic, with reason pessimistic about the value of the little attacks, hoping nothing from them but the luck of a nice wound. The Allies were bickering amongst themselves, saying in effect : " I've done this ; it is your turn to do something now." Schemes for moving the pressure from here to there, changing the point of attack, were proposed, championed, challenged, launched. The attack on the Dardanelles failed, in everything but individual courage, as it began, but failing was pursued as a scheme for many months. It was not a cheerful moment when the *Mauretania* in May, 1915, took her first load of troops to Lemnos.

She made three voyages with troops to Lemnos in May, July and August, carrying in all 10,391 officers and men. During these months she was, of course, a belligerent vessel since she carried troops ; she expected and looked out for enemy attack. She found the attack, and by the smallest possible margin escaped her sister's fate. The official account is, as it should be, terse. She was bound for Mudros when attacked by a submarine. Captain Dow saw the track of the torpedo approaching on the starboard bow ; he had the wheel put over hard-a-port. The torpedo missed the ship by a distance estimated at five feet. The great speed of the *Mauretania* enabled her to get out of range of the submarine's further attack.

The wheel went over smartly, that is certain ; the quartermaster spun the spokes as he had never spun them before. The ship did what she had done on her trials on the Skelmorlie mile, to the inconvenience of a cargo tramp astern, and the men in her blessed the builders, or should have done, who fashioned her to turn like that. In the moment of the ship's first swinging off her course, the men down in engine and boiler rooms, nasty places in which to be trapped, surely guessed at something ; as the order almost synchronising with the first swing, A.P.R., came down from the bridge the men down there obeyed it ; they gave every possible revolution. They gave her the steam to give all possible revolutions ; trimming or stoking or greasing, they fell upon their jobs with their own lives and the lives of their fellows as the prize of good work. Working below the water-line, in those narrow, electrically lit spaces from which escape was so difficult, they could only guess, but pretty shrewdly, at what was going on above. They gave her the revolutions, some part of their senses alert for an explosion, knowing that if the explosion came, the steam they were making for the revolutions would give many of them agony before it brought them death. The *Mauretania's* great speed took her to safety, but through some nasty moments.

After returning from her third voyage with troops, the *Mauretania* was docked and underwent her second War transformation. She became a fully equipped hospital ship. As such, it was considered by other persons as well as the authorities responsible for her transformation, there was need of her.

Merchant sailors who experienced it have a lot to say about the transport muddle of the Dardanelles. Their tales, humorous, tragic, often unprintable, sometimes unbelievable except for their staggering imprint of truth, would fill volumes. Merchant sailors, especially masters of merchant ships, are trained to hate waste of material or time. They would not command ships owned by companies or firms who expect dividends if they were not mightily concerned with economies and fearful of having to explain, to men intolerant of such explanations, delays or even minor extra expenditure. That ships carrying vitally needed cargoes should lie in ports where their merchandise is not required, that ships should be empty and idle when the need of them full and active is urgent, are to these men crimes. That a ship should proceed for orders to a port and find none when she gets there is, in their view, sheer unthinkable mismanagement. When a merchant ship's master, seeking orders or making legitimate demands as from master to agent, is patronised by an officer from another service, then there is trouble and jealousy. Get them in the right mood and the right company, and the merchant skippers will tell strange tales of the incredible muddle of transport at the Dardanelles. Many of the tales have been told, many of them in the interests of the future should be told, but the *Mauretania* is not directly concerned with them. She carried her troops and returned for more without figuring in any outstanding muddle. She was trooping, and she was a class of ship which even the most muddle-headed transport official could scarcely overlook. But she was concerned with spectacular muddle because in her second War transformation she came to rectify it.

The transport of medical stores and staffs occupies a prominent place in the muddle. It is recorded that a ship so loaded was forgotten, lying at anchor for ten whole days, while other unequipped ships a few miles away dealt with wounded as they could, clamouring for supplies and staffs which they could not get. The story of the " Black Carriers " does not adorn history. These were merchant ships which carried troops to the Gallipoli beaches and, having landed them, loaded up with wounded. In the earlier stages of the muddle the medical staff aboard most of these ships consisted of the surgeon, and his stores were the routine stores. When the wounded came aboard the surgeon, with one of the other officers as an amateur anæsthetist and stewards as dressers, had to perform such operations as could not be postponed. Then the ship would sail for, say, Alexandria, where presumably she had something in the nature of a hurried wash and brush-up to make her a little more fit for carrying wounded men, and where medical officers and nursing sisters came aboard. And so, in many cases, home with her damaged freight to England, there to pick up a fresh cargo of the undamaged. "Black Carriers," the name which they were given, is certainly a good one since it describes them. They were neither troopships nor hospital ships, but both, and medical science and humanity cry out at the combination. The accommodation which is adequate for a healthy man is seldom adequate for a broken one ; bad wounds and makeshifts do not go comfortably together. In a fully equipped hospital ship with cots nicely swung a cushy wound can prove itself a nuisance when stirred by the sea over a short Channel crossing. Speculation on the amount of unnecessary pain caused by those makeshift carriers is not pleasant. They had, not a narrow channel, but more than two thousand miles of sea to cross. How many times each of them must have paused in her passage home to drop into the sea freight which need not have been dropped had she been properly equipped to carry it is not an agreeable topic. But it was not an agreeable muddle.

These vessels were not hospital ships, but

sometimes when loaded with wounded they sailed
under the Red Cross flag. Often they were not
allowed to do that. Sometimes—and the incredible
thing is fact—they combined their dual rôles and
carried at the same time wounded and able-bodied
fighting men. It is recorded concerning one of these
vessels that while taking wounded home she also,
under orders, took on board 120 naval ratings at
Gibraltar, active men on active service. Some
genius had thought of economy ; perhaps—for
stranger things did happen in the war—he received
a decoration for his brilliance. There was space
available in a ship, so it was filled. Fighting men
and wounded travelled together, but not, of course,
under the Red Cross. The Black Carriers were
hirelings and had to earn their keep. The Germans
knew of the Black Carriers and the brilliant economies
practised in them. The English were in the habit of
carrying wounded and troops in the same ship. That
went back to Germany as a fact which could be
proved. The step to the belief—probably a perfectly
genuine belief in many German minds—that the
English sought to shelter troops under the Red Cross
was a short one. Muddle your troops and your
wounded together and you can scarcely blame an
enemy for refusing to give you the benefit of any
doubt. You can proclaim and protest that you only
do that in special cases in your Black Carriers, when,
of course, you do not use the Red Cross flag, but
will you be believed ? War does not make for such
generosity. At a later stage, when a base hospital
was bombed in France and wounded and women
were killed, there was terrific outcry. But along that
tract of sandy country where the outrage took place

there was another fine confusion—base hospitals, base depots for reinforcements, base dumps were nicely mixed together. Our shooting, the Germans excused themselves on that occasion, was not as accurate as we could have wished, but when legitimate targets are so mixed up with hospital areas these things must happen sometimes. It was horrible that those wounded and the women who tended them were killed. But is there any sane man who had knowledge of the bull-rings in those base camps or who lay in the hospitals adjoining who can honestly place blame for the tragedy on German brutality rather than English folly? War is not nice; if its few niceties are to be observed, there must be observance on both sides. The Black Carriers, under orders, but only much against the will of their commanders, did not concern themselves with observance of niceties. They practised economy; they established muddle and confusion when in the interests of wounded men either was indefensible. Those 120 naval ratings mixed with wounded from Gibraltar to England, the other cases of the same amazing folly were proved facts. The English were playing funny games. Right, there was an answer to that, and it was supplied by the *Mauretania* and other great ships. Properly equipped with wards and operating theatres, an adequate medical and nursing staff, painted white with a green band round her hull, with red crosses upon her sides illuminated at night, she and the others advertised themselves for what they were, hospital ships only. The Black Carriers were superseded, but a little too late. The harm had been done. The funny games had been proved. If they were played in one case, why not in another? So the *Britannic*, 47,000 tons, painted and illuminated with the red Cross, was torpedoed and sunk in the Ægean. Her sinking is not to be excused. That thenceforth hospital ships could no longer be considered exempt from the danger of attack was a dreadful happening. But English official stupidity, the gross folly of mixing in the Black Carriers, cannot reasonably be absolved from some hand in the sorry business.

The *Mauretania*, commanded by Captain Rostron, was admirably adapted for the transport of wounded, and did good service in her new sphere, making three voyages to Mudros and back home. She did not mix her job with any other ; she was a carrier of wounded pure and simple and was at pains to advertise the fact. It was her custom to coal at Naples, and on one occasion, when she was doing so, the enemy consuls were invited aboard and asked to inspect the ship as thoroughly as they might wish, even to the extent of having any bale or case of stores selected by them opened for examination. It was demonstrated that the *Mauretania* then carried nothing which it was not proper for a hospital ship to carry ; the enemy consuls admitted on that visit to her as she lay in the bay of Naples that that was so. But perhaps they wondered why England was so particularly anxious to demonstrate that at a particular moment her hospital ships were what they were supposed to be. Perhaps instead of allaying suspicion this request to come and see for themselves only aroused it. Anyhow, it was shortly after this enemy inspection of the *Mauretania* that the *Britannic* was sunk.

The fitting out of the *Mauretania* as a hospital ship

MAURETANIA
In War Time.
Destroyer Escort.

was well done at considerable cost. A huge sum was spent upon the job, and all that could be done was done for the comfort and welfare of the wounded. In October, 1915, she sailed from Liverpool for Mudros with her crew and her medical staff ; in November she returned from Mudros to Southampton with wounded. Sailing again the same month, she returned home with wounded in December. In January she started on a third voyage, and, Gallipoli having been evacuated successfully—the one real success of the whole venture—she brought back the last consignment of wounded. In all she transported 2,307 medical staff and 6,298 wounded.

So on those homeward voyages she was a full ship ; with her crew, her medical staff and her wounded she would equal or exceed her peace time load; she would have a good three thousand men and women aboard. But the accommodation of the three thousand marked the occasion. The big public rooms of the *Mauretania* were wards, packed closely with swing cots, her promenade and shelter decks, where they could be so utilised and when weather permitted, were also wards. She carried her damaged passengers as high up as she could get them, as handy for the boats as possible. When it had been established that Red Cross ships were not inviolate, that they must be prepared for the risk of being sunk by enemy attack, the thought of the alleyways of the lower decks in emergency must have shaped like a nightmare to those responsible for the ship and her freight. The ship listing and sinking, disabled and helpless with men to be transported along narrow passages, was not a pleasant picture. So the *Mauretania* carried her two thousand wounded as far as she could where alleyways would not have to be used in emergency; and emergency action was planned and replanned, practised and repractised.

It is easy to hear in imagination the walking wounded grousing at the boat drills and the emergency regulations. To the wounded, generally, the *Mauretania* was comfort and removal from immediate danger ; to the walking wounded she was luxury. Good food and hot food, warmth, hot baths, soft lying, she brought them those things which so many of them were growing to appraise as the only things of real value in life. Very few of the wounded would take the danger of the ship being sunk seriously ; it was too much of an outside chance to cause worry. A few men might worry, men with broken nerves, but to the majority just removed from close and constant association with death the ship shaped like a palace of safety. They groused about the boat drills and the emergency regulations as they groused about other regulations which prevented them from buying a drink when they wanted one, or from escaping being washed in the early hours of the morning when their tired but unaccustomedly comfortable bodies cried aloud for more sleep. These regulations were simply red-tape business, but, like the rest of the regulating and treating wounded soldiers as irresponsible children, had to be accepted with a grouse. It is impossible to picture the wounded, all but a very few, regarding the great ship as a place of danger or accepting the arrangements for their safety, or for some possibility of safety, with anything but toleration.

The nursing sisters would be indefatigable in practising emergency action, stern disciplinarians in striving to force their charges to take an intelligent interest in the performance ; and their charges, because they admired and were grateful to the women who looked after them, would do their best to please. It was the plain duty of the commander, his officers and crew to make arrangements for emergency and to provide for them being carried out ; it was the job of the medical officers to advise as to the least harmful way in which their patients could be handled. Both departments worked together to prepare for a danger which, in theory, a hospital ship ought never to have to face. Enemy fire on the Red Cross was an abomination ; the disaster, if the *Mauretania* should suffer it, was something too ugly for casual consideration. The two departments made their preparations with care and with anxiety, but it seems at least doubtful whether in doing this work they did not realise that the mixing in the Black Carriers was to some extent a contributory cause of the work being necessary. Discussing what had been happening so recently in those seas, indignation at the answer it had evoked was not wholly directed to the Germans. There was a war on, wars in themselves were abominations, so there was no sense in men engaged in one parting with all sense of justice and proportion.

So a picture forms of the *Mauretania* carrying wounded, facing the danger of encountering enemy attack, with only one section of her company wholly agreed as to German guilt and that the danger had to be faced. That section was the women, the nursing sisters, the stern disciplinarians in emergency drills. They were not unduly concerned for the safety of their own skins ; that was not the reason that gave zest to their driving men to prepare for danger. They were women, and they were not going to have anything at all to do with dispassionate consideration of causes. In defiance of all the decencies, helpless and suffering men under their charge might be attacked. It was vile and abominable. Any suggestion that there could be any excuses concerned with it was an outrage in itself. Fine haters, those sisters, tending their bad cases with care, coaxing or bullying their less bad cases into being sensible and doing what they were told without grumbling, probably the only complete haters in that mixed company.

Having returned from her third voyage to Mudros, the *Mauretania* paid off. Her elaborate hospital fittings were dismantled and she was never again used as a Red Cross ship. Taking into consideration the cost of fitting and dismantling it was an expensive phase. She had given comfort to hurt men, but not to a very great number of them. Having equipped her for a purpose which she performed satisfactorily, the authorities decided that, the affair of the Dardenelles being a thing of the past, she had better try something else. A few thousands more in war, what are they? Terrible things were happening to wounded men in Mesopotamia, but the elaborate fittings came out of the *Mauretania* and others went in.

She became a transport for troops for the second · time. She made two voyages from Halifax to Liverpool in October and November of 1916, carrying something over six thousand Canadian officers and men. For the battle of the Somme had exhibited a large appetite ; collecting more men to satisfy battle appetites was then, scarcely half-way through the war, a very urgent business. On her way over the Atlantic to collect one of these two loads of Canadians the *Mauretania* had a trying experience.

After more than two years of fighting nothing could be run with the smooth routine and the established, trained staffs of peace. The *Mauretania* coaled at Liverpool for that voyage ; when her bunkers had been filled the coal ports were closed and reported, amongst other routine matters, to and later by the chief officer as correct. The ship sailed, and two days out was rolling, but not heavily, to a moderate sea and a fresh breeze. That night the Staff Chief went round the engine and boiler rooms the last thing before turning in. He was Mr. Andrew Cockburn, who as senior second engineer had sunk with the *Lusitania*, but had been picked up after some hours in the water. Later he was to command the *Mauretania's* engines for more than thirteen years ; after he had already seen considerable service in her. He noticed on that night round that sea-water was oozing slightly from under the bunker doors. That had happened before within his knowledge ; the watch-keepers concerned reported the time of the first appearance of oozing sea-water and that it had not increased. Mr. Cockburn was " not exactly easy " about that ooze ; he ordered that it should be watched carefully and any increase immediately reported. Then he went to bed and slept—one assumes—a sailor's sleep. He was roused by the Chief shaking him and telling him to go to the Commander and get the ship stopped at once. With that order, but with no explanation, the Chief went off. Mr. Cockburn is a Scot ; native caution suggested that he would be in a better position to deal with the Commander if he had some explanation to give. Before going topsides he had a look below. One look, and that from the ladder of the engine-room hatch, was sufficient. The ship was listing : below him, inside the *Mauretania*, the Atlantic was rising and falling. He said to himself :

" I've seen the *Lusitania* go down. Am I going to see the *Mauretania*? "

And then he did not wait.

Captain James Charles was commanding. He was a sound sleeper, and appeared as he got out of bed not inclined to stop his ship. But Mr. Cockburn admits that, except for the essential fact that the Atlantic Ocean was finding its way in large quantities into the ship, his explanation may have lacked detail. The Commander went to the bridge, the staff chief to the engine-room. The *Mauretania* was slowed down but not stopped.

The ship was listing. There was a considerable depth of water in all four boiler-rooms. The lower fires were out. On the side to which the ship listed the pumps were choked with coal and cinders and would not suck. Engineers, up to their necks in water, sometimes plunging head under, fought desperately to free the ends of the suction pipes. Under the electric lamps the water gleamed, swishing and rushing with the ship's movements. Half-drowned men stuck to their jobs, but the water brought back the silt as soon as they had cleared it ; they could not keep the pumps sucking. But unless they could do that and so keep abreast of the inflow from the unlocated leak they could not save the *Mauretania*. The chief officer came down to view the situation ;

he had a look at the heads appearing and disappearing in the water and did not wait long. Captain Charles turned his ship round so that her list was towards the fresh breeze, and she was brought on to a more even keel. That gave the pumps on the other side a chance to help, but the engineers were taking no more chances with the silt of coal and ashes. They disconnected the pipes and refixed them, screwed them, lashed them and even held them by man-power just below the surface of the water, lowering them as the level of water dropped. It was not easy work, but the workers were tough and knew necessity when they saw it. They climbed up through the bunkers and found the leaks and packed them ; that, again, was not easy work. There was, indeed, no easiness about that night. With the situation—in that simple phrase—in hand, with the *Mauretania* taking in less of the Atlantic than she was sending out, the bridge telephoned down a message.

" Surely," they inquired, " you must be ready by now ? "

And the Chief replied gravely :

" I won't forget to tell you when I am."

Which bright sayings at such times pass for wit.

In due course the message that he was ready did not escape the Chief's memory, and the *Mauretania* proceeded on her way. They cleared more than two hundred tons of coal and dust and cinders from her bilges. The pumps were rigged again as they ought to be, and worked, though with a minor task, until the ship got to Halifax. She had looked her end squarely in the face and stubbornly refused to meet it. The coal ports, those convenient doors in the ships' shell for the entry of coal, but those excessively deadly

apertures in the ship's sides for the entry of the
Atlantic, had not been screwed home in Liverpool
by some unknown war worker, who had, however,
declared his job well and properly done.

After she had carried those Canadians, the authorities who ruled her fate were beaten. She was a very
expensive ship to run ; she was too precious to risk
without good cause. Her speed had saved her, but
it might not do so again. The seas were becoming
more and more dangerous for English merchantmen.
There were possible uses for her, but no obvious
necessity for a ship so large, so fast and so expensive.
So she was dismantled once again, and laid up in
the Clyde.

On her way to be laid up she became unmanageable and went ashore. She left her buoy in the
Sloyne on a winter afternoon when it was blowing
a south-easterly gale, dropped down river and
anchored, to wait for the flood tide. When, later
in the darkness, the port anchor was being weighed,
the cable parted. The ship, Captain Rostron,
then commanding her, relates, was not in a position
to use her starboard anchor, and her situation
in a river crowded with shipping had become
serious. The pilot tried to turn her downstream
and the starboard anchor was then let go to assist
the manœuvre. This cable also parted immediately.
The *Mauretania*, a ship of 38,000 tons displacement,
with a length of close on two hundred and seventy
yards, was unmanageable in a gale on a strong spring
tide in rain and darkness, broadside on in the
navigable channel of a wind-swept river which was
crowded with shipping. They could not turn her ;
she was out of hand. She simply took her own way,

and it was a good way. Drifting on to a sandbank " she sat down to await better conditions." They got her off with tugs later and proceeded to sea without anchors, cruising about till daylight. Returning to the river in the morning, the weather was too bad to make the buoy, so the *Mauretania* had to put into the Gladstone dock, where she awaited the recovery of her anchors.

Not a pleasant night. Captain Rostron states that it was simply good luck that they did not crash into half a dozen ships as they drifted, and that it was too much for the pilot, who never went on to a ship's bridge again. He does not mention his own feelings, but they can easily be imagined. The presence of a pilot on the bridge does not lessen the captain's responsibility. Accidents at sea demand payment, and the master concerned is not infrequently made to foot the bill. In the rain and the darkness and the gale one can imagine Captain Rostron wondering whether his ship alone was going to be laid up after the night's work was finished.

The *Mauretania* lay up at Greenock during the whole of 1917. Anyone who is unable to invest inanimate things with the idea of animate feelings must be a strange being. A motor car, a pen, a spade, anything that has given a man good service, can scarcely be separated from some qualities of living character in his imagination. A ship to many of us is of all human constructions the most vital and the most individual. It is sheer impossibility to think of her as wholly without feeling. The *Mauretania* was a worker ; she stood up to the hardest jobs ; she was happy in being driven and driven again. The picture of her laid up doing nothing for a whole year at a time when doing nothing was a black disgrace is not pleasant. One wants to find excuses for that idleness lest the ship should be blamed for it. The excuses are not hard to find. It was not the *Mauretania's* fault that auxiliary cruisers of her size and fuel consumption had been proved impossible to maintain at sea. It was not her fault that the cost of hiring her for war work rendered even the heartiest of war spenders chary of using her when some other less costly ship could be hired in her place.

According to the agreement under which she had come into being, the Government had the right to hire any or all of the Cunard ships at rates specified in the agreement. These rates of hire were calculated on the speed of the vessel. The *Mauretania*, having a speed of over twenty-two knots, was hired at the top rate, namely twenty-five shillings per ton gross register per month. That was for the plain hire of the vessel, when the Company did not provide and pay the officers and crew. In the event of the Company providing and paying the officers and crew the rate for hire rose to thirty shillings per ton gross register per month. The gross ton register of the *Mauretania* was 32,000, so that the plain hire of her by the Government cost £40,000 a month, over £1,300 a day. In addition, when hiring her in war-time, the Admiralty bore all risks in respect of loss or damage and all expenses of ship and stores. That did not end it. When the ship was hired by the Admiralty the Company were allowed seven days at the stipulated rate of hire in which to dismantle fittings not required by the Admiralty, and a further ten days at the same rate at the end of the period of hire for replacing these fittings. This work of dismantling and

replacing was to be performed by the Company at
the expense of the Admiralty. But that again did
not end it. If the Admiralty decided to alter the
arrangements of the ship—and the arrangements of
the *Mauretania* as a passenger liner would require
extensive alteration to prepare her for trooping or
for carrying wounded—they had the right to do so
at their own expense provided that, at the end of the
period of hire, the ship should be handed over in
the same condition as she was in when hired. She
was not cheap. Two years of continuous hire would
yield in rent alone close on the cost of her building
and fitting, with no risks taken by the Company and
everything put back free as it had been before.
It is no wonder that the Admiralty gave anxious
thought to her re-employment; even paying her off,
taking out all the hospital fittings, removing the cots
from public rooms, dismantling the operating theatres,
putting everything as it had been before at £1,300
a day plus the cost of the work, would impress those
reckoning up the bill as genuine expenditure. In
Admiralty offices where men worked for a wage and
were expected to give value for money, the expression
" white elephant " might have been used in connection with a great ship in wartime. Clerks, checking
up the monthly bills, for all accounts for hire were
settled monthly, possibly regretted that they had not
investments in shipping shares.

But upon the other side the Cunard Company
had to repay annually a twentieth of the money
which had been advanced by the Government for
the building of the *Mauretania*. They also lost the
amount of the annual subsidy payable only while
she was upon her legitimate business of carrying

passengers and mails on the North Atlantic. The annual repayment was roughly £65,000, the loss of subsidy £75,000 a year. So the ship idle, refused by the Admiralty, unused as a mail ship, became a considerable source of expense to the owners. But to employ her at the Company's risk, to try to make her earn her yearly repayment of capital and a bit over was a gamble. The *Lusitania*, her nearest peer for speed, had been sunk ; the *Mauretania* might follow. That would mean greater loss. The mail service to New York could be supplied with less precious ships. Records of speed, except when running for safety, were not in men's consideration for the moment ; passengers had to take what they could get. One thousand tons of the precious substance coal a day was too much. The ship which had been designed for a particular service in war was required for none. In the charge of a caretaking party at Greenock, she lay empty, silent, waiting.

As the *Mauretania* got to the Clyde at the end of 1916, the first, abortive, peace talks had begun. In France Joffre had been superseded by Nivelle, who had fine plans for the future. During 1916 Verdun had proved to the Germans, the Somme to the English and French that the idea of breaking through into open warfare was next door to fanciful. Jutland had immobilised the German battle fleet, but had not left the seas to the Allies. In 1917 the Nivelle plan failed disastrously on the Craonne Plateau in April. Russia had collapsed in revolution in March. For the remainder of the year, although America came into the war in April, the weight of fighting fell upon the British troops. They took Vimy Ridge in April, Messines in June. In July the dreadful business of Passchendaele was begun. History is not yet agreed as to the value of that long slaughter. It is maintained by some that it achieved its purpose. But to all men who took part in it, to the comparatively few who, taking part, survived, it is the weariest, the bloodiest, the most heart-breaking of all the happenings of the war. Mud and hopelessness, small, tired bodies of men calling themselves battalions of infantry staggering to attack, little handfuls of grey men, bemused and pitiful, plodding out again ; that, to the men who survived, is the lasting impression of Passchendaele.

In October the Italians collapsed at Caporetto. There was bad trouble in the French army. The Americans were still a long way from having trained troops. England had much to do. Tanks, having failed on the Somme, proved themselves at Cambrai in November. In the air there was much activity. The Zeppelin, which had been largely used for German raiding in 1915 and 1916, had been superseded by aeroplanes. Air raids were giving people in England some acquaintance with war's reality. With many people in London and elsewhere in the raided zone these raids had become a principal subject of conversation ; they affected many nerves. But the damage they did and the lives they took were negligible, and the Allies were doing their best to square the account by raiding enemy towns and killing enemy civilians. In the air, as elsewhere, England was busy, making progress, but the effort was tiring her. Everywhere in 1917, bearing her heavy burden of fighting, she was making progress, but everywhere she was showing signs of fatigue.

On the sea—where the *Mauretania* had no part—

this year of growing fatigue finished with solid achievement. Stark disaster marked the beginning of it. Their peace proposals having failed, Germany followed them with unrestricted submarine warfare. She did so with regret, conscious of the gravity of her action ; but she did so. She instructed her submarines to sink " without trace " all ships, whether enemy or neutral, which they might suppose, without having searched them, to be carrying either munitions or supplies for the Allies. She did so because her armies were exhausted after the Somme and because, in her view, it was the only action left to her by which she could win the war. It got within sight of winning the war. It commenced in February, 1917, and it certainly decided the matter of America's entry into the war. But between America declaring war and taking an effective part in it there must be a long gap. On that gap Germany certainly banked. Her submarine campaign was so successful at the start that in April her submarines sank 900,000 tons of Allied shipping, of which 540,000 were British. Tonnage, carrying capacity, equal to thirty times that of the *Mauretania*, gone to the bottom in a matter of four weeks. It was obvious that if that were to continue the Allies must be starved out, and quickly too. That huge loss of April was not equalled again, but for many months the danger was acute and deadly. The courage of sailors, organisation, " Q " boats, depth-charges, air and sea patrols, all manner of devices were factors in removing the danger, but the convoy system stood out amongst them all as the real means of escape. It was far from being a novel system of safeguarding merchant vessels, it had been used in many other wars ; in this war,

when the submarine menace had first appeared, it
had been discussed and rejected as impracticable.
Two main objections had been raised against its
adoption. The first, which was a good one, was the
insufficiency of destroyers. We had not enough
destroyers to supply escorts for the merchant convoys.
The second objection, which was a singularly bad
one, was that merchant captains could not be expected
to learn the complicated manœuvres required when
zig-zagging in convoy with destroyers. That sounds
good hide-bound, regular-service stuff, and one
wonders how in a time of stress it could ever have
carried any weight. But, apparently, it did and
carried it through months of extreme danger.
Merchant captains who fail to exhibit good seamanship lose their jobs ; as a class they are not conspicuous
for stupidity nor incapable of adapting themselves to
changed circumstances. Their most abiding tradition
is to handle ships when and where and how they are
ordered to handle them. Of course, when they
were told to learn these complicated manœuvres they
learned them. America helped with the destroyers.
The convoy system, with the merchant captains
zig-zagging, succeeded. By the end of 1917 the
submarine menace was broken.

From April until October in 1917 there had been
peace talks ; they ended with Lord Lansdowne's
letter in the *Daily Telegraph*. Nothing came of them
except the knowledge that the nations were growing
very tired and that most men longed for peace. The
year finished with a British success, the capture of
Jerusalem ; but elsewhere there was confusion and
growing weariness. The year 1918 began with
quarrelling between politicians and soldiers on the

Supreme War Council and off it ; there was no decision and much confused absence of set plan. Lloyd George and his Cabinet were convinced that there would be no break through on the western front until, at least, the weight of American numbers was felt ; and the weight of American numbers was not expected until 1919. Therefore in 1918 nothing offensive should be attempted in France and Flanders, but all troops not required for defence in the west should be sent for offence to the east. Haig did not agree ; France did not agree. There was conflict of ideas which resulted in no plans. Haig had to take over new ground, to defend a line reaching to the Oise. The Supreme War Council asked him for thirty divisions for the general allied reserve ; he said that it was not possible for him to give them. He foretold a German attack upon his right, where the British line joined the French. That Germany was about to attack again, and not lightly, on the western front became certain ; but there were no real plans for defence and no certainty as to the point of attack. The French thought Champagne, Haig thought St. Quentin. Without plans, without prepared defence, the one sure thing to do was to collect more men for any contingency which might arise. On the morning of March 21st, Haig and not the French command was proved right. In a few hours the Allies faced defeat. But when that foggy spring morning came the *Mauretania* had finished her long idleness and was at work again ; she was bringing American troops to the western front.

When she played her first part in the war the moment of her entry was not cheerful ; when, after a year of doing nothing on the Clyde, she came back to work again the moment was disastrous. Many things had changed. When she brought her first load of American troops to Europe the war had reached a stage when men, who had been long in the fighting line, could hopefully apply for special leave on the score of being war weary—a very long cry from the days when the only tonic for tired troops was considered small, useless attacks and still smaller and more useless raids. That men like metals have a breaking strain had been admitted by those in high command.

Men were needed and the *Mauretania* brought them. It was a job which she could do well, at high pressure as in her peace-time days ; but while doing it she played the part of hybrid. She sailed with Cunard officers, Captain Rostron commanding, under the White Ensign ; she was under Admiralty orders and mounted guns for her defence. The guns for which provision had been made at her building were at last in place, but still she was not an auxiliary cruiser ; she was an armed transport. At times, going eastward, she was that ; at others, going westward, it is difficult to know what to call her except what she had always been in service : a swift carrier of human beings. From Liverpool to New York she carried whomsoever she was ordered to carry, not ordinary paying passengers, that would not go with her White Ensign, but official passengers and, often, their wives and womenfolk as well as their staffs. Because she was the fastest merchant vessel sailing the sea, and because the submarine danger, though diminished, was not completely dead, official persons having business in America used her extensively. In order that she could accommodate large numbers of

American troops, she was stripped and fitted as a transport, but she kept part of herself fit to receive distinguished persons, whose devotion to duty and readiness to admit that war enforced sacrifices on everybody certainly did not run to the length of being willing to cross the Atlantic in anything but reasonable luxury. The picture the *Mauretania* presents in these months is a mixture ; at one time she was crammed with troops, feeding and housing them sufficiently, but not overdoing the comfort of the quarters or of service, at another she was supplying a much smaller number of much more particular people with the food and service and comfort which they expected.

On the first voyage to New York as an armed transport early in 1918, the *Mauretania* had a British mission aboard ; amongst its members were generals, Government officials and powerful representatives of big business ; they would expect and be given comfort. There were also some hundred and fifty English warrant officers and N.C.O.'s going to the United States to act as instructors to the American army : they would be capable of finding comfort for themselves. The *Mauretania* made a record voyage, but it is unlikely that anybody aboard could have found excessive comfort. She took over eight days to cross to New York ; the first and last time in her career when she was as long as a week about the business. Leaving her escort of destroyers off the north west of Ireland, she ran into westerly gales with very big seas. Before reaching New York she was very nearly out of coal. Even butting into full gales and terrific seas, it is not easy to understand how the *Mauretania*, who was accustomed to both, managed to achieve that record of slowness. That the ship was slowed down in the interests of the British Mission is a wild assumption, which might even by some be considered as bordering on irreverence. The more likely explanation is to be found on the return voyage with troops to Liverpool. Then, owing to the inferior quality of the coal supplied she could not steam more than 19 knots instead of the 25 she wanted. Inferior coal at not inferior prices on both sides of the Atlantic, was that the war-time explanation ? Steaming eastward for Liverpool at 19 knots when she wanted her full speed, the *Mauretania* carried 3,662 American officers and other ranks, with her own crew she might be considered to be full ; but that was the smallest number of troops she carried until the war had finished. On one of her voyages she bettered it by more than two thousand. At last she had found war work which she could do as well as any vessel on the seas, when she was given the chance. As she made that first voyage eastward with American troops, it was known when she left New York that the need of men was urgent ; as news reached her of the German attack on March 21st and the Allies' retreat she could not, because of that inferior coal, steam at more than 19 knots, although the need of men had become desperate. For the men tending those wonderful engines it was sheer heartbreak. Down in the engine and boiler rooms they would feel their failure very bitterly. Sweating and labouring to work up revolutions, they would find time to say things about war-time contractors which it might have been good for some contractors to hear.

The *Mauretania* made seven passages from New

York with American soldiers and on the first of them
only she failed to justify herself and her staff
below. Upon the others she kept close to her 25
knots whatever the weather. From off the coast of
Ireland she was escorted by five American destroyers.
After the Armistice Admiral Sims stated that she had
done more damage to his destroyers than any other
ship, since her escort zig-zagging while keeping in
touch with her had been nearly driven to pieces.
Sometimes in heavy weather the speed of the
Mauretania was too much for the destroyers; they
could not face the seas and had to ease down while
she went on alone. The guns which she mounted
are discreetly stated not to have been of the latest
pattern; the four mounted on the forecastle are said
to have been under water half the time in bad
weather. They were fired, but never at an enemy.
Once, her purser tells, they opened in practice and
caused something like a panic to the women and
children, nearly three thousand of whom she was
taking back to Canada before fetching a new consignment of American troops from New York. Sir
Robert Borden is said to have been almost submerged
on this occasion by excited children, but to have
managed to keep his head above the tide of youngsters
and to have assisted them materially in the recovery
of theirs.

Backwards and forwards at express speed across
the Atlantic, that had become the *Mauretania's* job
again. Once she did the round trip within a fortnight, and in June she brought close on eleven
thousand troops over from New York to fight. But
hers was not a fighting job; returning westward,
often empty except for diplomats and politicians and

officials, it was a hybrid occupation. That term, which is repeated, is used with reason. At this time the *Mauretania* had changed her name. Nobody aboard her, from her Commander down, knew that she was going to change it or even that she had changed it until after the event. Captain Rostron was, he states, considerably surprised when on arrival at Liverpool from New York he received an official letter addressed to the Commanding Officer of a ship unknown to him and was assured that the letter was being delivered to the right man and ship. But the authorities loved a little mystery in war and had the prettiest taste in fancy names. Men of the 7th Infantry Division will not forget that, preparing for Loos, when they first handled the abominable stuff which was to kill more of them than of the Germans, they had particular instructions never to mention the word gas but to refer to the poison by the singularly chosen title, " Roger." The Admiralty, seeking a new name for the *Mauretania*, was less exotic in their choice ; but they would have their joke. They called a great sea beauty, the fastest merchant vessel on the seas, H.M.S. *Tuberose !* Now it seems scarcely necessary to follow them in their flowery fancy.

The *Mauretania* had her troubles, apart from inferior coal, in these days. As she lay in the Mersey waiting for orders for her next voyage, no night leave was granted to any of her company, except her captain, although many of her men had their homes in or near Liverpool. The Cunard Company provided a tender to take leave men ashore and back, but it was not used. No leave except for her captain was granted. That seemed unreasonable to many men

in her crew, and there were not a few deserters, who
were duly arrested ashore, brought back and punished.
What were actually the rights and wrongs of the
trouble belongs to the past ; there is no evidence on
which to base an opinion.   But the incident was
typical of the moment.   Tired men were finding
grievances   frequently.   One   wishes   that   the
Mauretania could have been shown to do her war
duties without desertions, like a figure of romance.
One wishes that in all British ships and all British
regiments there had been no desertions.   But war
is not romantic and tired men are human.   So the
Mauretania had her share of the unromantic realities
which were current.

The troubles were less than the successes.   Things
were never easy ;   there were always difficulties to
be faced.   Her oddments of passengers westward,
distinguished but like the crew human, were not
easy.   They disliked the regulations for their safety,
and had to be handled with tact.   There was
trouble because, when returning eastwards, the ship,
carrying Amercian troops, was officially " dry," but
diplomacy on the part of the staff got round that arid
corner.   With two nations involved and two sets
of regulations, there was of necessity always need for
tact, but the successes not the troubles won.   The
Mauretania organised herself so as to feed five thousand
men in three-quarters of an hour.   She had eighteen
separate canteens, or buffets, for the troops, where the
men could collect their food and take it to the place
assigned to them for its consumption.   Not a small
task of organisation for all concerned.   By practice
and insistence that a better show could be put up,
finally by sounding the alarm so that all hands

imagined the emergency to be real and not supposed, she got the five thousand troops to their boat stations in three and a half minutes. Not bad going. That established, she held it to be a precedent which must be followed on other voyages ; and it was. The hybrid was not idle.

The American troops did not proclaim that they were going over to win the war. They seem to have accepted their part of inexperienced newcomers frankly and readily. Otherwise they were as the other troops which the *Mauretania* had carried. They laughed, they groused, they were eager, with occasional inevitable exceptions, for the great unknown adventure ahead. Some of them, as the proprietors of Crown and Anchor boards, did good business at the expense of their fellows, and the decks of the ship sounded to " Clickety-Click " and the other cries of that curiously beloved game " House." They were, these Americans, in all things English-speaking troops going in the English-speaking way to war.

The epidemic of what passed for influenza, which raged towards the end of the fighting and after the Armistice, is said to have taken more lives than all the bullets, shells, bombs and torpedoes of all the belligerents. It is curious that the *Mauretania* did not experience a single case of this disease.

For seven months the *Mauretania* carried American troops. First, to help in a desperate endeavour to stave off defeat ; then, more hopefully ; then triumphantly to make defeat. The last consignment was, except for the troops concerned, accompanied with real comedy. The ship was at New York where a false Armistice day was celebrated in that city on

November 7th. Rumour got ahead of truth, and after much public rejoicing had to admit that the war was still a fact. The *Mauretania* sailed for England with troops. On the seas, on November 11th, she received official news of the Armistice, but her orders were to take her troops to Liverpool, and she did so. On her passage over she sighted a German submarine on the surface, steaming eastward, which signalled, " I have no hostile intentions." That must have been practical proof to the troops aboard that the fighting was over, and, being human, their mixed feelings about the great adventure ahead must have turned to disappointment that they had missed the show. But to their considerable relief they were being taken to England, not being returned to New York without having set foot on any European shore. They were landed at Liverpool, qualified for a medal, sent to Knotty Ash Camp. Within a matter of hours they were brought from the camp back to the *Mauretania* again, and re-embarked for New York. They were the last American troops to leave New York, and the first to return there from overseas. New Yorkers were determined to mark the occasion of the first return of the war veterans ; they prepared a civic welcome. The veterans in the *Mauretania* were, naturally, not a little shy of this welcome, but they had to go through with it. Marching along the decorated streets of New York with the horrors of Knotty Ash still fresh in their memories, they must have needed a robust sense of humour to see the funny side of the plaudits of the populace. But, to their credit, they did proclaim themselves the Knotty Ash heroes.

For a few more months the *Mauretania* carried

troops back to their homes.   Her last outward voyage
on Government service was not an occasion of any
comedy ; she carried a consignment of some thousands
of crippled Canadians back to post-war crippledom.
On May 27th, 1919, she was finally paid off from
war service.   In all she carried 70,000 troops and
more than 6,000 wounded ; and she carried them
without a single man losing his life through any fault
of hers.   That she never did the work which had
been originally expected of her, that there were
gaps and pauses in the work which she did do are
matters for which neither the ship nor the men who
manned her can be blamed.

CHAPTER VII

DIFFICULT AGE

THE extreme confusion which enhanced the terrors of what had to be called Peace was not absent from shipping companies nor the affairs of ships. Except that most people assumed that a new age was dawning and that, with Mr. Lloyd George, they would like it to be fit for heroes, confused hopes of better things had to do duty for policies and faiths. America had become incredibly rich ; all the other belligerent nations were close to bankruptcy. Some individuals had made large war fortunes, many of the others, having had practical experience of the uncertainty of life, had evolved out of chaos a creed whose principal doctrine was to have a good time while living lasted. The new age did not increase their happiness so rapidly as it did their overdrafts. Perhaps it was the growth of these almost universal possessions which gave the Atlantic shipping companies a wholly false impression. Profiteers, although sufficiently numerous, were still a small minority ; the majority of men found the business of living on their incomes a difficult and most unpleasant performance. Carrying pre-war shibboleths into the confusion of peace, shipowners decided that the time must be close at hand when ordinary people would wish to live again with credit, not debit, balances at their banks ; they assumed, without any justification whatsoever in fact, that luxury ships, floating

palaces and the like would, on account of the high
fares which had to follow their high-running costs,
not be required for some considerable period. Business on the Atlantic was good in the sense that more
people wished to travel than the ships available
could accommodate ; but the ships which could be
used were mostly in very poor trim. In ordinary
times the large, fast liners of the world are treated
much as racehorses are, looked after with the most
careful attention ; four years of rough living or of
lying up had not improved their condition. Most
of them demanded the expenditure of much money
before they could be associated with real luxury
again. It seems fairly certain that that expenditure
had something to do with the shipowners' estimate
of what the public would want. Anyhow, they made
their plans for building to replace the ships lost in
the war and their arrangements for dealing with the
passengers who wanted to cross the Atlantic on the
basis that moderately fast and moderately comfortable
ships of medium size, charging comparatively moderate fares, would be in demand. Not having these
medium and moderate ships, the Atlantic companies
had to charter from other companies. Ships designed
for the tropics had to cope with the cold of northern
seas, and with passengers' complaints. But shipowners' false estimates of the requirements of the
future were not exceptional at a time when people,
outside nurseries, were solemnly talking of hanging
the Kaiser and at Versailles the foundations of the
next war were being well and truly laid.

The *Mauretania* was finally paid off from war
service just one month before statesmen and soldiers
assembled in the Hall of Mirrors at Versailles to put

their signatures to an amazing document. She had carried across the Atlantic, at various times, many of the men present at the signing of the Peace Treaty ; she was to carry many of them again when they were anxiously trying to undo some of the harm which had been done on that June day in the Palace of Versailles. As the greatest transport link between Europe and the United States, her decks and her public and private rooms were to hear much talk about the results of that disastrous Treaty both from contributors to it and sufferers from it. But while she waited her turn for refit amazing action at Washington, not Versailles, prepared practical changes and very material difficulties for her and for all Atlantic ships. The people of the United States had turned down their President, the League of Nations which he had managed to force on other people, and the Treaty of Versailles itself. Collective security, with or without collective power, was something with which they refused to have any truck ; they were going to keep themselves to themselves and be free. As a means to that end their legislative assemblies passed the Volstead Act ; and President Wilson, abandoning idealism for other nations in favour of sound practical consideration for his own, stepped in to do some turning down himself. He vetoed the Volstead Act. That, it may well be considered, was the wisest and, had it been allowed to stand, would have been the most beneficial to his country of any act of his career. But the Eighteenth Amendment to the constitution of the United States prevented it from standing. The people of the United States had determined that they would not get mixed up again with other nations' troubles, a perfectly vain determination. They had a fine fancy that prohibition of alcoholic drinks would remove many of their domestic troubles, a perfectly majestic mistake. Having made the mistake in October, 1919, they were obstinate about it. It became obvious to themselves and to the world that the result of interference with such primary liberties as a citizen's right to select his own food and drink was far wider than the obvious one of forcing normally law-abiding persons to obtain bad and expensive drink by underground methods. The underground methods spread into a vast complication of underground organisations defying the law and exercising a species of terrorism. The whole structure of American government suffered and was brought into disrepute, but prohibition remained. How long it will take to remove the evils nourished by this attempt at social reform is a question which the future has to answer ; but the immediate effect of the Eighteenth Amendment was apparent in ships on the Atlantic. A type of passenger appeared, not in small numbers, who was much concerned with drinking against time. The opportunity of obtaining good liquor at moderate prices was not to be missed ; not missing the opportunity, but not abusing it, was too much for many people. It is certain that in a very short time after its passing the stewards in the *Mauretania* and other liners could have given the promoters of this singular law much valuable data about its effect.

Americans making short business trips to Europe had so much to get in in so short a time that they had to employ concentration. Here is an illustration of the attitude. The *Mauretania* had just sailed from New York and an officer, seeking a breath of air, had gone forward on the boat deck. The Statue of Liberty was a short distance ahead, and there was a passenger leaning on the rails staring at it with an almost anxious concentration. As the officer walked over to the passenger to pass the time of day the ship's whistle sounded and continued to sound. It was a fine whistle, electrically controlled, with a key on the bridge upon which, if desired, tunes could be played ; but occasionally, like all intricate mechanism, something went wrong with it. As the evening was fine and no craft, small or large, in the *Mauretania's* way, the officer assumed that the whistle was playing games again ; but the passenger seemed impressed. He turned from his intent watching of the statue.

" I'll say," he said, " that's fine. This great ship saluting that great statue. Yes, I'll tell the world that's fine."

The officer, not wishing a sentiment so admirable to suffer harm, murmured without committing himself. The whistle ceased sounding, and a figure in overalls, greasy, oil-stained and dishevelled, climbed down from the funnel casing.

" Fixed the damn thing. Good night," an electrical engineer stated, and passed on his way.

The officer regretted the bursting of the fine sentiment, but the passenger showed no disappointment. His gaze, concentrated and eager, was on the great effigy of Liberty. He watched it pass astern ; then he turned, alert and purposeful.

" Say," he said, " that statue's gone. The bars will be open, won't they ? "

With regret the officer had to inform him that the land of liberty was not yet officially astern.

Ship-building and repairing yards could hardly deal with their orders. Things had to be taken in turn and the best made of what was possible. Some strange things came out of the yards : ships which had been already in the building when the war began, which had been commandeered by the Government and had become the victims of changing official ideas. As they grew on the stocks uncertainty as to their use and war-time disregard of expenditure marked them. At one time the obvious use of one of them might be considered a carrier of troops in the tropics and work hurried on to that end ; at another some man of ideas would recognise in the same unfinished vessel an ideal hospital ship, so the necessary alterations would be made to produce the ideal ; before these were completed an economist in high places might step in and decree general utility, entailing, of course, more structural alterations. The ending of the war found many of these uneasy victims of changing ideas still in process of being changed. They were handed back to their owners with not illiberal compensation. The compensation was often used in fitting them with expensive cabin accommodation, and they were hurried into service as passenger liners, for which their owners had originally laid them down. Many of the great companies were handed back one or more of these changelings ; some still possess them. Passengers very often like them because their fittings are so good. But the men who try to guide them across the seas, or drive them or work them do not share that liking. The Suez Canal has been nearly blocked by them, dock gates have been removed, pierheads and jetties pruned, other ships endangered and many heads turned greyer. That these victims of official changes of ideas should have occupied good yard space before they were turned out to perform their antics on the high seas, when yard space was very precious, is only one of their minor performances ; but it was annoying at the time for shipowners trying to get good ships back to hard-working order.

After her handing over from Government service the *Mauretania* was not put into service until the spring of 1920. The yards were so full ; she was so expensive to run, and she did require, after seven years of brilliant work and six of only such attention as was imperative, considerable overhaul. Her famous woodwork was carefully reinstalled, her cabin accommodation was renovated and improved, but her engines did not receive more attention than was barely necessary. They were wonderful engines, and they could do the work required of them at a time when so many things had to be made to do. Her home port was changed from Liverpool to Southampton, and on March 6th she sailed, calling at Cherbourg, for New York. She made seven voyages that year, four only in 1921, all at, for her, very moderate speeds. She did not once during those two years average for a passage, either outward or homeward, as much as 22 knots, and on several occasions she could not maintain as much as 20 knots. Those two years were, without doubt, the least glorious of her long life ; they must have been near to misery for the men serving her, who knew her for the ship she was.

In the list of voyages one which she made at this period, No. 119, the second outward passage after the war service, can hardly fail to attract attention. An average of 17·81 knots for the *Mauretania* calls for some explanation. The explanation is not weather

MAURETANIA
Outward Bound
(" The Swinging Ground "),
Southampton.

or ice, it is what one may call fatigue. One of her low-pressure turbines was disabled temporarily, and for the rest of that passage she had to drag the propeller on that shaft through the water. It could not revolve because the turbine was out of action, so it acted as a brake. The *Mauretania* had already made reasonable speed with three propellers driving her ; she was on more than one occasion going to do so again, but even her gallant engines could not ignore a brake. The incident is a small one of no great importance ; mishaps occur in all engine-rooms, but it does illustrate facts. That sort of thing was liable to happen in those years. The ship did need, like all hard workers, a period of rest and recuperation.

The public was beginning to give her less attention. To many people it seemed that her great days were done. The lure of size, whatever the shipowners had hoped, still attracted passengers. She had been passed in size by not one but several ships, the *Olympic*, the *Aquitania*, then the two huge Germans, *Imperator* and *Vaterland*. She had become, by comparison and for those people concerned with that peculiar reckoning gross tonnage, a small ship. But she was still the *Mauretania*, very easily the world's fastest liner, with an unrivalled record of consistent performance. Germany having been deprived of her large merchant ships, the Allies redistributed them. The Cunard Company and the White Star between them bought the *Imperator* and the *Bismarck*, taking half shares in each. The *Imperator*, removed from Hamburg, where she had been lying idle since 1914, became the *Berengaria* and flew the Cunard flag ; the *Bismarck* was completed and became the *Majestic*. In the reshuffle the United States took over the *Vaterland* as the *Leviathan*. Germany was left, without ships of the first size, to plan her re-establishment amongst Atlantic fleets as she was planning her re-establishment amongst the nations. The big ex-Germans—to use a prefix then enormously in vogue—with the *Aquitania* and the *Olympic* had not been designed for record speeds, a comfortable 23 to 23·5 knots was about their mark. Under ordinary circumstances the *Mauretania* could watch them drop astern until the horizon hid them without increasing her own economic speed by a single revolution. But the circumstances were extraordinary ; owing to her condition the *Mauretania* was forced to part with her speed ; she could not even average 22 knots. To maintain that she was beautiful and still the world's outstanding merchant ship, that she still had it in her to regain her first place as the fastest and hardest of workers, was of mighty little use. The men who served her then knew that to be the truth, but they also knew how hard it was for them to make her show even the moderate performance she was showing. The latest and the biggest equalled her in speed and surpassed her in popular attraction. Her great name belonged to years that had become immensely far away ; so many of her old regular passengers, the men and women who by their enthusiasm bred enthusiasm, were dead. She was never, with her great power, anything but expensive to run. With coal troubles increasing it appeared that running her was going to be difficult as well as costly. She ran for four months in 1921, that was all.

The coal strike of 1921 hit both the Cunard Company and the *Mauretania* hard. It also brought changes. Returning from the third of her four voyages in that year, the *Mauretania* was ordered to go to Brest to fill her bunkers with what was alleged to be mixed Welsh and German coal. She did so ; and the chief noticed as the lighters came alongside that there was grass sprouting amongst the coal. Normally a certain proportion of the fires are cleaned each watch, but the *Mauretania* should have been able to make the passage from Brest to Southampton without any cleaning. With that grass-grown mixture making a feeble show of burning she had, during the short passage across the Channel, to clean 110 out of her 192 fires, and even then could scarcely maintain sufficient head of steam to keep the propellers turning. Before reaching Southampton the chief went to the commander and reported that with the coal in the bunkers he could not take the ship to New York. That was a serious matter. Captain Rostron warned him of the possible consequences, but Mr. Cockburn stuck to his opinion. With that coal the passage to New York was impossible. So a wireless message was sent to the management, and commander and chief, working together, prepared to face the trouble which met them at Southampton. The ship was due to sail within a few hours, and she was going to sail as advertised : that was the managers' attitude. She could sail if she supplemented the muck in her bunkers with 1,000 tons of good Welsh coal, other-wise not : that was the chief's attitude, and he sup-ported it with facts about the steam-raising capacity of the muck. The managers, convinced by facts, pointed out that it might have escaped his attention that the country was enjoying a coal strike. Where could 1,000 tons of good Welsh coal be obtained at short notice? The chief could not answer that question, but the managers did. They got the good coal from the Admiralty; but that was a long way from the end of the trouble. Organised labour took a hand; the ship had been coaled at Brest, so the coal heavers refused to touch it except on their own terms. They demanded three pounds for each man, by way of premium, as the only condition on which they would begin work. The passengers were due to come aboard in a few hours; the *Mauretania* was advertised to sail that evening; if she did not sail the passengers would have to be looked after and fed and steam kept up for an extra day. The manager in charge of the proceedings did not like that demand, and said that he did not, but he agreed to it. Loading the Admiralty coal commenced and, in spite of the three-pound premium, went forward strictly according to the standard rate. At five in the afternoon, when whistles sound in Southampton and a flood of men on bicycles stream from the gates of the dock, it was estimated that another two hours of the unhurried labour would see the job finished. But the coal-heavers stopped work with the whistle; they had reached another stage of demand. They refused to do a single minute overtime work unless another premium, this time of five pounds for each man, was paid. That was too much even for managers anxious that a famous ship should keep her appointments. The passengers came aboard and eat their dinners and slept alongside in Southampton. Next morning loading coal was resumed and finished comfortably within two hours. When the *Mauretania* had sailed for New York, without calling at Cherbourg, the manager told the coal-heavers something of what he thought about them. He said that they would repent such action. Those of them who preferred employment to unemployment did, although many of them complained bitterly of injustice when in a short time the big ships came to Southampton and were fed with their fuel through a pipe.

The *Mauretania* went off to cross the Atlantic very sedately, although her mixed coal did not alone account for that. Her black squad was not what it had been ; men simply could not be found to do the work as it had been done before the War. The firemen and trimmers did their job, or were replaced by other men, the engineers saw to that ; but the old pride in their job which had helped them to overcome the enormous demands of giving the ship her steam for fast passages was not there. Most of the engineers who knew exactly the size of those demands seem astonished not at the post-war attitude, of doing the job and no more, but that the other attitude, of giving the ship what she demanded, should ever have existed. Labour difficulties at this time were appearing everywhere. Ships had to face them as did factories and mines and railways. The ships, of course, were in an individual position, as nobody amongst their crews, except an occasional fool whose folly would earn small sympathy from his fellows, would refuse work while at sea ; but once the crew was paid off at the end of a voyage a ship with a bad name might be boycotted by the men who knew their work, the only sort of men the *Mauretania* could afford to employ. She never had anything but a good name ; men said of her that in her they could always get a hearing ; but even with her good name her supply of labour was then a constant anxiety.

Of one thing all the officers who handled that difficult labour seem agreed : most of the officials of the men's union and particularly the leaders, Havelock Wilson and his immediate staff, were of very real assistance. If some individual were causing trouble, stirring up ill-feeling without cause, making what the unions considered illegitimate demands, by reporting the matter to the officials, the officers could rely on effective treatment. In most cases, certainly in most cases in the *Mauretania*, union officials and merchant officers were on excellent terms. There is a little story about that. The ship was at Halifax ; one of the union officials had looked in to have a chat with one of the senior officers, but had not been offered the customary drink. The facts were that the ship's bars were closed at that hour and by a mischance, which did not often occur, the private store in the cabin locker had run short. Next day, when the union official was aboard again, the officer apologised for his lack of hospitality, explaining the circumstances.

"Red tape everywhere," said the union man. "But d'you mean to tell me that the chief steward closes down the bar on you ? "

"Definitely, he does," the officer told him.

"Does he ? " the official of labour replied. "I'll soon fix that for you. How would this do ? I'll go to the steward and tell him that if it occurs again I'll call all his men out and keep them out. That ought to help."

A pleasant, friendly spirit which helped difficult times but could not cure them. The union officials sought to control a machine which was liable to take charge ; the staff of the *Mauretania* had to make

do with a ship in bad need of thorough overhaul
with a crew grown difficult. It was a bad patch.
The ship was being caught up by new rivals, not
by her own fault, but, as the men who served
her then will say, because she was not being given
the quarter of half a chance. The owners had only
one answer to the plea that she needed thorough
attention : she was still getting a full passenger list
and the money for large expenditure was not there.
Undoubtedly she was still attracting passengers, but
as undoubtedly she was losing ground. To have
claimed for her, as she made her last voyage that
year, averaging 18.23 knots in summer weather, that
she was the greatest steamship in history with an
amazing future before her would have sounded simply
silly.

She got back to Southampton at the end of July,
and found luck. She caught fire. Captain McNeil,
who had been her first staff-captain and was later
to command her when she made her most famous
voyage, was at the time the Cunard Marine Superintendent at Southampton. He and Sir Arthur
Rostron, then commanding her, both describe the
incident in their books of reminiscences. The ship
had docked on her return from New York the day
before, and was coaling ; other work, naturally, was
going on aboard. On E deck, in the first-class cabins
below the dining saloon, some bright worker, whose
name should surely be remembered with gratitude,
was using an inflammable spirit for cleaning carpets, a
practice very much against the Company's rules. As
a result—although he does not say this in his book—
Captain McNeil, who had just finished lunch aboard,
had to risk an attack of indigestion by exhibiting

great activity immediately after a meal. The fire got a good hold, because without adequate smoke helmets the fire-fighting party could not get at the seat of it, but had to concern themselves with preventing it spreading throughout the ship. This, with two commandeered passenger tenders pumping water in through the portholes on one side, and the local fire brigade doing the same thing on the other, they managed to do. The fire burned fiercely for six hours before it was subdued, and had to be watched, and occasionally fought, throughout the night. All the first-class cabins on E deck were gutted, and the deck above (the floor of the dining saloon), was buckled. The daily papers had gone to press that night with the news that the *Mauretania* was burning. Captain Rostron read of it at his home in Liverpool in bed in the morning and, one presumed, did not eat the leisurely breakfast he had planned for the first morning of his shore leave. With Mr. Cockburn, the chief engineer, and representatives of the management, he left at once for Southampton. The damage was considerable, but there was no real hurt to the structure. The management had in mind the fact that all available passenger space on the Atlantic was being eagerly booked. The Cunard Company had a big building programme ahead to replace the heavy losses of the War. A large increase of ordinary share capital was close at hand, together with the flotation of a big debenture loan. Profits from the hiring-out of that much demanded passenger space were very necessary financially. It was important for the balance sheet that the *Mauretania*, although she might be overdue for careful attention in order that she could give of her best, should not miss her turn. There was no question at all of her not being safe to go to sea ; any suggestion of that sort was purely fantastic. She was merely like a car that is badly in need of decarbonisation ; she would get there, but not in the time and with the smoothness which she should. If the gutted portion of E deck were boarded off so that passengers could not see the effects of the fire, she could well go on her next scheduled voyage. That was the first decision of the management. There was opposition to it. It is interesting to picture the situation as the damage caused by the fire was surveyed. On the one hand, the management, largely concerned with finance and their duty to shareholders ; on the other, the men who served the ship, who had in fact learned to love her, who were bitterly disappointed that she had been steadily falling from her high place. Captain Rostron, as the commander, voiced the opposition ; he did not lack backing from the chief engineer and from the marine superintendent, who had served her and was going to command her. The opposition's case was based largely on the bad effect which a boarded-up space, a bandaged wound, might have on passengers. The case was won on the fact that the lower floor of the first-class dining-room could not reasonably be used by first-class passengers whose demands for comfort had not been stifled by the War. The *Mauretania's* next voyage was cancelled. That cancellation led to the taking of a long view. If immediate profits had to be foregone, why not make provision for larger ones in the future ? The coal situation was very difficult. The opportunity for the change which had always been in view since the ship was designed seemed at hand. It was taken.

Captain Rostron took the ship up to the Tyne to her builders instead of to New York. The bright worker, with his inflammable spirit and his disregard of rules, had done a great ship a valuable service at a moment when she needed it. Popular favour, once it begins to turn away, has a trick of keeping away. Americans had always liked the *Mauretania* ; from her first voyage she had taken their fancy and held it. But American favour was turning from all things British ; it might well turn from an elderly coal-burner.

When the Treaty of Versailles was signed, the amount of money which Germany was to be expected to pay by way of damages to the Allies was not fixed Under duress she signed a confession of war guilt, and then the Allied experts began to make the wildest shots at estimating her capacity to pay. They began by fixing on the sum of twenty-four thousand million pounds, and at the General Election in England, which followed close on the Armistice, that bill for damages was dangled in front of the electors. Quite shortly afterwards doubts arose as to whether there was not something a little wrong with that estimate. The experts had another try, and in 1921 reduced their figure to one quarter of the original. Later it came down to one twelfth of the original, and finally to the fact that Germany could not make any further payments at all. Most of the money which she had by then paid had been borrowed from the United States. That borrowing from the creditor to pay the creditor led to complications, since ultimately every nation involved in the War was due to pay the United States money because they had all borrowed from her. But bitter reparation quarrels started

directly the experts' estimate of Germany's capacity to pay was found to be faulty. France was consistent, she declared that, if Germany did not pay her, she certainly would not attempt to pay anyone else. If one debtor defaulted let all default. England tried to negotiate. The United States demanded full payment whatever happened to Germany. On both sides of the Atlantic, amongst ordinary people, there was considerable bitterness. It was urged that America had done uncommonly well out of the War; that she had collected already vast sums of money; that by sending Wilson to Versailles as her accredited representative, and then repudiating him and his League of Nations and refusing to sign the Peace Treaty, she had added enormously to the difficulties of her late Allies, who had suffered immeasurably more than she had. To that America replied that she wanted her money and was going to have it, while a certain section of her population, though not those who had had experience of fighting, maintained that England and France had failed to conquer Germany, but that the United States had succeeded and expected payment for it.

The happenings in Ireland in 1920 and 1921 did not improve the feeling between England and the United States. That miserable business of murder and reprisals and weak hand-to-mouth handling could not remain as a domestic quarrel within the British Empire, but was duly advertised as an example of incompetency in government throughout the world. The thousands of Irish in America made use of it to inflame opinion against the English.

Before the Irish Question was appeased, though hardly settled, by the grant of Dominion Home Rule,

the United States had made a proposal for a naval
holiday, and the first of many disarmament conferences sat at Washington.   It proved, like its successors
that agreement about disarmament was scarcely
likely to be reached ; but it led to the breaking-up
of the British-Japanese alliance and a new arrangement whereby Britain, France, Japan and the United
States agreed to settle by mediation differences which
might arise between them. To many people that
seemed hardly consistent with membership of the
League of Nations ; but then, in the opinion of
many people, the League had been still-born. The
confusion of peace was as thick as the fog of war ;
there were troubles everywhere. In 1922 Egypt
passed to independence from a curious form of
British rule ; there were growing difficulties in India.
Then Mr. Lloyd George backed a loser ; he sup-
ported the Greeks against the Turks, who had been
somewhat left out of count in the Versailles Treaty.
The Chanak crises forced him to appeal to the
Dominions for military support, in case he should
need it for his Greeks. To the surprise of many
Englishmen who do not give much thought to Empire,
except that it is vaguely connected with jingoism,
the Dominions claimed that they were Dominions
and not Colonies, and so entitled to some say in the
foreign policy of the Empire which might involve
them in wars. That was a horrible claim to many
conservative souls in England ; it suggested that the
mother no longer had full control of the children ;
she could not spank them when she considered they
had been naughty, nor command them to do this
or that. It was more than a score of years since
some of the colonies had become Dominions, yet the

implications of the new status had not penetrated to the minds of quite a lot of people at home. With America, an English-speaking nation, becoming estranged and the Dominions becoming uppish, it was a great time for those people who found no virtue except in past days, and a species of comfort in predicting that their country was going to the dogs. Something had to be done. The dictatorship of Mr. Lloyd George had worn threadbare. In the same month, October, that Mussolini marched on Rome, there was a famous meeting at the Carlton Club in London, and England returned thankfully to a spate of party politics. A General Election followed and the Conservatives came into power. Mr. Bonar Law became Prime Minister, and Mr. Baldwin was sent to America to make arrangements for some settlement of the bitter reparations quarrel and for the funding of our debt to the United States. What he arranged was a considerable shock to many of his countrymen.

It was a time of important comings and goings on the Atlantic. The *Mauretania* was an expert in that sort of carrying. She could claim success at her job, when real success was very rare. But her success was limping a little. Really, the bright worker with the inflammable spirit seems to have timed his effort well. American feeling at that moment might almost have welcomed the chance to call the slight limp of an old favourite lameness, and turn to some other ship which was not dry.

The cost of converting the *Mauretania* to an oil-burner was something over a quarter of a million ; in addition, the damage caused by the fire had to be made good—a heavy bill. The *Aquitania* had already been converted to oil. The prices of labour and material were very high. Although the Cunard Company had increased their share capital by one million pounds and issued a four million pound debenture loan, they had a big building programme ahead of them. They decided to restrict expenditure on the *Mauretania* to boilers and the fire damage. Her turbines were examined, her engines were tuned up as they normally were on annual overhaul, but nothing extensive was done to them. She was put back into service in March, 1922, and worked steadily and regularly through that year and till the autumn of 1923.

In 1922 she made eleven voyages in nine months ; in 1923 twelve in ten months. That was getting back to work again. As an oil-burner, directly her engineers had got used to the ways of the new fuel, she began to show better averages. On both the outward and homeward passages of her first voyage burning oil, she managed to maintain for the open sea run more than 24 knots. The boiler rooms had become different places in which a different race of men worked—a handful where there had been hundreds before. Interested passengers could be taken round and shown the surroundings of furnaces as clean as the decks. She burned plenty of oil—somewhere around 4,400 tons of it on each average passage—and oil is not a cheap commodity ; but the advantages of the change were enormous. Maintaining a constant pressure of steam was a simple affair, no longer largely dependent upon the skill and the appetite for work of a type of men brutalised by the nature of their job. The old black squad had done magnificently in their day, but their departure from

the ship had not made her a less pleasant place.
Refuelling was a clean, simple and rapid business.
Above all, the *Mauretania*, fourteen years old and
with many large new rivals, had followed fashion.
Passenger pleasing is a delicate business ; more than
one good ship has been barred from success as a
carrier of human freight because she had not the
number of funnels demanded by popular taste.
Particularly on the Atlantic Ferry where, except in
abnormal times, there are more ships and more
passenger space than can be filled, a small thing—
an indifferent orchestra or a temporary shortage of
caviare, say, in the first class, something of more
account like too many four and more berth cabins in
the other classes—may send customers into a rival
hull. Her conversion to burning oil improved the
Mauretania as a steamship ; it opened the way to
taking her out of the class of famous ships into the
small company of those which history will not forget ;
at the same time it gave her a better standing with
new passengers. She was then in the difficult middle
period : she was not new, but she had not acquired
the glamour of the veteran. One of her characteristics
was that she could always hold the affection of those
who knew her ; former passengers would come back
to her regularly. But it was enormously important
at this time that she should attract new passengers.
Oil prevented people, the possible new passengers.
from saying what people were saying then : " Coal
for a big liner ! It's really the stone age."

So the *Mauretania* left the stone age, but by no means
for any easy age for Atlantic shipping companies.
In 1922 the United States Government brought in
the quota system for immigrants, which was a strict

rationing of the number of alien inhabitants whom
the country would accept. Immigrants to the United
States had always been a paying trade even when
great ships like the *Mauretania* had reduced the fares
of this class of passenger to six pounds or less for the
passage, and lesser ships to the neighbourhood of
three pounds ten shillings. There was danger that
the third-class accommodation would be empty.
Something had to be done. The Cunard managers,
with other managers, gave the matter thought, because
the third-class accommodation was not small. Out of
this thought there came a new term which is very
familiar to-day—" tourist." Call it a comfortable
third class, a third class without too many restrictions, a class very far away from that now obsolete
description, " steerage." In 1922 and 1923 the
Mauretania was busy with considering what would
have to be done about this new class. Right at the
other end of the scale, in that not easy time, she tried
another form of attraction. She went cruising.
To-day almost every ship which can substantiate a
decent claim to comfort makes a cruise or so a year.
Then it was not so common, though the Germans
had started it and made the idea popular with big
ships some years before the War. The crews of the
ships concerned do not call it cruising ; they speak of
it as yachting. For most of them it is relaxation, a
change from routine, comfortable speed without
driving, frequent stopping at unaccustomed ports.
To the steward's department it is probably much extra
labour, handling and pleasing and entertaining
passengers of whom the majority, unlike the regulars
of routine passages, are strangers to the sea ; the
shore excursion racket makes it often a nightmare ;

but there is compensation in the tips. The *Maure-tania*, seeking profits wherever they could be found, made her first acquaintance with this cruising business in a fashion which left its mark upon the memories of her crew.

Early in 1923 the American Express Company chartered the ship. There was then a lot of money in America, and this travel agency seems to have had designs upon a sizeable lump of it. They chartered the whole ship for a cruise from New York to the Mediterranean, and so could fix their own fares ; the *Mauretania* and her crew were rented for a few weeks. Luxury cruises had been much advertised already ; there was nothing of the appeal of newness about them. The American Express Company went one better. They hired the world's fastest liner and appealed exclusively to sheer extravagance ; they arranged the prices so that no man or woman who could not lay their hands on considerable sums of cash could possibly go upon that cruise. They trailed not a luxury lure but one of real squandering upon a majestic scale. Passengers could say proudly—and one assumes that only people who could be made proud by such a claim were passengers —" I was in the *Mauretania* when she was the millionaire ship. We did splash it round." Judge Garry, head of the Steel Trust, appears to have had the distinction of heading the list of fares ; he paid twenty-five thousand dollars for his suite. The cruise lasted six weeks. So no one of the proud company aboard could point the finger of scorn at him and say that he was hiring cheap accommodation. That airing of wealth certainly impressed the officers and crew of the *Mauretania* deeply. The cruise was, naturally, fully advertised. So, probably, it impressed others deeply too. Many people were finding peace, at least, a more hungry business than war ; several heroes were homeless ; ex-colonels could, as it were, be picked up round about two a penny. So fine a collection of men and women with money to waste had possibly never been assembled before in the hull of one ship. It was, almost certainly, a record, but it hardly ranks as one of the most glorious which the *Mauretania* made.

The *Majestic*, which as the Hamburg-American *Bismarck* had been uncompleted at the beginning of the war, was put into commission by the White Star Company in 1922. Judged by the standard of registered tonnage she was getting on for twice the size of the *Mauretania*. Her 56,620 tons appealed considerably to those people who always want the biggest. She was designed for a speed of 24 knots and perhaps could do even better than that. So could the *Leviathan*, whose speed on her trials when she was taken over by the United States Government had been impressive but not unassisted by the Gulf Stream. Both these big new ships were giving the *Mauretania* trouble, they were making faster passages although they could not take away the old ship's record. But the Cunard Company, like all other shipping companies, was facing difficulties ; they had spent a large sum on converting the *Mauretania* to oil ; she was doing reasonably fast passages, sailing with reasonably full lists and would have to go on doing so for the time. That was the answer to her engineers who, pleading minor troubles in the engine room, begged for a complete overhaul of her turbines. Given that, they urged, there could be no more talk about the *Majestic's* rival speed. But the begging and the urging were not fruitful. Then the White Star Company made a slip ; they advertised the *Majestic* as the world's largest and fastest ship. The Cunard people were at them immediately and made them take the " fastest " back. To make certain that the inaccuracy should not slip into being fact, the *Mauretania* was taken out of service at the end of her one hundred and fifty-first voyage early in November, 1923, and put into Thornycroft's hands at Southampton. The overhaul had come at last.

Her great turbines, still the most powerful in the world, were dismantled and examined, where required new blades or new segments of blading were put in. That, with the four ahead and the two astern turbines entailed a big job, but it was carried out carefully and was proceeding well. The stage of reassembly had been reached ; the renovated rotors were in place. These rotors in the low pressure turbines weighed each one hundred and twenty tons and in the high pressure ones over seventy tons ; the tops of the casings, of which the smallest component sector of any one weighed thirty-five tons, were in the lifting gear ready to be lowered into place. These figures of weights of parts of machinery are necessary description, otherwise the picture of the *Mauretania's* engine room at that moment cannot be conveyed. The whole place was in a mess, a job and a job entailing the moving of enormous weights in a curtailed space was being finished. The tops of the turbine cases—call them huge curved steel lids, composed of thirty-five ton segments bolted together, each of a total weight of about one hundred tons—were swung in position for lowering on to the bottom casings. It was at that moment that organised labour took a hand ; the men engaged on the job put down their tools and walked out.

The Cunard Company had spent and were spending a lot of money, somewhere around a third of her original cost, on the *Mauretania*, with reasonable hopes of her yielding an improved return. Thornycrofts had taken on a contract. Neither the Company nor the contractors had any intention of allowing that strike to defeat them. If English labour refused to finish the job, French workmen should finish it. That was the decision : the ship was to go over to Cherbourg to be completed. It was a big decision because with her turbines open she had, of course, no means of steaming. She took on board a crew ; down below the chief and his officers and the Cunard and Thornycroft foremen who had not walked out, on the bridge the commander and the watch-keepers. The turbine top casings were shored up and wedged so that, it was hoped, they would not damage either themselves or anything else. Having seen to that, the engineers had nothing more to do but hang around and await arrival at Cherbourg. The chief maintains that it was an amusing experience, smoking his pipe and observing how they got the ship across without her engines. That sounds well, but not at all convincing ; that either he or his assistants found any considerable amusement in the prospect that the engines, which were their pride, were in danger of severe injury is hard to swallow. Anxiety and not a little bitterness with organised labour accompanied them on that cross-Channel passage, because a hundred tons of metal taking charge can do a bit of damage.

Six Dutch tugs—the moment did not seem at all an English occasion—took the *Mauretania* in charge. When they had got her down the Water, past the Nab, and out into the Channel, the weather began to breeze up. During the night it blew; and the great ship resented being towed. By common consent the Dutch skippers handled their tugs magnificently and showed themselves skilled, in the highest degree, at their jobs; but they very nearly lost the *Mauretania*. In the dark and the wind, in the short confusion of a Channel sea hawsers parted; the tugs could not nose and push her against the weather. It rained as well as blew. There was a moment when it seemed that the ship, powerless to help herself in any way, might drift on to a lee shore. But the Dutch skippers kept their tugs at it; they refused to take defeat from that bad night at sea. The *Mauretania* got into shelter at Cherbourg without even damaging the turbine casings. But without a bit of luck over and above the obstinate attentions of skilled Dutchmen it is, in the view of the men who passed that night in her, unlikely that she would have got there. The seas can make a rough game of it with eight hundred feet of helpless ship, when they set their mind to it.

French workmen, under the *Mauretania's* engineers and Cunard and Thornycroft foremen, finished off the job. It took them six weeks. For the first time, probably, the engine room smelled of garlic and caporal tobacco; but that was not the only souvenir of Gallic assistance which the ship took away with her.

The actual closing of the turbines was an anxious job. There had been cases in other ships where a small tool or even a chip of metal had been forgotten and closed down in a turbine with most unhappy results. When the turbine was revolved the stranger inside it played the devil with the blades. A small piece of carelessness at the end of a long job had on two or three well authenticated occasions, resulted in most of the blades being stripped off and the turbine wrecked. That meant a job which, with engines of the *Mauretania's* size, with dismantling, replacing damaged material, reassembling, might run into many weeks and cost not hundreds but thousands of pounds. An engineer who allowed that little piece of carelessness could form a very accurate estimate of his owners' attitude as they reckoned up the cost of it. The chief of the *Mauretania* superintending the finish of the work at Cherbourg had not the slightest intention of facing that reckoning. He evolved a procedure which almost amounted to a drill for eliminating any possibility of carelessness occurring. When a turbine was ready to be closed tools were counted and removed from its vicinity. The workmen were all ordered to stand back. The chief and his officers formed a cordon round the turbine, examined everything finally, and remained on guard, as it were, while the lifting gear lowered the top casing into place. That had been done while five of the six turbines were closed ; it was certain that no strange bodies had been shut up in them. The drill was carefully repeated around the port low pressure turbine. The French workmen stood back, the engineer officers after making sure that there had been no carelessness formed their guard circle while the top casing, weighing more than a hundred tons, came slowly down. As the space between the upper and lower casings lessened, there was a light metallic tinkle. The chief's mind located and diagnosed the sound. He turned to his staff-chief.

" You heard that ? "

" Aye."

" What was it ? "

" Something metal falling on the rotor."

" Where ? "

" About there." The staff-chief pointed.

That was confirmation. None of the engineers had seen anything, they had only heard ; but they agreed as to the spot from which the sound had come. The top casing was raised again. Very slowly the rotor was turned in the hope that whatever had dropped on it might be discovered. Nothing appeared ; so, since it was clear that something was there which should not be there, the turbine was dismantled. The rotor, weighing one hundred and twenty tons, had to be lifted out ; not a quick or easy job. While it was going on a very careful watch was kept on all the workers ; and speculation as to what would happen to the man discovered to have been careless was probably active. Not carelessness but a brass trouser button, of French manufacture, was discovered. It is unfortunate but researches do not make clear exactly what was said by a Scots chief and a Welsh staff-chief when the button was found. A French workman, either a humorist of the misguided order or a thrifty soul who did not like to see the finish of a lucrative job approaching, had flicked it from the rear rank when he and his mates stood back. His skill as a flicker, it seems, was never rightly appreciated in the *Mauretania*. But his button, which could have wrecked, very effectively, that low pressure turbine, is preserved. It is embedded in a silver cup presented to the chief by Sir John Thornycroft, who would not have liked a wrecked turbine to have resulted from a contract given to his firm.

After the work provided by the funny stuff with the button had been completed, the *Mauretania* left Cherbourg for Southampton and service again. She had then made one hundred and fifty-one voyages ; she was going to make close on two hundred more, putting in to them steadier, better and faster work than she had done before. On May 31st, 1924, she sailed from Southampton, her difficult middle period over. She was then between sixteen and seventeen years old, an elderly ship ; but she had had her rest and recuperation. The men who took her out westward did not doubt that any nonsense about the *Majestic* was finally finished.

On the first day out from Cherbourg of that passage, the commander was giving a tea-party and the chief was president at a session of the *Mauretania* Bridge Club of which he was the founder. In this club there was heavy gambling, they played for stakes of as much as one penny a hundred and the debts incurred were seldom settled as they should be. While the commander entertained passengers over a cup of tea and the chief gambled, the rejuvenated *Mauretania* was pushing ahead in style. Everybody concerned with her was pleased, because the old ship had been given her chance. Then she shook with a curious slight jar and slowed down. The commander went on with his party, knowing that the message which was coming to him must not be allowed to disturb passengers. The chief stopped playing bridge and was ready to meet the messenger who was coming to him. The governors fitted to a turbine would prevent any serious damage when a shaft went, but he was anxious to be down below to make certain of the full amount of damage. One of the outer shafts had snapped off where it emerged from the stern tube ; the propeller, of course, was in the Atlantic. There was no water coming in through the glands. Within ten minutes of that slight jar the *Mauretania* was going full ahead again on three screws. She did not make a good passage, but she kept on time and did not make a bad one. She came home at an average of over 24 knots and made another voyage at quite respectable speed before the damage was repaired. With only three propellers she could do steady work on the Atlantic as she had proved before and was to do again. Machinery is liable to play these games however carefully it is tended; but it was disappointing because she had to keep the confounding of her critics until her third voyage after overhaul. Then she made no mistake about it ; she made all other ships on the Atlantic give up for several years the idea that she could be beaten. England in that month had got rid of her first Labour Government, though not, despite the devout beliefs of many diehard minds, of any perceptible portion of her troubles. The *Mauretania* had then seen close on seventeen years of service. For an express liner she was no longer elderly but old. The affairs of the nations in the forthcoming years were to go from bad to worse.

It is comforting—except for the confirmed pessimist, who is, anyhow, a creature of small account—to find in this old ship something English which defied the trend of those years. Nobody can deny her that defiance ; it had a most astonishing vigour about it.

CHAPTER VIII

TRIUMPHANT DEFEAT

THE *Leviathan* as well as the *Majestic* was at that time occasionally, when the weather promised well, being driven all out and making fast passages. Competition was keen, and the chance to take from an old ship the record she had held for so long, looked better than it ever had before. It was, of course, known to Atlantic shipping that the *Mauretania* had been in dock to have her turbines rejuvenated ; it was also known that on her first voyage after the refit she had dropped a propeller. There is about as much chance of a famous ship keeping her affairs from being discussed in other ships as there is of a village parson escaping criticism from his parishioners. She had been tuned up, that was common gossip, but so was the fact that, being in tune, she had not yet showed her pre-war form. There were gossips who said that, whatever they did to her, she was past showing that. So on August 9th, 1924, she was sent off from Southampton on her one hundred and fifty-fourth voyage expecting to stop the gossips' silly talk. She did stop it. Taking the long westward lane, she crossed from Cherbourg Breakwater to the Ambrose Channel Light-vessel in 4 days, 20 hours, 2 minutes, at an average speed of 25·58 knots. Going westward, feeling the throb of her, passengers wanted to know whether she were out for a record ; going eastward again, feeling the same throb, which produced less vibration than when she was steaming at ordinary full speed, knowing that she had made a record outward passage, another crowd of passengers wanted to be told whether she were at it again. If they had asked a horse dealer what he had paid for a horse, they would have had the same slender hope of getting a positive answer as they had in asking sailors about attempts on records. She was going ahead : that was the extent to which her crew would commit themselves in words. But the faces of her crew, particularly that of the chief, might give the discerning further information. The barber—it is curious but a fact that the barber in the *Mauretania* was traditionally supposed, by passengers, to have inside information about the day's run—was asked for tips ; he attempted to maintain his reputation. In the smoking room of the first saloon where the tickets for the next day's run were auctioned in the evening, big numbers and the high field got most of the bidding. The *Mauretania* was going well, more than half the passage was over, there was no weather in prospect that could delay her, everybody concerned with her was pleased and proud. Her four funnels, her slender lines of speed, her own unmistakable action marking her, she was tearing eastward, restored to her first place on the Atlantic, the most striking and the best-known ship's figure on those seas, when she met a little tramp wallowing and pounding westward. The little tramp made her number, and then her master, watching the great liner through his glasses, had an inspiration ; he made another signal.

"What," he asked, "ship are you ? "

It worked. The *Mauretania* did not proclaim her identity with a hoist of flags. Up on her bridge inspiration failed the watch; with another record almost safe in their pockets, they could not think of a suitable retort to the wallowing humorist's insufferable impertinence, until it was too late.

The *Mauretania* completed that passage in 4 days, 19 hours, at an average speed of 26·16 knots. She had then been sailing the seas for close on seventeen years. It was the fastest voyage, both ways on that route, which she had ever made, but a long way short of the fastest which she was to make. The *Leviathan* and the *Majestic* and the others had to drop out of the competition; it seemed useless to go on with it.

During 1925 Winston Churchill brought England back to the gold standard with results which were not quite those for which he had hoped. Coal miners and owners got at each other once again, and Government intervention could not settle their disputes. So the principle of State subvention of wages was introduced; it cost the taxpayer £20,000,000 and failed to prevent the General Strike of the following year. At the end of the year Britain, Germany, France, Italy and Belgium signed the Locarno treaties. They agreed never to resort to war with one another, but if one of them should, then the others should combine to hit her hard. The League of Nations was still in existence. Some people had high hopes of the Locarno treaties and also of the League. Industrially it was an uneasy year. But the *Mauretania*, being no longer concerned with coal miners or owners, only suffered general interference with her business. She made fifteen voyages, and showed herself again on two of them as a pleasure cruiser and not a mail ship.

In 1926, on her first regular voyage after a Mediterranean cruise, she gave marine history further proof of her quality. She left Southampton for Cherbourg and New York on March 27th, carrying six hundred and eighty-one passengers and precisely the same number of crew. For those who like signs of the times it may be of interest that she carried only one hundred and fifty-three persons in the third cabin, a far cry from the days when emigrants were one of her paying lines. Until March 30th the voyage was uneventful ; then the weather began to change. At 2.20 p.m. the log records a heavy westerly swell and revolutions reduced from 180 to 160 per minute. At 8.0 p.m. there was a strong breeze and rough sea, as well as the heavy swell. Snow and hail squalls were frequent, and the ship was pitching and spraying over all. An hour later extra ice look-out was placed. Twenty minutes before midnight the *Mauretania*, putting her nose into it, shipped a heavy sea forward, which did a fair amount of damage. At 2.50 a.m. on the 31st, revolutions were reduced to 100, but that was only while the damage on the forecastle head, caused by shipping the heavy sea, was being secured. Throughout that night, at short intervals, she was altering her revolutions, increasing when she got the chance, slowing down when the seas bade her. When the forenoon watch came on duty a moderate gale was recorded ; there were snow squalls, and the ship was pitching and shipping water forward. During a temporary lull revolutions were put up to 140, but the weather would not let her exceed that, nor keep to it for long. At noon the moderate gale was still blowing, and there was a high, confused sea, with a heavy W.N.W. swell. The log, not given to exaggerated statements, adds to the record of pitching and spraying over all the word " heavily." It was no weather for records of speed, or comfort, or pushing a ship without testing her severely. After the noon position had been fixed, Captain Rostron sent a wireless message informing New York of the exact time at which he expected to arrive. Here four subsequent entries in the log are worth recording as they stand :

3.25.   S O S call received from s.s. *Laleham* in Lat. 39° 06′ N. Long. 55° 18′ W.

3.30.   Proceeded full speed to assistance of *Laleham*.

4. 0.   Strong breeze. Very rough sea and swell. Cloudy and clear.

4.24.   Received amended position of s.s. *Laleham*— Lat. 39° 06′ N. Long. 56° 16′ W.

There is no record of revolutions, because full speed in answer to an S.O.S. call means, in the tradition of the sea, all the revolutions which the engine-room staff can give. There is no record of pitching and shipping water, because in that same tradition of the sea discomfort to passengers and minor damage to the ship had ceased for the moment to have much importance.

The *Mauretania*, when she received that S.O.S. call, was 180 sea miles from the vessel calling her. The *Laleham*, actually, was then on her beam ends, with all her boats carried away, very near to her end. The *Mauretania* had no details of that—all that she knew was the urgency of the need of assistance. To most passengers the " Strong breeze, very rough sea and swell " looked like a real storm, to the crew of the *Mauretania* the weather showed itself more than menacing for any vessel in distress. So they gave her all the steam they could give her and reached a speed of 29 knots. When the old ship was driving through those seas, answering the call upon her in a fashion which earned real love from the men who served her, she got another meesage. The log records :

8.35 p.m.   Received report that s.s. *Shirwan* had rescued crew of *Laleham*. No further assistance required.

8.38 p.m.   Course set for New York.

So within three minutes of the receipt of that message the engines were back to more normal revolutions, and at a speed more comfortable for the people she carried on that very rough sea the ship proceeded about her ordinary business. By steaming for five hours at that high speed she had got a long way off her direct route to New York and she had done nothing to assist the *Laleham* ; but the dash to answer that call had not entirely failed in achievement ; it had shown, and the showing is remembered on the Atlantic, what manner of ship she was in her old age. Captain Rostron had informed New York of the probable time of his arrival before the *Mauretania* had left her course. After she had finished with going out of her way, knowing his ship, he allowed his message to stand. The *Mauretania*, although she was encountering a fresh gale until she arrived at the Ambrose Light and did not reach at any time her normal full-speed revolutions, reached New York two minutes ahead of the time given in her Commander's message. Her day was very far from being over.

The General Strike was, and still is, declared by the Trades Unions not to have been an attempt to force their demands upon the country by direct action. The country, however, did not at the time accept that declaration. It took the view that a section of the community was holding a pistol to its head, and in a manner altogether English it knocked the pistol away and told the holder not to be a blamed fool. For eight days it muddled through complete dislocation of its ordinary life without anything very spectacular happening. The first, and it is to be hoped the last, English official daily newspaper, the *British Gazette*, had a brief existence, and showed the Government to be very far from success in that line of business. Young people, undergraduates and the like, and others not so young, worked hard and thoroughly enjoyed a brief change from routine. Businesses of all sorts suffered a setback and lost money. Generally, a crisis which could have produced revolution and bloodshed aroused a stolid, not ill-tempered determination to get through with such foolery as soon as possible, and something like real national conviction that, on the principle of trying everything once, general strikes could be tolerated without rancour, but that after the one trial they must be stopped. Vituperation was welcomed in party politics, somehow it missed a welcome in that strike. After eight days the country got back to its routine, and the holders of the pistol, reckoning up their depleted funds and their miscalculation of the British spirit, considered their stupid folly. The miners alone continued a die-hard policy, and by November found it extremely expensive. In the exact middle of that eight-day test of what could or could not be done in England, the *Mauretania* sailed from Southampton on her advertised date. Had she still burned coal it is unlikely that she would have sailed ; as it was, she suffered amateurish attentions before she got away. When she did sail on May 8th, she carried, amongst the crew, men who were saying all sorts of fiery things about new eras and others whose criticism of the fiery talkers was not in itself tame, and, amongst her passengers, persons who had inside information about England being really in a very bad way. When she arrived home again, sixteen days later, England was still really in a very bad way, but the General Strike was over, and the country was getting along with the bad way and anxiously considering what horse to back for the Derby. A most tiresome country for those who like to take their troubles seriously.

The year of the General Strike in England stands out in Atlantic history. There were many changes, new appearances and plans, all of which affected the *Mauretania*. The Compagnie Générale Trans-atlantique launched the *Ile de France*. She was only a 23-knot ship, with a gross tonnage of under 44,000, so she had no claims to first place, either in speed or size. Her special appeal was made to luxury and to modern French art in decoration. Answering the situation arising from American restriction of immigration, she was designed to carry less than five hundred third class passengers. Making a bid for something which publicity could emphasise as without question a new feature in mail ships, she was provided with an aeroplane and a catapult launching gear. The aeroplane, leaving the ship at a considerable distance from her terminal ports, would, it was hoped, enable express mails to be delivered a day or more ahead of those entirely sea-borne. The experiment was costly and not at first wholly successful, but it marked a stage. When the *Ile de France* made her maiden voyage in 1927, she did, very definitely, so far as fittings and decorations were concerned, show up the *Mauretania's* age. There were plenty of people who considered that the old ship, with her sober, ungaudy woodwork, was more restful and more pleasing than her new French rival ; there were others who found the taste in decoration of twenty years before rather too near to the dawn of civilisation for their young fancy. To answer the claims put forward by the *Ile de France* the Cunard Company did much redecorating and redesigning of state-rooms and suites, wisely they did not attempt anything in the nature of face-lifting by changing the appearance of the public rooms ; but the simple fact remained that in her twentieth year of service the *Mauretania* was showing in appearance the wrinkles of old age.

Italy was designing and launching new ships to attract Atlantic passengers. The *Augustus*, a ship of roughly the same size as the *Mauretania*, not designed for speed, but making her mark as the biggest motor ship in the world, could not be ignored as a lure for lovers of the latest.

During the war the International Mercantile Marine, the Morgan Combine, which had had so much to do with the building of the *Mauretania*, had got into a bad way and had been placed in the hands of a receiver. It had largely recovered ; but soon after the war negotiations had commenced for the purchase from it of the White Star Line. The Royal Mail Steam Packet Company had made an offer to buy all of its ships which flew the British flag ; but President Wilson had stopped that. Early in 1926 new negotiations for the sale of the White Star Line were begun and broke down. A little later the Kylsant-controlled group of companies made the purchase and thereby became, though without ultimate advantage to the financier at the head or many of the shareholders, the largest ship-owners in the world. After many years the Oceanic Steam Navigation Company, which was the White Star's official name, came back to English ownership, and to ambitious plans which dated from the days before the Morgan Combine had absorbed it. For thirty years Harland & Wolff had been concerned with the designing and redesigning of a ship for the White Star having a length of 1,000 feet. After the Kylsant purchase, this ship was laid down ; work was begun, suspended, and finally abandoned in 1929, when Germany had re-established herself on the Atlantic.

German plans for her re-establishment were the event of 1926 which had most effect on the *Mauretania*, for during that year the North German Lloyd, in spite of the difficulties in which Germany was involved, without direct subsidy from the government, decided to do what they had wanted to do since 1907. Two ships were ordered for one especial purpose : to cross the Atlantic in a shorter time than the *Mauretania*. For nineteen years, really unchallenged except by her sister, the old ship had held her record of speed ; for three more years, while the new German challengers were being built with much secrecy, she showed her pace and her reliability, while, also in secrecy, she made her own plans. It is a tribute to the quality of the ship, which needs no emphasis, that at her age, when her style and her decorations were so clearly dated, the Cunard Company, having a century of experience of ships on the Atlantic, should have made those plans.

In July, of 1920, Captain A. H. Rostron was knighted and left the *Mauretania*, which he had commanded since the last year of the war, for the *Berengaria*. Captain E. G. Diggle took his place.

At the end of 1926 the *Mauretania* was taken out of service for six weeks. When she went back to her job on February 9th, 1927, she had two new propellers, but they were given very small publicity. Amongst the records of the old ship there is a pamphlet, folder, brochure—anyhow, printed paper advertising that voyage. It is in gold and black, with a fine blue silk ribbon attached to it. It reads on the outside :

Cunard

R.M.S.

" Mauretania "

NEXT SAILING FEBRUARY 9TH

New decorative schemes

100 Magnificent new Staterooms and additional rooms with private baths

Lounges, Dining Saloons, Smoking Rooms and Veranda Café redecorated and refurnished

Miles of New Carpets, Curtains, Silks and Chintz.

The interior of the folder or brochure or pamphlet

contains a picture of the *Mauretania* above a blue ribbon steaming out of a golden background with a list of sailings beneath. Another page shows the first-class lounge and gives some description of the work of redecoration carried out to prepare the " 1927 *Mauretania* " for this voyage. Three miles of new carpet are mentioned, amongst other things, also the likeness of the Veranda Café to the Orangery at Hampton Court. The number of yards of costly silk and chintz used in the overhaul is given ; the restoring and repolishing of the woodwork is described. It is a good advertisement, which catches the eye. The machinery is not forgotten ; in three short lines the fact that it has not been overlooked is pointed out, and the information that the famous turbines have been overhauled and two new eighteen-ton propellers have been fitted, is supplied. That quite effective advertisement has significance : except for the blue ribbon it does not mention speed. All the world of shipping and the people who travel in ships knew about the speed. With its thousands of yards of silk and its miles of carpet and its new bath-rooms it sought to convince the public that the *Mauretania* was wearing clothes in the fashion. A most expensive overhaul and most significant. Until the two new German ships came into commision neither sailors nor those of the public who were interested in ships could conceive of the *Mauretania's* speed record being taken from her, so other features had to be advertised. Mention of bath-rooms on the outside of that advertisement describing the 1927 refit is really significant, because bath-rooms, later, had so much to do with her going to the breakers.

The General Strike was followed by much internal quarrelling in the English Liberal Party and the retirement of Asquith from its leadership. Legislation designed to remove the threat of general strikes in the future was introduced in 1927, then the country settled down to face the uncomfortable fact that there was no employment to be found for vast numbers of its citizens, nor, apparently, much likelihood of creating employment. In June the Naval Conference at Geneva, to which the *Mauretania* brought delegates, came to an end with something like a real first-class row between the United States and Great Britain. Disarming and preserving peace led, as was becoming usual, to the creation of ill-feeling. A year later, on July 18th, 1928, another conference seeking to ensure peace did not break down. The Kellog Pact established, on paper and in theory, agreement that war must not be used as a legitimate instrument of policy. Great nations agreed that threatening to go to war as a means of bringing an opponent to heel should be against the rules ; many people sighed with relief, and found the agreement good ; but, once again, no provision was made for effective action if somebody broke the rules. Ordinary people were becoming steadily less enthusiastic about expensive conferences, more pessimistic about collective security, more sceptical about international agreements which were based, sincerely but hardly firmly, on the nations' solemn assurance, " We will be good." Unemployment, trade depression, the high cost of living and dying, the growing obesity of taxation, kept most men and women supplied with worries.

The innumerable expensive conferences of those

years were good in a small way for first-class shipping on the Atlantic, for, naturally, delegates to conferences would not look at anything but first-class accommodation in first-class ships. The *Mauretania* had her share, and it was in the nature of a lion's share, in that delegate carrying ; but it was a small, intermittent carrying at best, and during those years she had her own particular difficulties. As an answer to the White Star coming back to British ownership with an ambitious building programme in view, the Cunard Company increased its capital by £1,000,000, and made plans for the future. The mistake, which shipowners had made when the War ended, of imagining that luxurious, first-class ships would not be needed was by then decently interred. The *Ile de France* and the great new ships building or planned provided, as it were, a suitable memorial over that buried idea. But with the quota system regulating immigration into the United States these great ships were deprived of the large consignments of third-class passengers which had made in times past such a large contribution towards paying their fuel bills. The demand for comfort was singularly robust, and higher standards of living were the talk and the hope of millions. Shipping companies had to meet that talk and those hopes. By 1928 the cabin ship had established itself and was giving shipowners plenty to do and plenty to think about. Broadly, there was a large public who could not afford or did not intend to pay the high rates of really comfortable accommodation in the great first-class liners, who also objected to being put out of the way in the after part or the lower decks of the second cabins of those big ships. This public wanted, being the public of its day, ships which would allow them the run of their best decks, which would supply them with first-class, as distinguished from extremely luxurious, food and accommodation at second-class fares. Since it was a large public, capable in the aggregate of paying shipping companies large sums annually, it got its way. The *Duchess* class ships of the Canadian Pacific proved that it had got its way. All companies had to come into line. The Cunard converted the *Carmania* and *Caronia* into cabin ships ; and made plans for otherwise meeting the new demands. That left the big first-class ships without much demand on a large part of their space. It was scarcely to be supposed that many passengers would book cabins in the *Mauretania*, somewhere nicely situated over her long counter where the pitching and the throb of the propellers were somewhat noticeable, simply for the sake of travelling in a famous ship. There were passengers willing to do that in the *Mauretania* because they knew and liked her, but they were not many and certainly not an increasing number. The cabin ships were filled and the second cabins of the first-class ships began to go empty. It was not an exact parallel to what had already happened to the railways ; for they had abolished the second class altogether. Shipping companies, however, had provided complete, separate transports for their second-class passengers, and that forced them to another step. It had to have a name, so they called it tourist. More comfort and considerably more freedom from minor restrictions at the old fares : that was the tourist class. But the raising of the standard of living, having got to work on ships, carried the business right through.

A number of liners were still to carry third-class passengers, but they were forced to carry those bed-rock creatures more comfortably lest a rival should step in and grab their insignificant but desired fares.

The 1927 *Mauretania* of the pamphlet or brochure with the blue ribbon had advertised how, to celebrate her twenty-first birthday, she was falling into line. The next years show her continually keeping abreast of demands. Her millionaires and her great ones of the earth naturally got the first consideration, but the small continual improvements for comfort went throughout the ship down to the patrons of the Kosher kitchen. In that she was doing neither more nor less than other well-managed ships were doing. Her individual contribution to the demands of those years was exact timekeeping, harder work, and steadily increasing speed.

In the yards at Bremen and Hamburg, where the two new German ships were building, the performances of the old ship were watched with care ; and the builders of the new ships had plenty to watch. The appearance of cabin ships, taking a whole class of passengers from the first-class liners, had had the effect of increasing attention to speed, which for so long had been almost the exclusive possession of the *Mauretania*. Great size, luxury and, above all, speed, it was considered, must be given to passengers who paid the high rates. That the supremacy of the old Cunard ship was going to be seriously challenged by the Germans led to other schemes for challenges from other quarters.

One scheme from America was at least ambitious. It was proposed to run a daily service between

Long Island and the English Channel ports. A daily service across the Atlantic requires a ship or two : ten, it was considered, ought to be sufficient. They were not to be big ships, according to the latest standards of size, just modest 20,000-tonners to take a modest number of passengers, 800 each. But the idea was that with them speed should really be speed, no fooling about with an attempt to beat the *Mauretania* by half a knot or, at best, a knot. An average of 32·5 knots would, it was held, be sufficient. Ships capable of maintaining that average are not cheap to build, that was recognised ; so a price of round about £3,500,000 per ship was provisionally named. Four days to cross the Atlantic, a full, leisurely twenty-four hour day in which to turn round at one of the Channel ports, then four days back again : that was the outline of the pro-gramme. But the French, with the *Ile de France*, had started the aeroplane business, so this really speedy American proposal could not leave the air out of count. Each ship was to carry aeroplanes, so that when she got within a comfortable flying distance of either eastern or western shore, she could shoot several of her passengers, at any rate, into the air and save them a day or so of the slow business of moving on the sea at 32·5 knots. The scheme created quite a lot of interest and attention in the United States. There was much talk about it, because half-measures and just scraping home with a bare record had no place in it. It was suggested that the name of the company which should own and manage the ten £3,500,000 ships should be the Blue Ribbon Line, presumably because the legendary Blue Riband of the Atlantic would be safe in its possession and might be expected to be there for as long a period as the old *Mauretania* had held it. There were really only two difficulties in the way of the scheme : the one engineering, the other financial. Marine engineers and architects mentioned the difficulties of their side of the business ; but they never really arose. To launch the scheme successfully, it was considered, Government subsidy would be required. If the United States Government would lend to the company three-quarters of the capital required—£35,000,000 for building the ten ships and a bit beyond that to get the show running—and give them an annual subsidy of not quite as much as £2,000,000, it was confidently expected that difficulties would vanish. The United States Post Office would benefit enormously by this new rapid mail service, the navy would have at its disposal ten really fast ships which could be used in time of need as auxiliary aircraft carriers. It was hoped and anticipated that the Post Office or the navy, or both, would bite, but both lacked enterprise. So the scheme did not call upon the engineering difficulties ; it crashed on finance. That daily service of 32·5 knots was not propounded or discussed as a joke. It was a perfectly genuine proposal, which attracted much attention. From it emerges very clearly the fact that attempts to end the *Mauretania's* long reign as the fastest of the world's liners were not half-hearted at that time. The Blue Ribbon Line having failed to get born, Germany, broken and squashed by the War, was left to do the real challenging. So Bremen and Hamburg watched the doings of an old ship, and, watching, had to consider improving their secret designs.

In the midst of steady, reliable and singularly efficient work the *Mauretania* let off from time to time a firework, just to keep the Germans guessing. On June 23rd she left Southampton and before tying up at New York was considerably delayed by fog, so that she could not average more than 24·26 knots for the westward passage. That was unfortunate, as it was the busy season. She turned round in New York in thirty-two hours. Nothing, of course, that could compare with the plans of the Blue Ribbon Line, or what she had already done in the past or what she was to do in the future. But it was not slow. She returned at 25·37 knots, and docked in Southampton less than twelve and a quarter days after she had left. That, again, was not her best ; but, again, it was not bad. Add to that the fact, which certainly reached Bremen and Hamburg, that when she left New York there was a waiting list running into three figures of persons hoping that some passenger would not take up his berth in the first class, and so give a waiter the chance to sail in her. Neither in speed nor in popularity at that time could it be reasonably claimed that she was falling back.

In 1928 she again changed her commander. Captain E. G. Diggle went to the *Aquitania* and Captain S. G. S. McNeil, who knew the old ship well, took over. During that year she just kept the Germans guessing, constantly improving on the best that she had so far done. A record passage now and then, a particularly fast day here or there, a short burst of high speed, she was very busy with these. The reports of them duly went into the papers ; the American press, for most Americans took a pride in her, gave her plenty of space. All the reports went back to Bremen and Hamburg for careful consideration. In July of 1929 she was making a record westward passage when the Kellog Pact was signed ; she made another two months later. It was a busy year for her. The Americans were saying that only an aeroplane could beat her ; the Cunard people were saying very little, except that she was doing quite well. The Germans were busy with their two new ships and also said very little. They had taken on the job, on which the whole of Atlantic shipping outside the Cunard seemed agreed, that the *Mauretania* must, after twenty-one years of dominance, be beaten. But the veteran— for by press and public she had by then been accepted under that title—was making it exceedingly difficult. for them to know exactly what they had to beat. The two new ships had not been conceived with quite the same imagination as the Blue Ribbon Line, they did not hope for an average of 32·5 knots ; if the *Mauretania* were to go on improving her speed it was possible that they might not be equal to the job they had undertaken. The normal life of an express liner is not more than twenty years. The *Mauretania* had already passed that normal life and was throwing off these disconcerting fireworks without effort. She was throwing them off, moreover, without any special attention, in the course of her ordinary service, without a refit. There were rumours, of course, that the Cunard Company had something up their sleeve, but the fact was indisputable that the old ship was steadily in service doing these fine performances without the something coming from the sleeve. So that, it was to be supposed, when the carefully considered something did come out of hiding her performances must become finer still. At Hamburg and at Bremen there was anxiety as well as assurance.

In the middle of November, 1928, the *Mauretania* was taken out of service and docked. She was only out of commission for six weeks, but during that time strangers were not encouraged in or about her engine-room. It was known that the something was being produced from hiding, but questions concerning its nature simply were not answered. There was secrecy at Bremen and Hamburg and Southampton. Even now there is a good deal of the " hush, hush " business about what was done to the *Mauretania* during those six weeks. New condensers were fitted, new pumps, and " something " was done to the turbines ; that has since become common knowledge ; but details of the condensers, the pumps, and the " something " are not readily supplied. At the time, of course, the whole refit was carefully clothed in mystery. The shipping world was much interested, but unsatisfied. The interest spread from men of ships to the general public. The business shaped itself into a sporting event, and so claimed the heart of the million. The world had taken up an old ship's challenge and appointed Germany its champion ; the old ship, making nothing of her years, and equipped with some mysterious gadgets, was ready to put up a fight for what had been hers for so long. No one not even the most ardent champions of what is new, could maintain with complete assurance that the new must beat the old.

England was much concerned with mounting

unemployment figures and industrial troubles ; the
United States was facing a slump which was neither
a small nor a temporary set-back. Other nations
could claim plenty of difficulties. Yet, on both sides
of the Atlantic and far beyond, indeed, on all the
seas and in most of the countries of the world, men's
interest turned to the forthcoming fight between an
old ship and a new.

The *Mauretania* returned to service, carrying her
mysteries, on January 2nd, 1929, and took well over
six days to cross the Atlantic at an average of
19·38 knots. That was nothing but the fortune of
the seas. It was not expected that, in that winter
weather, she would find the chance to try out any of
her gadgets. But the voyage is interesting because,
on that westward passage, she shipped one of the
biggest seas she had ever taken aboard in all the
years of her facing of Atlantic storms. That sea did
a lot of damage ; so did another which she took
aboard on January 6th, when she was slowed down
to 100 revolutions before a whole gale. Later she
had to reduce to 90 revolutions, and she carried
bad conditions to the Ambrose Light vessel, so that
her slow passage shows as a fine performance for
that weather. Her glass and crockery bill for that
winter passage was very heavy ; and she reached
New York with her boats and deck fittings visibly
scarred. Some of the damage done by the first big
sea she took aboard on that passage is of interest.
Several windows of the bridge and of the wheelhouse were smashed, the chart-room was flooded,
and up on the Monkey Island above four feet of
solid teak rail was torn away. The *Mauretania's*
bridge was not near to her water-line ; it required

something of a sea, a real mountain of a fellow, to reach up to the Monkey Island with sufficient weight to play with that teak rail as though it were a matchstick. With seas of that size to be encountered, only a fine ship, finely handled, can reach an average of 19·38 knots. Having more than twenty-one years of experience, the *Mauretania* did it ; but the trying out of her " hush, hush " gadgets was a performance which even she could not accomplish on that passage of real storm.

She did a cruise in February, starting from New York, calling at Southampton, and then going off to Mediterranean ports. After that, she got back to regular work. She was then calling at Plymouth, homeward bound, making three ports—Plymouth, Cherbourg, Southampton—on her last day, giving her navigators and her crew something to keep them from idleness, but conveniencing her passengers. On one occasion during these early months of 1929 she left New York two hours after the *Leviathan*, which had some pretensions to being not a slow ship. The *Leviathan* was carrying the United States mails, which was an annoyance to most of the *Mauretania*'s crew. Before the Atlantic was half crossed the *Leviathan* saw the old ship's light astern ; then she saw them abeam ; then the old ship saw the *Leviathan*'s lights astern. On that eastward passage the *Mauretania* called at Plymouth at 7.0 a.m., went over to Cherbourg, and crossed back to Southampton, where she berthed early in the afternoon. She was in the hands of the shore staff at Southampton, with her passengers disembarked, and most of her officers and crew in their homes ashore when the *Leviathan* arrived at 11.0 p.m. That was a Tuesday ; the *Leviathan*'s mails were not delivered in London till Wednesday. The old *Maure-tania* could have had them delivered on Tuesday afternoon. Yet the *Leviathan* considered herself a fast, reliable ship.

With her secret gadgets, however, the *Mauretania* was putting up no fireworks. She was just going about her job, and waiting. Nothing at all was to be given away which could possibly assist the anxious men at Bremen. Whether the mysteries she carried really gave the results hoped from them must not leak out. That period of waiting was undoubtedly trying. One guesses at something like frayed nerves aboard the old ship, which usually maintained her tradition of being happy. There was some dis-agreement between commander and chief as to suitable moments for trying, secretly of course, what speed she could reach. There was a dash in the Channel which gave an impressive figure, but a favourable tide made it of little real value. Nerves, for men who were waiting for the trial with the new German ship, which meant so much to them, could not be anything else than strained. But the strain, showing itself occasionally, did the men and the ship no harm ; it was all an inevitable part of the sporting event which, in troubled times, was attracting so much public attention.

On June 22nd, 1929, the *Mauretania* sailed from Southampton about her ordinary business and a few hours later she left Cherbourg. Between the Casquets and the Bishop's Rock she met the *Bremen* returning after lengthy trials. News that she was approaching went round the ship before the German was sighted. Another ship passing at sea seldom fails to bring decent attention ; the passing of the *Bremen* brought attention that was absorbed, eager, almost painful. It was a summer night. Many passengers would not disturb their rest or their amusement to gaze at the lighted shadow of a distant ship, but from the bridge, from the forecastle, from port-holes, from the nearest spot they could reach from which to see, men and women of her crew did. To these men and women, for there were not a few stewardesses in the *Mauretania* who had proper pride in their ship, that passing of the *Bremen* in the night was a tremendous happening. They could not see much of her, not a tenth part of what they wanted to see of her ; they had to guess at much of what they only saw dimly ; but there were many eyes straining to get some idea of her. She was there, actually steaming the seas, almost ready for the contest : that was the fact of tremendous importance. How she had looked, how she had moved—particularly how she had seemed to move—would supply conversation for bridge, engine-room, bars and galleys for the passage to New York and back again.

It is a perfectly safe assumption that very few of those of the *Mauretania's* crew who had that hurried glance in the night at the *Bremen* considered the new ship a beauty. The two squat, stream-lined funnels, the cut-away stem, the cruiser stern, the enormous and seemingly too heavy deck erections would hardly find favour with those who loved the *Mauretania's* lines. There may have been one or two of her crew who found the *Mauretania* suddenly grown old-fashioned after that sight of the *Bremen*, who saw in the new ship some pleasing suggestion of power ; but they would certainly keep those heretical views to themselves. The point for discussion, long

discussion, seamen's discussion, was that the rival
was at last upon the sea.   She had been designed and
built with one object primarily in view : to show
her heels to the *Mauretania*.   She had 50 per cent.
more tonnage than the old ship, was a hundred feet
longer and had more than twenty feet greater beam ;
her designed shaft horse-power of 130,000 was nearly
double ;   her four propellers were turned by geared
turbines.   She was, at that moment, the latest and
the best which German marine engineering and
German ships' architects could produce ;   and the
Germans had always been the Cunard's most successful rivals.   She looked workmanlike—that could not
be denied her.   Could an old ship, with nearly
twenty-two years' of hard work and close on two
million of sea miles behind her, resist her challenge ?
—that was the question discussed in the *Mauretania*
and in many places up and down the earth, wherever
men have interest in the sea and ships.   It seemed
too much to expect of old age ; yet it was not only
expected, but believed by many well-informed persons and by a host of others knowing nothing at all
about ships, of whom thousands had never seen the
Mauretania, nor ever even gone to sea.

There was a slant of excellent weather across the
Atlantic at that time.   On that voyage, at the start
of which she had first seen her new rival, the *Mauretania* made an excellent eastward passage home at
close on 25½ knots.   It was the busy season and she
carried a large, mixed crowd, who had much to say
about the trial which lay ahead of her.   On July 13th
she took her regular sailing again from Southampton,
the fastest liner in the world.   It was very perfect
summer weather, smooth sea, light airs, and she

carried it with her all the way to New York and kept it while she was turning round. It was, by the common consent of her officers and crew, really exceptional weather, a fine spell such as, with long experience, they had not often seen before on the Atlantic, perfect speed conditions which they might well have to wait years to meet on that ocean again. As usual, the *Mauretania* left Southampton on Saturday and was due to dock at New York the following Thursday, so she was not pushed, but steamed across a sea in settled summer mood at her comfortable full speed, making an easy 180 revolutions. She was herself a servant and served by servants of the owners ; her orders were to arrive at the hour advertised, not to waste fuel by getting in before, and she obeyed her orders. To some men—to one, certainly—it is a real tragedy that those were her orders for that westward passage, that she was not sent out from Southampton on July 13th into that wonderful slant of weather to do the best she could, not knowing, of course, what she had to beat, but to do the best she could. For the North Atlantic is not often for very long a mild and placid ocean, so to make no use of one of its moods of uncommon geniality seemed to some men, certainly to one, the tragic missing of a heaven-sent chance. When the old *Mauretania*, doing her comfortable full speed, was three days out she received news that the *Bremen* had left Cherbourg. The fight, which had been preparing for so long, was at last begun—the challenge to the old ship was actually being made, for no one could expect that the commander of the *Bremen* would miss the opportunity of that weather. From Captain McNeil and Mr. Cockburn down to the bell-boys, the news of the *Bremen's* departure roused a common thought : " If she, too, carries this weather across ? " That would mean making what had to be done, what they were determined to do, harder than the hard job it already promised to be.

The old ship got a good reception in New York. Americans were loyal to an old friend. Although they had a fondness for the latest and a love of records, they wished the old *Mauretania* luck. The *Bremen* was doing well—that was clear from messages received ; she could hardly fail to do well in that wonderful weather. The *Mauretania* discharged her passengers and got on with her business of turning round. Aboard her the strain was high : waiting to know whether she were still the fastest liner in the world was not comfortable, speculating as to what she would have to beat if she were no longer the holder of the Blue Riband was not easy. That wait was not a long one. The description of its ending may well be given by the picture of one man.

One of the officers, not on duty, had slept well during a night in port ; getting up not too early, without any news of the morning, he paid a visit, after dressing, to his near neighbour, the chief engineer. In the chief's cabin he saw Mr. Cockburn seated at his writing-table with his head on his hands. He asked what the trouble might be ; his reply to that was not words, but an outstretched arm and a finger pointing towards the window. The officer, paying a morning visit to a friend, looked out of the window and saw, at the opposite berth across the dock, a large liner with two squat, stream-lined funnels and cut-away stem. So, being a man of reasonable tact, he left the chief to his bad hour.

Mr. Cockburn had been in charge of the *Mauretania's* engines for over ten years—a decent slice out of any man's life. He had, for that long time, nursed them, driven them, taken an enormous pride in them. Before he took charge of them he had known them well. During the difficult middle period after the war he had worked for them and pleaded for them, believing in them. He had found and removed a French humorist's trouser button from them. More than anyone else in the old ship he knew their strength and their weakness, what they could do and what was beyond them. Being an engineer, for a long period of his life he had been able to tell himself that he was in charge of engines that knew no rivals in the world. That period was ended. There was not much gaiety aboard the old ship on that July morning in New York, because the record held for close on twenty-two years had gone. The chief in his cabin, alone with his bad hour, realised, better than all the others who were not gay, how difficult recovery was going to be.

Captain McNeil, observing the niceties of a decent rivalry, had gone over early to visit Captain Ziegenbaum of the *Bremen* and to congratulate him on his ship's performance. The new German vessel had made the crossing in that fine slant of weather from Cherbourg to the Ambrose in 4 days 17 hours 42 minutes, at an average speed of 27·9 knots, which was faster by more than $1\frac{1}{2}$ knots than the *Mauretania* had ever done. That was a staggering margin, something which would take much covering. The visit of defeated captain to victorious captain passed successfully. Lately the countries of both captains had been at war, but there was no bitterness on that account. Indeed, throughout the short struggle between the old *Mauretania* and the new *Bremen* there seems to have been an entire absence of any bitterness ; two fine ships, finely served, struggled for supremacy, and amongst their companies few members, if any, descended to blackguarding each other. Captain McNeil says that he considered the *Bremen* a very fine ship, but he could not admire the decorations. There is a delightfully humorous touch there. As a sailor he had to admit her quality, as a man, hurt in his pride and affection for the last ship and the greatest which he commanded, he must have hated the sight of the new supplanter. The *Mauretania* sailed from New York on July 24th and, still carrying good weather, at comfortable full speed, passed the Eddystone in 5 days 1 hour 1 minute, at an average of 25·58 knots. Aboard her, making that familiar passage unfamiliarly as no longer the world's fastest liner, they had, as Captain McNeil has written, " something to think about." To be exact, 1½ knots average margin was in their thoughts.

On August 3rd the *Mauretania* sailed again from Southampton on her two hundred and twenty-seventh voyage. She had orders from her owners to do the best she could : the gadgets, the " Hush-hush " improvements were to be tried out. She sailed at noon in very fine weather and crossed the Channel at 26·40 knots. She left Cherbourg at 6.0 p.m., and as she cleared the harbour the throb of her informed the men and women in her that the old ship was obeying her owners' orders. From Cherbourg she met a spring tide against her for four hours, which added a good twenty minutes, when minutes were precious, to her passage. At midnight on that Saturday the weather report in the log reads :

"Strong breeze. Rough sea. Heavy rain at times."

The fair slant of weather had gone. Passing the Bishop's Light she was shipping heavy sprays over the bridge, where the watch, which included the commander, were wearing sea-boots and oilskins, and she was pitching enough to lose speed. At midnight commander and chief—there was not going to be much sleep for either of them for the next few days —had a talk. The engines were making 205 revolutions, some twenty-five more each minute than the designers had intended. Captain McNeil decided, although conditions were not good, to keep her going at that until the morning when, he told the chief, unless things had improved, he would ease down. Next morning the weather showed slight improvement, so the old ship was driven on. Visibility had not been good and taking any sights had been impossible. At noon on Sunday, August 4th, the position, by dead reckoning, gave a run of 498 miles at an average of 26·11 knots. That was very far from good. Nobody of the men responsible for the ship was happy ; it is on record that Mr. Cockburn was the unhappiest of them all. His engines were turning as they had never turned before ; but the good weather had gone and the ship was pitching and increasing the propeller slip. At midnight the sea had moderated and the officer of the watch was getting a hazy horizon at times.

On Monday, August 5th, it was clear enough to

take observations. The noon position gave a run of 680 miles at an average of 27·20 knots. The passengers, getting a thrill from taking part in a sporting event which had been so anticipated throughout the world, received news of the run with enthusiasm. They had no need to ask whether the *Bremen's* record was being attacked—the feel of the old ship told them that. It was agreed that when she was fully extended, except right aft over the propellers, where some of the second class cabins were feeling it, she had curiously little vibration. The passengers were very cheerful on the Monday afternoon, but that cheerfulness was not with the bridge and engine-room staff. The sea had dropped to moderate, but so had the barometer. There was a swell, and the outlook for good steaming was poor. Revolutions had been raised to 210, but the propeller slip had increased by 100 per cent. On Tuesday the 6th, at noon the weather report in the log reads : " Strong breeze, rough sea, cloudy, clear, moderate S.W. swell." Conditions had got worse again as, had been anticipated. But the old *Mauretania* had made a run of 687 sea miles, at 27·48 average. Although the wind was freshening, the sea temperature had risen to 75° and the Gulf Stream was against her, she was still being driven as hard as they could drive her. One of the ship's humorists met the occasion with a remark, which stamps him as a man of small understanding. " It ought," he said, "to be reported to the R.S.P.C.A." But the fact was that the twenty-two-year-old ship seemed to be enjoying it ; she caused her passengers, except those right aft, singularly little discomfort ; amidships there was no vibration perceptible, although the propellers were turning at thirty revolutions a minute more than the designers had intended ; there was no strain or labouring.

At noon on Wednesday the 7th, when the log gives " fresh breeze, rough head sea, westerly swell," the run was given as 676 miles at 27·00 knots. From that Wednesday noon position, against a head sea in warm water, she ran to the Ambrose Light vessel, a distance of 621 miles, at 26·90 knots. She had made her ocean passage from Cherbourg to the Ambrose, a distance of 3,162 sea miles, through weather that had never been really good for fast steaming and upon most days definitely against good times, in 4 days 21 hours 44 minutes. The average speed had been 26·90 knots, and the mean revolutions of the four propellers 208·6 a minute. She had beaten her own record for the westward passage by five hours, and had been beaten by the *Bremen* by four and a half hours.

In New York she had a wonderful reception. The Press found plenty of space for her in spite of the demands of the slump. The public were stirred by a decent sentiment. Her failure fixed passengers' affection on her as much as her success had ever done. Some prominence was given to the circumstance of an operation for the removal of a passenger's appendix having been performed in midocean without slowing the ship down. Those were facts : the passenger parted with his appendix while the *Mauretania* was being driven all out. He suffered no additional discomfort from the driving, neither did the old ship. She had been asked to give more speed than she had ever given before ; and she gave it. While giving it, something had to be done for

the benefit of a passenger ; it was done. Her job
had always been many-sided ; but she could always
do it.

She left New York at noon on Friday, August 16th,
having turned round in leisurely comfort. But
down below in the engine-room they were not idle,
nor content. The old ship had failed to beat the
Bremen westward, but the voyage was not over and
she had been ordered to do the best she could on it.
Homeward she found no better conditions for fast
steaming than on the outward passage. At first the
sea was moderate, but the water was warm though
there was no helping current. The revolutions were
kept up and things below grew warm, so warm that
some of the junior engineers anticipated receiving
orders to slow down, but did not get them. On
Saturday, at midday, the run was 611 miles at 26·56,
not good. In the early morning of Sunday it was
blowing half a gale, and when that blow passed
there was fog hanging about. But the Sunday run
was 630 miles at 27·40, which cheered the passengers
considerably. On Monday, owing to the weather,
the position was fixed by dead reckoning and showed
an average of 27·56 knots. The temperature of the
water was getting cooler, and passengers were very
pleased. On Tuesday, although the log records
" fresh breeze, rough sea," the run was 636 miles at
27·65 knots. The *Bremen*, for the fight was cleanly
fought, wirelessed good wishes on that day. Aboard
almost everybody was pleased. But from the Tuesday
noon position to the Eddystone, conditions were bad.
There were heavy squalls and heavy rain, which
necessitated slowing down, and for several hours an
adverse spring tide delayed the ship. She anchored

at Plymouth in the early hours of Wednesday, August 21st, having made the ocean passage from the Ambrose to the Eddystone, a distance of 3,098 sea miles, in 4 days, 17 hours, 50 minutes, at an average of 27·22 knots, the mean revolutions of the propellers being 211·5 a minute. That again was some hours slower than the *Bremen's* eastward passage.

Passenger tenders came alongside at Plymouth at 5.0 a.m. The *Mauretania* arrived at Cherbourg at 11.30 a.m. By 5.0 p.m. she was tied up in her berth at Southampton. At 5.45 p.m. the passengers were all ashore. At 6.30 p.m. the crew were paid off and signed on again. On the following day, public interest in her lost fight being very considerable, the old ship was heard for the first time " on the air." Following a short statement by Captain McNeil to the effect that she had done her best, she sounded her whistle. Two days later, on Saturday, August 24th, after three days in port, she sailed for New York again. She had tried and failed ; but she still had her job to do.

To-day controversy as to her chance of beating the *Bremen*, had she been allowed another attempt, is not dead. It is said that she could have done so given the same weather conditions as the new ship, that her commander and her chief only wanted to have definite orders to try again, that the owners fearful of the enormous strain on an old ship, would not give the orders. Lots of things are said. The weather which the *Bremen* had might not have come again to the Atlantic for a very long period. With new propellers and with her bilge keels removed—which would not have been comfortable for anyone aboard— the *Mauretania*, finding the weather, might have averaged 28·0 knots. When she had done that the *Bremen*, a new ship designed to beat her, might have done better. There are lots of possibilities ; but the facts are good enough. After twenty-two years of hard service, having been designed for 25 knots, the *Mauretania* did not lose the Blue Riband without fighting to retain it. She made a voyage, taking both passages together, at an average speed of 27·06 knots. That performance alone, at her age, would have given her a place apart in the history of ships. Speculation about that performance being improved is answered by Mr. Cockburn, who, if any man does, knows what she could have done. He says of that August voyage that on it the old ship did all that she could do.

CHAPTER IX

THE BLACK HULL PASSES

THE men who served her undoubtedly took the defeat of the *Mauretania* hardly ; they could not have been expected to do otherwise. But, although she had had more to do with speed records than any other ship in Atlantic history, her reputation, never having been based simply on her size and pace, actually grew after she had passed to the position of a comparatively small ship with not only one but several rivals who could beat her in a race. The people who had assumed that, if the *Bremen* beat her, the old ship would pass quietly out of account, were badly wrong. For the remainder of her service, five years, she continued to do hard work and fast work. She had then no lure to attract the public except that she continued to be herself ; but that was often a sufficient lure.

During a rough passage when the after end of the old ship had been as lively as usual in that sort of weather, one of her officers, being of an enquiring mind, asked an American passenger why he preferred to travel second in the stern of the *Mauretania* instead of comfortably somewhere amidships in a cabin ship.

" Well," the American replied, " I guess it's sentiment and enthusiasm before my innards. For many years I've planned a trip to Europe before I died and before the *Mauretania* died. And, believe me, I'm right glad to have done it."

That was the spirit which brought new passengers to the *Mauretania* in her old age. Throughout the United States in the East and South, the Middle West and West there were thousands of American citizens who had that fixed and settled ambition, to make their long-planned trip to Europe in the ship which carried the greatest name on the Atlantic. That and the Eighteenth Amendment to the Constitution of the United States of America, had a good deal to do with the very hard, fast and exacting work which the *Mauretania* was ordered to do in the last three years of her life.

At the end of 1930 she made her two hundred and fiftieth voyage. She took just twenty-three minutes short of a full seven day week to make the ocean passage to the Ambrose at an average of 18·37 knots. That crossing illustrates the way she did her work ; it explains the reason her name was great and why thousands of passengers still wished to travel in her. She had, as she had so often done before, brought passengers over to Europe three days before Christmas ; she had had her Christmas at home and sailed again from Southampton at noon on Saturday, December 27th. The barometer was falling and the thermometer rising, not good signs. She left Cherbourg at 7.13 p.m., carrying 377 passengers and 564 crew. Clearing the breakwater at Cherbourg, she ran straight into bad weather and carried it across the Atlantic. At midnight, when the Lizard was abeam, she was meeting squalls of gale force, and the log records gales moderate, fresh and whole, for the rest of the passage. The entries in the log become monotonous with the repeated report that the ship was pitching and spraying over all. At midnight on

MAURETANIA
The Last Landfall.

December 29th, and again at noon on January 1st,
that monotony is varied by the very expressive
statement that the ship was labouring. Once she
is described, when the head sea had become a beam
sea, as lurching—another expressive term. During
the whole of that week she was constantly increasing
and diminishing the engine revolutions, sometimes
at intervals of a few minutes, seizing whatever slight
improvement in the weather she could find. During
one period of eight hours, sixteen alterations of speed
are recorded ; and twice she was forced down to
70 revolutions a minute. On the second day out,
Sunday, the usual church service was not held ;
instead she shipped a big sea, which did a fair amount
of damage. Throughout the passage she was
shipping water fore and aft.

That is the description of that passage which the
log gives. A picture less terse is possible. From
Southampton to New York there was wind and
greyness, never a recorded gleam of sunshine ; from
the Nab Tower to the Ambrose a welter of grey
wind-lashed, white-capped water, never anything
but angry, rising at times to the fury of full storm.
Noise, wet, cold, violence of movement across three
thousand miles of sea. In it the *Mauretania* laboured,
lurching and pitching and spraying over all.

Pitching and spraying unexpectedly had always
been one of her individual tricks. Many great
characters have something of the urchin in them ;
that sudden dip of hers was an urchin performance.
She could perform her trick in very slight seas,
without any warning. Pushing her stem into nothing
bigger than moderate hummocks of water, she could
dip her nose without warning and send a whiff of

spray high over her navigating bridge. She caught
her commanders that way time and again, although
they knew her and her ways. In nice quiet weather,
not once but often, she would wait until her master,
nicely arrayed in blue and gold with a gleaming
boiled shirt prominently displayed, appeared to have
a look round before going below to show himself to
passengers at dinner and so advertise the fineness of
the weather. Very often she got him, for the movement was quick ; a dip, a whiff, a spatter of spray
on starched, glazed linen, and the commander of a
great liner not referring to her as a lady. How often
the officer of the watch found diversion from the
Old Man's face as, caught again, he went below to
put on another shirt is not recorded, but it was not
too infrequently. That, of course, would not count
as anything but the ship's sanctioned jest. When
pitching came into the entries, the spray which came
over was more than a whiff.

"Labouring, pitching, lurching, spraying over all,
shipping water fore and aft," meant not urchin tricks
but a real fight with something mightier than herself.
There were no boiled shirts up on the bridge then,
but the commander was there. Oil-skins, sea boots,
sou'westers, mufflers and gloves, that was the rig of
the men up there, and in it they were cold and wet.
Often they were blinded. The stem, that keen blade
like affair would dive into a great white-capped,
roaring sea and water would come streaming, tearing
and foaming aboard. It poured in solid sheets down
the windows of the wheelhouse, obscuring all outlook,
sometimes it smashed the thick plate glass of those
windows ; it fell with weight upon the men peering
over the dodger, finding its way through their thick

clothing, stinging their faces and making their straining eyes smart. It rattled against the funnels. It even sent out its advance guard to the two men gyrating wildly through the air in the crow's nest. As the stem lifted again tons of sea cascaded and spouted noisily from the forecastle head and swished violently about the well-deck. The Atlantic hammered and beat upon the plating ; the wind whistled, whined, shrieked, tore and shook ; water thrust aside came back to the attack. Seas crept up for a flank onslaught and came aboard over the quarters ; the stern rose high and enormous strain was put upon the shafts as the propellers were lifted to the surface. The whole ship plunged and lurched and quivered, diving into the great hills of water and dragging herself from the heavy hold of them with a straining effort ; she was labouring. From time to time, seen from her high bridge and from her higher crow's nest, she was just a smother of driving white with the four funnels and the masts alone emerging : she was spraying over all.

The streaming decks were deserted except by men having business on them. Inside she was warm, though not always in places, for the seas were searching her, dry. She was scarcely comfortable, since no ship in a storm ever is. The alleyways were hard to walk, the saloon and the public rooms required careful crossing. Inexperienced people progressed by short runs between clutchings of furniture and fittings, experienced men and women paused often, balancing, waiting for the roll or pitch. The damage to crockery was not slight ; men and women having bought drinks had to swallow them quickly or keep a watch upon their glasses. The fiddles were on the

tables in the saloon, and baths had to be half filled.
There were some people in beds envying seamen their
stomachs, and others, being hurled about in their
forecastle bunks envying passengers amidships quarters in which seamen's stomachs and seamen's tired
bodies would get a chance of sleep. Down in the
engine and boiler rooms men kept up the head of
steam and dealt with the constant demand of the
bridge for changes of revolutions, anxious lest with
that labouring and pitching they might have to meet
that mishap common to steamships in storms, a
broken shaft. Throughout, despite all the patent
gadgets and the seasoned woodwork, there was
creaking and chattering.

That went on for nearly seven days, sometimes a
little easier, sometimes very much worse, never for a
single hour anything but really bad. The ship was
running late, making a poor average, 18·47 knots.
An eastern going mail-ship, the fastest of them,
would have considered that average a gross exceeding
of the speed limit ; but the Atlantic demands a
service of its own. The *Mauretania* tied up at New
York at 4.58 p.m. on the 3rd of January, 1931, very
much behind her scheduled time. That necessitated
a good deal of hurried and hard work, for she was
due to sail next day. She did the work and sailed for
Southampton at 1.0 p.m. on January 4th, the hour
which had been advertised.

That is a picture of her at her work. The circumstances of that passage were not quite usual, but
they were those which in the course of her long
service she had very often met before. They were
part of her job ; and she could do her job. She had
lost all records then and she was getting very old,

but she was still an express Atlantic liner and the most efficient worker of them all.

The Atlantic in storm was a power to whose dictation the old ship had to bow. She had to run late on these occasions, but it is a fact that, being the ship she was, in defiance of her old age, the men who guided her and the men who drove her were able safely to make sure that she was not so late as faster ships under the same conditions would have been. The Atlantic in fog, and it is often in fog, could, of course, dictate to her as masterfully as in storm. But there again her own qualities helped her ; given any clearing of the weather she could pick up speed and get away in her stride as few ships could. Of the minor troubles of that troubled ocean she had her share, during her last years, but as in her earlier ones she made no song and dance about them.

She broke another shaft ; this time while her chief, still Mr. Cockburn, was standing in the tunnel watching it revolve. It cracked in the stern gland and the propeller joined others of hers down below ; but it did no other damage and did not let a drop of water into the ship. For a time, once again, the *Mauretania* managed very well with three propellers.

She was in collision, in the New York river. Captain McNeil, who was then still in command, has written the story of that mishap in his book, " In Great Waters." The *Mauretania* left dock at midnight and half an hour later had a difference of opinion with a railway-car float crossing over from Brooklyn. There were two floats with a tug in between and, too late, the cumbersome outfit decided to cross the liner's bows. So the *Mauretania's* bows went off with one float and the tug with the other ;

when the float had been cleared and taken back to where she belonged, which was not where the navigators of the liner wished her, the *Mauretania* went back to dock. She had a twisted stem and several plates forward holed. The job of repairing the damage was started at 6.0 a.m. and the old ship sailed at 9.0 p.m. Twenty tons of cement were put over the holed plates and new plates were secured over that. It was putting on the cement which took the time, and it was considered rather an unnecessary precaution. Without it she could have sailed at 6.0 p.m. She made the passage to the Eddystone at 25·09 knots, but, of course, she was late again.

All sorts of little difficulties occurred, but she met them and dealt with them as they came. There was the case of Anna Mauretania. The mother was an American subject, who had been taken as a child by her parents back to Czechoslavakia, where they had been born. In due course the girl, still an American subject, married a Czech and decided to return to the United States so that her first child might be born there, and acquire citizen rights. But a south-westerly gale spoiled these plans and the infant was born in a British ship three days out from Cherbourg. The proud parent had been well cared for in the British ship and insisted on making suitable acknowledgement. So the log registered the infant with the Christian names of Anna Mauretania. And at New York Anna Mauretania gave the immigration authorities a problem which delighted officialdom. Father a Czech, mother an American with papers in order, child British because born in a British ship : all very difficult. A further complication was that Anna Mauretania had no passport. The careful decision was that the mother should go to hospital ashore, the infant either to Ellis Island or should remain in the ship, technically the land of its birth. It took much forceful argument and appeal to higher authority before the separation of mother and child or their permanent residence in the ship was prevented. Before the *Mauretania* sailed eastward again the investigation authorities had studied the extremely difficult problem once again and Anna Mauretania was in enjoyment of full citizen rights.

The call at Plymouth homeward bound was a considerable convenience to passengers but a considerable addition to the *Mauretania's* work. Three ports in one day was not easy going for the ship or for the crew, but she started the business some time before she lost the speed record and she kept at it to the end.

In 1931, when so many people in England were passing through a stage of mild economic panic, trying to sell their homes and find smaller ones, getting rid of servants, talking endlessly of economies and depression, the *Mauretania* made her concession to the hard times by dropping the description second class, making improvements in the accommodation in the stern and adopting the style tourist for passengers who were neither first saloon nor third. Soon after this change she made four passages of the Atlantic, steaming twelve thousand four hundred miles, in one month. That was not a bad performance for a ship with close on twenty-four years of service behind her. She stood up to that sort of high pressure work well, so she was given more of it.

Normally she left Southampton on Saturday, arrived at New York the following Thursday, and lay there doing nothing but turn round easily until the next Wednesday when she sailed again for home. With depression gripping the world, shipping in a bad way and dividends uncommon hard to earn, the Cunard Company realised that something better could be done with a ship, which never broke down under hard work, than letting her lie idle in New York from Thursday until Wednesday. So she was sent off week-end cruising. She sailed from New York on Friday evening, arrived at Nassau in the Bahamas early on Sunday morning, gave her cruising passengers a run ashore, sailed again in the evening, arrived back at New York on Tuesday evening, disembarked her cruise passengers, took in oil and had a general clean up, sailed with her express liner human freight for Plymouth, Cherbourg and South-ampton on Wednesday. Quite a full week-end which allowed none of her crew real idleness. It required a fast ship to carry out those cruises between passages ; the *Mauretania* in her old age was faster than she had ever been before. So they set her to it and kept her to it for a long time. Some-times, to show her cruise passengers that she could do better than potter along at the 25 knots which the week-end programmes demanded of her, she did a hundred miles or so at high speed. With the Gulf stream favouring her, she reached 31 knots for a period. But that sort of thing was just a passenger pleasing stunt and has little real significance in the history of her hard life's work.

Soon after she started this cruise business Captain McNeil reached the Cunard age limit and retired. A last voyage can never be anything but trying ; his nearly ended in its last hour in the sinking of the

Mauretania. In the dog's leg channel between the West Brambles buoy and the Calshot light vessel, a French freighter nearly rammed her, missing her, owing to the old ship's ability to spurt ahead, by only fifteen feet. The Frenchman had touched the mud and been canted towards the *Mauretania.* It was a close thing, but close things do not count. What does count with Captain McNeil is that he had the honour to command the *Mauretania* on that voyage when she failed to get back the Blue Riband from the *Bremen* but failed so gallantly that the failure ranks as an unforgettable success. Captain R. V. Peel succeeded to the command. He was the last of the old ship's captains.

The Nassau week-end cruises were a great success. In a very short time they had become known as " Booze Cruises." That name gave a great deal of offence to some members of the *Mauretania's* staff and a considerable amount of amusement to others. It was not really an accurate description of those week-end runs to Nassau, but there was something of justification about it. The citizens of the United States, or many of them, had a great affection for the old ship and at the same time a decent regard for less corrugating liquor than, owing to the Eighteenth Amendment, they could purchase at reasonable cost in their own country. So they went cruising in the *Mauretania* in large numbers not without thought for the fact that as free and responsible beings they would be able to buy a good drink when they wanted it. But the old ship which held their affections, held her own influence over the thirstiest of them. She was the *Mauretania* and she exacted and maintained a certain standard of reticence in men and women celebrating their return to liberty. The popularity of these week-end cruises to Nassau led to other longer ones, twelve or thirteen day affairs round the West Indies. That was, in the common phrase, the beginning of the end. The *Mauretania* began to miss her turn in the regular sailings of the big Cunard liners.

Her hull was painted white for these longer cruises. Not long after she had been ordered to that new job—a cruise round the West Indies, a passage home and back, then off on a cruise again—she came to her berth in Southampton. She had white paint on her hull, but streaked and stained after the Atlantic passage. A man who had served in her and loved her, watched her coming up the Water with horror.

" My God ! " he said, " it's the old *Maury* looking like a wedding cake gone wrong."

That expresses concisely what so many of the men who had served her and still served her felt. She was called out West, "The West Indies Express." She earned the name because she was always up to time at each port at which she called, although her crowded programme demanded full speed, her full speed, between ports to get there. But her greatness and her glory were not associated with a white hull but a black.

Captain Peel has written a letter about those cruising years which must be quoted at length. With admirable simplicity it produces a very real picture. He writes :

" I was in command of her for the last three years of her career, most of which time was spent in running cruises from New York around the West Indies, chiefly thirteen-day cruises every fourteen days.

" In the West Indies she became to be called ' The West Indies Express,' as she was always up to time at each port, although full speed was required pretty well throughout the cruises. At some of the smaller islands, where no ships outside of the smallest ever called, I have been told that the *Mauretania*, passing every fortnight almost at the same minute, was looked forward to as quite an event by the inhabitants.

" Our first landfall after leaving New York was the tiny island of Sombrero, on which is a lighthouse and signal station, 1,420 miles from New York. Although the signalman on the island must have been perfectly certain whom we were, he never failed to hoist the signal : ' What ship is that ? ' Of course we replied, but thought we might just as well hoist, ' What island is that ? ' only thought our tourist passengers might lose confidence in our navigating abilities.

" The ship nearly always had a full consignment of passengers, and it was with a sigh of relief to all to leave New York on a bitter cold winter evening, knowing that next day everyone would be sun-bathing on deck and swimming in the open-air pools on deck.

" The rapid change in temperature is caused through running at a big speed due south out of the cold Arctic current into the warm Gulf Stream. Coming the other way we ran as quickly into cold weather. I have seen the temperature drop from 80° above zero to 17° below in a very few hours. That is not so good.

" It was with almost equal relief that we would

leave New York on a hot summer's evening and head down South for Trinidad, La Guayra, Curaçoa, Colon, etc., all of which places were considerably cooler than New York.

"Much was done on board to keep the people entertained and happy, even to going out of our way at times in order to avoid an approaching hurricane. But I used to wonder what the old ship thought of it, who for so many years would have disdained to turn aside from anything in the way of storms and hurricanes in the North Atlantic.

"The passengers we carried were people of all kinds, most would show a great interest in all they saw, and be on deck to see anything there was to be seen in the way of land, passing ships, flying fish, etc. Others showed less interest that way, and nothing would bring them on deck if they happened to be dancing, drinking cocktails, or making love. In the last amusement one can imagine them being oblivious to all else, but it was surprising in the other cases. However, they all believed in amusing themselves in their several ways, and seemed to succeed very well.

"It was a sad day when I made the ship fast in Southampton after her last voyage ; but I had some consolation, as a certain professor on board some time previous, before the ship started running to the West Indies, proved to me by the system of Numerics that the ship would end her days wrecked in the West Indies ; she was the only thing he knew of that had the same Numerics as the ill-fated *Titanic*. Whether he told me all this, kindly warning me against taking her to the West Indies, I do not know. I do not know that I am as superstitious as sailors are generally said to be, but when a learned professor expresses and claims to prove his convictions, it is a little disconcerting."

Half New York, as the saying goes, used to come down to see the *Mauretania* off on those cruises. She did not lack popularity. For some time, with her hull painted white, she gave many thousands of people agreeable holidays and the particular form of pleasure which suited their individual needs.

In 1932 she made seven voyages as an express liner on the Atlantic. In December of this year Mr. Andrew Cockburn left her and retired from the sea. For thirteen years he had been in command in her engine-room, and for many more he had served there in a junior capacity. Those engines had become the crown of his working life ; he knew, certainly, more of them, he had got more out of them than any other man. It is fitting that after he had left them they were not used again to drive the old ship on the express service to New York and back again. She made many more voyages ; she crossed the Atlantic at high speed several times again. But after Mr. Cockburn had left her she was taking passengers on pleasure cruises ; her work as a black-hulled mail ship was virtually done. When in 1933 Adolf Hitler seized power in Germany and a new dictatorship came into being, the old *Mauretania* had finished with carrying her mixed crowds between Europe and America. People going to or coming from the making of history no longer walked her decks. Mostly in the sunshine, going out of her way to avoid bad weather, she took persons on holiday to see sights or to drink cocktails or to make love.

The Cunard Company had made plans to meet the growing competition of new, big, fast ships with a huge vessel which should be an effective answer to the Italians, the French and the Germans. The *Bremen* and the *Europa* were good ; the *Rex* was good ; the *Normandie* when she appeared was expected to be more than good. On the Clyde the *No.* 534 was laid down in John Brown's yard. She would, when completed and named, restore, it was and is believed, England to the first place on the Atlantic ; she would do what the *Mauretania* herself had done so many years before. But things, with England off the gold standard again and struggling at the cost of all sorts of public and private sacrifices to become solvent, were against large expenditure on ships. The *No.* 534, partially built, lay on the stocks with her future in doubt. Then the public and private sacrifices took some effect ; the economic outlook began to improve. Men turned back to the old view that to make money you must spend money. There was a demand that the huge new Cunard ship should be finished, although finishing her entailed, as the building of the *Mauretania* had entailed, the assistance of the taxpayer.

At the time when public opinion was strongly in favour of the resumption of work on *No.* 534, as the *Queen Mary* was known before her launch, the Government were prepared to provide certain facilities, but on condition that steps were taken to eliminate competition between the British Lines engaged in the North Atlantic trade. This, in effect, suggested the merging of the fleets and personnel of the Cunard and White Star Lines, which had for so long been operated as independent companies.

Negotiations, in which the Government took part, were accordingly set on foot, and eventually, on March 28th, 1934, a tripartite agreement was signed between the Treasury, the Cunard Company and the Oceanic Company. This agreement was embodied in an Act of Parliament known as the North Atlantic Shipping Act, 1934, and provided for the merging of the fleets of the Cunard and White Star Lines in a new company to be known as Cunard White Star Limited, of which the shareholding of the Cunard Line is 62 per cent. and the Oceanic Company 38 per cent. In addition, facilities were provided by the Government, under certain stipulated conditions, for the advancing of monies to complete the new ship, and for the provision of other tonnage.

This merger of two great companies which had for so long been rivals on the Atlantic came as a surprise to many people. It aroused a good deal controversy and talk. But it did not become effective until after the *Mauretania* had made her last voyage in the service of her old owners.

On September 26th, 1934, after three months of cruising in the West Indies, the *Mauretania* left New York for the last time, bound for Plymouth, Cherbourg and Southampton. She made the passage in five days and twenty hours at an average speed of 24·42 knots. When she berthed at Southampton she had been in service for one month short of twenty-seven years. As a black-hulled mail ship, excluding her war service and her cruising, she had steamed two million one hundred thousand miles. She came home to Southampton on that October afternoon in 1934 in her wedding-cake disguise. Her work was done.

On the day when the old ship left New York for the last time, the new *No.* 534 was launched from the ways on the Clyde by Queen Mary, whose name from that moment she bore. So it is hoped and believed the tradition set by the old ship will go on.

While the *Mauretania* lay idle at Southampton during that winter and the following spring, rumours about her fate were born, grew, and created much indignation. It was said that after her long service the new Cunard White Star Company were going to sell her to a foreign power to end her life as a drudge. As well, horrified people said, sell an old hunter which has carried you brilliantly for many seasons into the station cab. But rumour lied. The new Cunard White Star Company had not that intention. The *Mauretania* was sold, but to the breakers.

She was sound, fast, efficient to the end. When she was broken up, her boilers, the boilers of 1907, which had made steam to drive her across nearer three than two million miles of sea, were in excellent sound condition. She was not failing; she was past the fashion. Bath-rooms and bathing pools had a lot to do with her going. Many rooms with private baths, bathing pools and swimming pools which were not makeshift affairs, those were what the cruising passengers wanted, and those she could not supply. So before the holiday-makers turned from her, before she suffered the last indignity of not being able to sail with a full list, her new owners decided, surely wisely, that she should not sail at all.

During May, 1935, aboard, as she lay at South-ampton, her appointments and fittings were sold by auction. Then she was stripped of what had been sold. On July 1st she left Southampton for Rosyth. The press gave that last voyage much illustration and much space, much genuine tribute of respect to the passing of a great figure. The public was stirred. Excursions were run to points on the East Coast where the old ship, white-hulled and stained, with masts cut down to stumps, could be seen passing. As she passed the Tyne the town which had built her turned out to pay its respects. Aboard her, in makeshift quarters in the tourist cabin, for her first saloon was stripped empty, there were a considerable number of passengers. She was given a civic farewell from Southampton. Her passing was made into a function. Captain A. T. Brown, who had not commanded her on service, took her to Rosyth. To have asked one of her old commanders to do so would have been to meet polite refusal. Captain Sir Arthur Rostron saw her off from the quay, but he would not go aboard to look at her stripped desolation. Mr. Andrew Cockburn would not go near her from the time she made Southampton for the last time, although he lives in that town. He had made his farewells before to the express, black-hulled mail ship. She left Southampton flying the Cunard flag, not that of the Cunard White Star : that was fitting. For the voyage to Rosyth fifteen knots were ordered, but she would keep on working up to eighteen : that was herself.

A model of her is preserved in Winchester Cathedral : that for many people is clear proof that the old ship is enshrined in English history. But her place in marine history is safe without that model. It was promised of her when Englishmen contributed their money to her building that she should do great things for them ; she did, and in doing them lived from one age of human history into another. But the great achievements alone, her speed, her reliability, her wonderful hard work do not explain her enduring popularity nor her peculiar place in the history of ships. She was an inanimate thing of steel, but her individuality was so near to personality as to be really living for very many thousands of ordinarily sensitive human beings. All ships passing at sea attract the attention of others. The *Mauretania*, coming from the horizon, would bring men from their work and from their pleasure to the rails to stare in wonder. That thrust and dip and drive of hers into the seas and through them, that trick of hers which could wreck the rails of the Monkey Island with solid sea or playfully spatter salt water on a commander's boiled shirt, did not belong to any other ship. The sight of her at work commanded and obtained wonder.

She was only known on two of the Seven Seas. She never crossed the Line. She never made a long voyage, as long voyages are reckoned. Yet wherever men go in ships her name is familiar as the greatest of her kind.

Does she want an epitaph beyond that ? Surely not. Should one, however, be sought it should be along these lines : " Pitching and spraying over all, she kept comfortably to time."

THE END

APPENDICES

MAURETANIA'S VOYAGES

No. of Voyage.	Outwards. Liverpool to New York via Queenstown.					Homewards. New York to Liverpool via Queenstown.				
	Date.	D.	H.	M.	Average Speed in Knots.	Date.	D.	H.	M.	Average Speed in Knots.
	1907.					1907.				
1	Nov. 16	5	5	10	22·21	Nov. 30	4	22	29	23·69
2	Dec. 14	5	0	55	23·00	Dec. 28	4	23	2	23·58
	1908.					1908.				
3	Jan. 11	5	9	10	21·52	Jan. 25	5	2	41	23·90
4	Feb. 22	5	3	24	23·41	March 7	5	0	5	24·42
5	March 21	5	16	44	21·13	April 1	5	1	46	24·08
6	April 11	4	23	59	24·08	April 22	5	1	14	24·19
7	May 2	5	6	17	22·89	May 13	5	11	23	22·32
8	May 27	4	20	15	24·86	June 4	5	1	44	24·10
9	June 13	5	5	4	23·11	June 24	5	3	17	23·78
10	July 11	5	2	41	23·56	July 22	5	5	23	23·41
11	Aug. 1	5	2	30	23·59	Aug. 12	5	5	22	23·40
12	Aug. 22	5	0	59	23·00	Sept. 2	5	3	3	22·81
13	Sept. 12	5	5	52	22·09	Sept. 23	6	18	08	18·72
14	Oct. 10	5	6	13	22·04	Oct. 21	5	5	42	22·33
	1909.					1909.				
15	Jan. 24	5	2	02	23·71	Feb. 3	4	20	27	25·20
16	Feb. 14	4	17	06	25·55	Feb. 25	4	20	2	25·28
17	March 7	4	17	15	25·53	March 17	4	18	35	25·61
18	April 3	4	19	32	25·04	April 14	4	19	26	25·42
19	April 24	4	18	11	25·33	May 5	4	18	11	25·70
20	May 15	4	16	53	25·62	May 26	4	18	28	25·65
21	June 5	4	17	38	25·44	June 16	4	17	21	25·88
22	July 3	4	15	55	25·84	July 14	4	18	35	25·62
23	July 24	4	17	04	25·58	Aug. 4	4	17	20	25·89
24	Aug. 14	4	14	38	25·16	Aug. 25	4	14	27	25·41
25	Sept. 4	4	11	35	25·87	Sept. 15	4	13	41	25·61
26	Sept. 25	4	10	51	26·06	Oct. 6	4	14	24	25·45
27	Oct. 23	4	15	40	24·92	Nov. 3	4	14	45	25·36
28	Nov. 20	4	12	40	25·60	Dec. 1	4	16	47	24·92
29	Dec. 11	4	12	21	25·68	Dec. 22	4	15	57	25·10

No. of Voyage.	Outwards. Liverpool to New York via Queenstown.				Homewards. New York to Liverpool via Queenstown.			
	Date.	Length of Ocean Passage.		Average Speed in Knots.	Date.	Length of Ocean Passage.		Average Speed in Knots.
		D.	H.	M.			D.	H.	M.	
	1910				1910			
30	Jan. 29	4	17	03	25·56	Feb. 9	4	20	10	25·24
31	Feb. 19	5	9	59	22·23	March 2	4	19	12	25·43
32	March 12	4	15	29	25·91	March 23	4	18	0	25·69
33	April 2	4	16	30	25·68	April 13	4	18	35	25·56
34	April 30	4	15	49	25·85	May 11	4	18	40	25·59
35	May 21	4	17	07	25·55	June 1	4	20	17	25·22
36	June 11	4	18	24	25·26	June 22	4	18	27	25·64
37	July 27	4	18	10	25·31	July 13	4	20	16	25·23
38	July 30	4	16	37	25·66	Aug. 10	4	19	50	25·32
39	Aug. 20	4	13	36	25·36	Aug. 31	4	15	42	25·13
40	Sept. 10	4	10	41	26·06	Sept. 21	4	14	44	25·38
41	Oct. 1	4	18	16	24·33	Oct. 12	4	15	43	25·14
42	Oct. 29	4	12	00	25·74	Nov. 9	4	16	28	24·96
43	Nov. 19	4	13	36	25·36	Nov. 30	4	15	50	25·10
44	Dec. 10	4	20	07	23·94	Dec. 17	4	15	57	25·07
	1911.				1911.			
45	Jan. 21	4	16	31	25·68	Feb. 1	4	19	48	25·32
46	Feb. 11	4	17	52	25·37	Feb. 22	4	21	00	25·06
47	March 4	4	22	35	24·36	March 15	4	19	35	25·38
48	March 25	4	16	59	25·77	April 5	4	19	44	25·33
49	April 22	4	21	02	24·68	May 3	4	20	15	25·22
50	May 13	4	18	32	25·22	May 24	4	20	40	25·13
51	June 3	4	17	01	25·56	June 14	4	22	16	24·79
52	June 24	4	20	42	24·76	July 5	4	21	43	24·91
53	July 22	4	17	22	25·48	Aug. 2	4	21	39	24·92
54	Aug. 12	4	16	34	25·66	Aug. 23	4	19	46	25·33
55	Sept. 2	4	13	36	25·36	Sept. 13	4	15	32	25·17
56	Sept. 23	4	14	27	25·21	Oct. 4	4	17	56	24·65
57	Oct. 21	4	15	35	24·92	Nov. 1	4	17	28	24·73
58	Nov. 11	4	15	29	24·95	Nov. 22	4	16	47	24·91
	1912.				1912.			
59	March 2	5	17	59	20·94	March 13	5	1	25	24·15
60	March 23	5	0	19	24·01	April 3	4	21	03	25·05
61	April 13	5	0	0	24·29	April 24	5	5	32	24·54
62	May 11	5	6	14	24·55	May 22	5	5	23	24·85
63	June 1	5	4	9	24·95	June 11	5	3	58	25·14
64	June 22	5	4	08	24·96	July 2	5	4	22	25·05
65	July 13	4	20	11	24·87	July 24	4	23	40	24·83
66	Aug. 10	4	21	45	25·06	Aug. 21	4	23	43	24·83
67	Aug. 31	4	23	36	24·66	Sept. 11	5	1	53	24·39

No. of Voyage.	Outwards. Liverpool to New York via Queenstown.				Homewards. New York to Liverpool via Queenstown.			
	Date.	Length of Ocean Passage. D. H. M.		Average Speed in Knots.	Date.	Length of Ocean Passage. D. H. M.		Average Speed in Knots.
	1912				1912			
68	Sept. 21	4	19	38	24·52	Oct. 2	4	20	49	24·55
69	Oct. 12	5	1	8	23·41	Oct. 23	4	23	6	24·08
70	Nov. 16	4	21	09	24·23	Nov. 27	4	23	7	24·09
71	Dec. 7	5	13	13	21·28	Dec. 17	4	23	33	24·02
	1913.				1913.			
72	Jan. 12	6	0	22	19·64	Jan. 22	5	5	52	23·62
73	Feb. 1	5	19	17	21·00	Feb. 12	5	5	49	23·61
74	Feb. 22	5	4	38	23·48	March 5	5	2	36	24·24
75	March 22	5	3	27	23·73	April 2	5	3	31	24·07
76	April 12	4	23	30	24·49	April 23	5	3	54	23·84
77	May 10	5	0	12	24·17	May 21	5	2	57	24·03
78	May 31	5	2	18	23·76	June 11	5	1	47	24·25
79	June 20	4	23	49	24·27	July 2	5	4	16	23·77
80	July 12	4	21	45	24·68	July 23	5	7	7	23·24
81	Aug. 9	5	3	59	23·45	Aug. 20	5	12	22	22·33
82	Aug. 30	5	2	27	23·75	Sept. 10	5	4	13	22·90
83	Sept. 20	4	22	49	23·66	Oct. 1	5	3	02	23·07
84	Oct. 11	4	21	00	24·03	Oct. 22	5	3	26	23·06
85	Nov. 8	4	23	40	23·49	Nov. 19	5	1	33	23·44
86	Dec. 7	5	2	44	22·90	Dec. 16	5	0	56	23·54
	1914.				1914.			
87	March 7	5	17	3	22·78	March 17	5	11	3	23·48
88	March 28	6	9	7	20·52	April 7	5	7	44	24·09
89	April 18	5	8	7	24·36	April 28	5	13	43	23·01
90	May 16	5	10	42	23·89	May 26	5	8	52	24·00
91	June 6	5	11	53	24·13	June 16	5	7	10	24·35
92	June 27	5	12	42	23·77	July 7	5	13	27	23·15
		Liverpool to Halifax				Halifax to Liverpool			
93	Aug. 1	4	21	10	24·00	Aug. 14	4	15	47	23·07
94	Aug. 29	5	5	7	24·02	Sept. 9	5	9	13	23·31
95	Sept. 19	5	7	21	23·59	Sept. 30	5	6	51	23·75
96	Oct. 10	5	6	49	23·64	Oct. 21	5	12	8	22·82

117 | During the War period and for some time afterwards the *Mauretania* was engaged on Government service. On June 1st, 1919, she sailed from Liverpool for New York via Halifax, and returned on June 14th from New York to Southampton, the time for the homeward passage being 5 days 17 hours 15 minutes, and the average speed being 23·42 knots.

No. of Voyage.	OUTWARDS. SOUTHAMPTON TO NEW YORK.				HOMEWARDS. NEW YORK TO SOUTHAMPTON.			
	Date.	Length of Ocean Passage. D. H. M.			Date.	Length of Ocean Passage. D. H. M.		Average Speed in Knots.
	1920.				1920.			
118	March 6	6	5	7	21·21	March 23	6 1 34	21·80
119	April 14	6	22	48	17·81	April 24	6 4 53	20·12
120	May 8	6	19	33	18·35	May 22	5 19 8	21·92
121	June 19	6	3	12	21·97	July 1	6 3 44	20·84
122	Aug. 21	6	6	23	20·12	Sept. 2	6 2 40	19·83
123	Sept. 18	5	20	36	20·50	Sept. 30	6 5 20	19·50
124	Oct. 16	6	4	50	19·40	Oct. 28	6 13 40	18·46
	1921.				1921.			
125	March 26	6	5	25	19·85	April 7	6 1 45	20·64
126	April 30	6	1	59	20·55	May 12	5 20 5	21·77
127	June 4	6	20	0	18·23	June 15	6 0 3	20·77
128	July 5	7	3	47	18·60	July 15	6 18 47	20·48
		Cherbourg Breakwater to Ambrose Channel Light Vessel.				Ambrose Channel Light Vessel to Cherbourg Breakwater.		
	1922.				1922.			
129	March 25	5	4	5	23·93	April 4	5 2 35	24·58
130	April 15	5	8	53	23·81	April 25	5 1 23	25·14
131	May 6	5	3	16	24·37	May 16	5 2 13	24·99
132	May 27	4	23	48	25·10	June 6	5 0 49	25·26
133	June 17	5	1	56	24·65	June 27	5 1 5	25·19
134	July 8	5	6	41	22·92	July 18	5 0 28	25·30
135	Aug. 5	5	1	34	24·41	Aug. 15	5 1 24	24·79
136	Aug. 26	6	6	57	19·66	Sept. 5	5 23 53	20·57
137	Sept. 16	6	4	54	19·32	Sept. 26	6 4 14	19·65
138	Oct. 28	4	23	47	24·08	Nov. 7	4 23 15	24·46
139	Nov. 18	5	3	53	23·36	Nov. 28	6 4 59	19·53
	1923.				1923.			
140	Jan. 27	On Mediter		ranean	cruise from	New York.		
141	Feb. 7	Cruise from		New	York.			
142	April 7	5	12	54	22·63	April 17	5 5 46	24·22
143	April 28	5	7	17	23·06	May 8	5 5 29	24·31
144	May 19	5	16	13	23·87	May 29	5 6 3	24·01
145	June 9	5	7	56	—	June 19	5 5 25	24·34
146	June 30	—			23·74	July 10	5 5 54	24·24
147	July 28	5	10	4	22·80	Aug. 7	5 6 29	23·78

No. of Voyage.	OUTWARD. SOUTHAMPTON TO NEW YORK.				HOMEWARD. NEW YORK TO SOUTHAMPTON.				
	Date.	D.	H.	M.	Average Speed in Knots.	Date.	D.	H.	M.	Average Speed in Knots.
	Length of Ocean Passage.						Length of Ocean Passage.			
	1923					**1923**				
148	Aug. 18	5	7	31	23·27	Aug. 28	5	5	48	23·91
149	Sept. 8	5	8	46	22·39	Sept. 18	5	2	28	23·79
150	Sept. 29	5	5	49	22·92	Oct. 9	5	5	9	23·44
151	Oct. 20	5	6	5	23·00	Oct. 30	5	2	53	23·80
	1924.					**1924.**				
152	May 31	5	12	35	22·67	June 11	5	5	50	24·25
153	June 21	5	11	6	22·09	July 2	5	5	54	24·24
154	Aug. 9	4	20	2	25·58	Aug. 20	4	19	00	26·16
155	Aug. 30	5	0	2	24·7	Sept. 10	4	18	20	25·69
156	Sept. 20	4	21	16	24·75	Oct. 1	4	18	23	25·68
157	Oct. 11	4	19	56	25·2	Oct. 22	4	19	1	25·54
158	Nov. 1	5	0	30	24·11	Nov. 12	4	20	19	25·25
159	Nov. 22	4	21	52	24·62	Dec. 3	4	20	25	25·2
	1925.					**1925.**				
160	Jan. 8	5	5	20	23·15	Jan. 17	5	5	0	25·04
161	Feb. 7	5	13	25	22·23	Feb. 17	Med. Cruise.			
162	Mediterranean Cruise.									
163	March 21	5	5	3	23·72	April 1	5	0	13	25·38
164	April 11	5	9	03	23·28	April 22	5	2	36	24·9
165	May 2	5	5	51	23·86	May 13	5	1	10	25·2
166	May 23	5	6	42	23·72	June 3	5	2	31	24·91
167	June 13	5	11	38	22·83	June 24	5	1	5	25·21
168	July 4	5	6	34	23·43	July 15	5	1	4	24·84
169	Aug. 1	5	5	39	23·44	Aug. 12	5	0	11	25·02
170	Aug. 22	5	5	45	23·6	Sept. 2	4	20	47	25·15
171	Sept. 12	5	4	55	23·26	Sept. 23	4	22	10	24·85
172	Oct. 3	5	4	57	23·26	Oct. 14	4	21	36	24·98
173	Oct. 24	5	9	48	22·34	Nov. 4	5	1	20	24·21
174	Nov. 14	5	7	22	22·80	Nov. 25	5	0	20	24·26
175	Dec. 8	5	4	18	23·36	Dec. 16	4	23	56	24·48
	1926.					**1926.**				
176	Feb. 3	5	15	45	21·84	Mediterranean Cruise.				
177	Mediterranean Cruise.									
178	March 27	5	7	55	23·83	April 7	5	0	59	24·86
179	April 17	5	9	43	22·86	April 28	4	23	12	25·23
180	May 8	5	3	30	24·02	May 19	4	22	44	25·34
181	May 29	5	14	9	23·56	June 9	5	5	14	25·06
182	June 19	—			23·82	June 30	—			25·00
183	July 10	5	5	41	23·60	July 21	5	7	21	23·62

No. of Voyage.	Outwards. Southampton to New York.				Homewards. New York to Southampton.			
	Date.	Length of Ocean Passage.		Average Speed in Knots.	Date.	Length of Ocean Passage.		Average Speed in Knots.
		D.	H.	M.			D.	H.	M.	
	1926					1926			
184	Aug. 11	5	1	29	24·45	Aug. 18	5	0	23	24·98
185	Aug. 28	5	5	27	23·64	Sept. 8	4	21	53	24·91
186	Sept. 18		—		23·62	Sept. 29	4	21	31	24·99
187	Oct. 9	4	21	31	24·69	Oct. 20	4	22	5	24·87
188	Oct. 30	5	3	17	23·53	Nov. 10	4	23	2	24·68
189	Nov. 20	5	7	38	22·74	Dec. 1	4	20	50	25·14
	1927.					1927.			
190	Feb. 9	5	6	48	23·00	Mediterranean Cruise.			
191	Mediterranean Cruise.								
192	April 2	5	7	2	23·35	April 13	4	23	41	25·13
193	April 23	4	21	31	25·02	May 4	4	23	49	25·10
194	May 14	5	6	27	23·45	May 25	5	3	57	24·30
195	June 4	5	4	50	23·76	June 15	5	0	50	24·89
196	June 25	5	1	42	24·37	July 7	4	23	22	25·20
197	July 16	5	0	9	24·74	July 27	4	23	42	25·13
198	Aug. 6	4	22	58	24·93	Aug. 17	4	23	5	25·06
199	Aug. 27	5	0	14	24·68	Sept. 8	4	21	37	24·97
200	Sept. 17	4	20	53	24·83	Sept. 29	4	23	53	24·48
201	Oct. 8	4	21	25	24·72	Oct. 20	4	21	32	24·98
202	Oct. 29	5	11	57	21·99	Nov. 10	4	21	26	25·00
203	Nov. 19	4	22	27	24·50	Dec. 1	4	21	26	24·90
204	Dec. 21	5	3	46	23·45	Dec. 31	5	4	12	24·36
	1928.					1928.			
205	Feb. 8	5	6	51	22·88	Feb. 21	Med. Cruise		
206	Mediterranean Cruise.								
207	March 31	5	3	51	23·50	April 11	4	23	59	24·65
208	April 21	5	3	18	23·97	May 2	5	2	27	25·30
209	May 12	5	1	0	24·51	May 23	5	0	9	25·04
210	June 2	5	3	25	24·10	June 13	5	1	55	24·70
211	June 23	5	2	22	24·26	June 30	4	22	39	25·37
212	July 14	5	3	17	25·63	July 25	4	23	13	25·25
213	Aug. 4	4	22	27	25·07	Aug. 16	5	1	46	25·43
214	Aug. 25	4	20	46	25·43	Sept. 10	4	19	51	25·36
215	Sept. 15	4	18	38	25·27	Sept. 27	4	21	10	25·10
216	Oct. 6	5	5	37	23·11	Oct. 18	4	20	8	25·3
217	Oct. 27	4	20	52	24·84	Nov. 8	4	21	23	25·04
	1929.					1929.			
218	Jan. 2	6	5	59	19·38	Jan. 12	4	19	55	25·38
219	Feb. 6	5	7	12	24·81	Feb. 16	Med. Cruise		

No. of Voyage.	OUTWARDS. SOUTHAMPTON TO NEW YORK.				HOMEWARDS. NEW YORK TO SOUTHAMPTON.			
	Date.	Length of Ocean Passage.		Average Speed in Knots.	Date.	Length of Ocean Passage.		Average Speed in Knots.
		D.	H.	M.			D.	H.	M.	
	1929					1929			
220	Mediterranean Cruise.								
221	March 30	5	7	56	24·69	April 10	5	3	44	25·04
222	April 20	5	14	5	23·7	May 1	5	4	20	25·25
223	May 11	5	19	52	22·84	May 22	5	3	40	25·38
224	June 1	—			—	June 12	5	3	55	25·34
225	June 22	5	12	19	24·15	June 29	5	3	16	25·47
226	July 13	5	5	16	25·35	July 24	5	1	1	25·58
	Record voyage.					Record voyage.			
227	Aug. 3	4	21	44	26·90	Aug. 16	4	17	50	27·22
228	Aug. 24	5	2	51	25·70	Sept. 5	4	23	38	25·30
229	Sept. 14	5	5	53	24·57	Sept. 26	4	23	10	25·38
230	Oct. 5	5	9	20	23·93	Oct. 17	5	0	0	25·22
231	Oct. 26	5	8	47	24·07	Nov. 7	4	23	44	25·29
232	Nov. 16	6	0	6	21·47	Nov. 29	5	0	46	25·09
233	Dec. 17	5	14	0	23·10	Dec. 28	4	23	3	25·42
	1930.					1930.			
234	Feb. 5	5	13	7	23·04	Cruising.			
235	Cruising.					Cruising.			
236	Cruising.					Cruising.			
237	March 29	6	13	48	20·03	April 9	5	3	48	25·02
238	April 19	5	5	21	25·21	April 30	5	2	45	25·25
239	May 10	5	12	56	23·76	May 21	5	2	46	25·23
240	May 31	5	5	28	25·2	June 11	5	2	31	25·27
241	June 21	5	9	38	24·37	June 28	5	1	58	25·39
242	July 12	5	7	6	24·85	July 23	5	1	18	25·53
243	Aug. 2	5	5	29	25·15	Aug. 13	5	0	24	25·72
244	Aug. 23	5	3	19	25·62	Sept. 4	4	23	16	25·37
245	Sept. 13	5	8	21	24·12	Sept. 25	5	0	13	25·17
246	Oct. 4	5	10	25	23·72	Oct. 16	4	23	26	25·36
247	Oct. 25	5	13	21	23·19	Nov. 5	5	4	19	24·34
248	Nov. 15	5	15	17	23·27	Nov. 26	5	3	5	24·57
249	Dec. 9	5	17	24	22·46	Dec. 16	5	3	27	24·51
						1931.			
250	Dec. 27	6	23	37	18·47	Jan. 4	5	1	37	24·88
	1931.								
251	Feb. 4	5	14	32	22·99	Feb. 14	4	23	38	25·31
252	Feb. 25	5	14	29	23·00	March 6	5	9	34	23·35
253	March 28	5	10	7	23·78	April 8	5	2	20	24·74
254	April 18	5	2	31	24·33	April 29	4	22	30	25·38

No. of Voyage.	Outwards. Southampton to New York.				Homewards. New York to Southampton.			
	Date.	Length of Ocean Passage.		Average Speed in Knots.	Date.	Length of Ocean Passage.		Average Speed in Knots.
		D.	H.	M.		D.	H.	M.	
	1931				1932				
255	May 9	5	9	25	23·31	May 20	4	23	26	25·19
256	May 30	—			25·57	June 10	4	22	19	25·45
257	June 20	5	3	41	25·55	June 27	5	0	16	25·01
258	July 11	4	20	34	24·88	July 22	4	23	36	24·58
259	Aug. 1	4	19	36	25·12	Aug. 12	4	23	29	24·57
260	Aug. 22	4	20	03	25·03	Sept. 2	5	0	8	24·41
261	Sept. 12	4	20	37	24·89	Sept. 23	4	22	22	24·81
262	Nov. 11	5	14	30	21·57	Cruising.				
263	Cruising.				Cruising.				
264	Cruising.				Cruising.				
265	Cruising.				Cruising.				
266	Cruising.				1932. Jan. 8	5	5	22	23·45
	1932.								
267	Feb. 17	5	4	55	23·24	Feb. 26	5	0	33	24·38
268	March 16	5	6	5	23·01	March 29	4	19	26	25·44
269	April 6	5	7	52	22·84	April 15	5	0	14	25·03
270	May 14	Cruise.							
271	May 21	5	4	40	23·82	June 1	4	22	41	25·33
272	June 11	5	9	29	23·06	June 24	4	23	15	25·20
273	July 2	5	7	38	22·86	Aug. 3	4	22	50	24·73
274	Cruising.								
275	Cruising.								
276	Cruising.								
277	Aug. 13	4	20	52	24·82	Aug. 24	4	23	3	24·67
278	Sept. 3	5	1	46	23·80	Sept. 14	5	0	11	24·58
279	Sept. 24	4	21	21	24·72	Oct. 4	4	23	24	24·59
280	Dec. 28	5	9	25	22·43					
	1933.				1933.				
281 to 288	} Cruising voyages from New York.								
289	—	—			—	April 21	5	4	31	24·88
						to Southampton.			
290	June 3								
291	June 10	} Cruising voyages from Southampton.							
292	July 1	4	21	0	24·81				
293 to 297	} Cruising voyages from New York.								

No. of Voy-age.	OUTWARDS. SOUTHAMPTON TO NEW YORK.			HOMEWARDS. NEW YORK TO SOUTHAMPTON.		
	Date.	Length of Ocean Passage. D. H. M.	Average Speed in Knots.	Date.	Length of Ocean Passage. D. H. M.	Average Speed in Knots.
298	1933 —	—	—	1933 Sept. 27	5 3 38 to South-ampton.	24·47
299	Nov. 15	5 4 50	23·27			
300 to 303	} Cruising	voyages from	New	York.		
304	1934. Jan. 17	6 3 17	19·7	1934.		
305 to 310	} Cruising New York.	voyages from	—	—	—	—
311	—	—	—	April 20	5 0 12	25·08
312	June 30	5 9 10	22·48	—	—	—
313 to 317	} Cruising New York.	voyages from	—	—	—	—
318 319	—	—	5	Sept. 26	5 0 20	24·41

Last voyage—July 1st, 1934—Southampton to Rosyth.
Distance run, 488 miles. Average speed, 12·51.

THE MAURETANIA'S CRUISES

In addition to her regular Transatlantic voyages, the *Mauretania* made fifty-four cruises, some of which are indicated in the table of voyages. On these yachting trips, which were mainly from New York, the ship travelled over a quarter of a million miles and carried over thirty-one thousand passengers. The complete list of these popular sea excursions is as follows :

LIST OF " MAURETANIA " CRUISES

From	Period of Cruise.	Itinerary.	Mileage.	Passengers Carried.
New York ..	Feb. 2–Apr. 7, 1923	Mediterranean	10,132	531
,, ..	,, 17–Mar. 18, 1925	,,	9,549	674
,, ..	,, 17– ,, 23, 1926	,,	9,549	702
,, ..	,, 21– ,, 27, 1927	,,	9,549	906
,, ..	,, 21– ,, 26, 1928	,,	9,549	964
,, ..	,, 16– ,, 22, 1929	,,	9,549	889
,, ..	,, 12–Feb. 17, 1930	Havana ..	2,334	843
,, ..	,, 20–Mar. 26, 1930	Mediterranean	9,549	774
,, ..	Apr. 24–Apr. 28, 1931	Nassau ..	1,922	804
,, ..	May 15–May 19, 1931	,, ..	1,922	693
,, ..	June 5–June 9, 1931	,, ..	1,922	421
,, ..	July 17–July 21, 1931	Halifax ..	1,186	407
,, ..	Aug. 7–Aug. 11, 1931	,, ..	1,186	700
,, ..	,, 28–Sept. 1, 1931	,, ..	1,186	510
,, ..	Sept. 18– ,, 22, 1931	,, ..	1,186	447
,, ..	Nov. 18–Nov. 30, 1931	West Indies ..	4,908	820
,, ..	Dec. 3–Dec. 15, 1931	,, ..	4,908	784
,, ..	,, 19–Jan. 3, 1932	,, ..	5,346	436
,, ..	Mar. 24–Mar, 28, 1932	Nassau ..	1,922	748
Southampton	May 14–May 19, 1932	Gibraltar ..	2,334	836
New York ..	,, 27– ,, 31, 1932	Bermuda ..	1,386	562
,, ..	June 17–June 21, 1932	,, ..	1,386	269
,, ..	July 8–July 16, 1932	West Indies ..	3,005	784
,, ..	,, 16– ,, 29, 1932	,, ..	4,908	720
,, ..	,, 29–Aug. 2, 1932	Halifax ..	1,186	269
,, ..	Jan. 7–Jan. 19, 1933	West Indies ..	5,318	300
,, ..	,, 21–Feb. 2, 1933	,, ..	5,318	384

From	Period of Cruise.	Itinerary.	Mile-age.	Passengers Carried.
New York ..	Feb. 4–Feb. 16, 1933	West Indies ..	5,318	513
,, ..	,, 18–Mar. 2, 1933	,,	5,318	628
,, ..	Mar. 4– ,, 16, 1933	,, ..	5,318	350
,, ..	,, 18– ,, 30, 1933	,, ..	5,318	319
,, ..	Apr. 1–Apr. 8, 1933	,, ..	3,005	287
,, ..	,, 9– ,, 18, 1933	,, ..	3,078	230
Southampton	June 3–June 9, 1933	Casablanca ..	2,380	568
,,	,, 10– ,, 16, 1933	Madeira ..	2,674	553
New York ..	July 8–July 21, 1933	West Indies ..	5,296	719
,, ..	,, 22–Aug. 4, 1933	,, ..	5,296	744
,, ..	Aug. 5– ,, 18, 1933	,, ..	5,296	762
,, ..	,, 22–Sept. 4, 1933	,, ..	5,296	742
,, ..	Sept. 9– ,, 22, 1933	,, ..	5,296	708
,, ..	Nov. 25–Dec. 8, 1933	,, ..	5,277	379
,, ..	Dec. 9–Dec. 22, 1933	,, ..	5,277	204
,, ..	,, 23–Jan. –, 1934	,, ..	5,277	330
,, ..	Jan. 27–Feb. 9, 1934	,, ..	5,223	409
,, ..	Feb. 10– ,, 23, 1934	,, ..	5,223	540
,, ..	,, 24–Mar. 9, 1934	,, ..	5,223	509
,, ..	Mar. 9– ,, 19, 1934	,, ..	4,417	460
,, ..	,, 23–Apr. 2, 1934	,, ..	4,417	632
,, ..	Apr. 6– ,, 16, 1934	,, ..	4,417	459
,, ..	July 7–July 20, 1934	,, ..	5,241	609
,, ..	,, 21–Aug. 3, 1934	,, ..	5,241	648
,, ..	Aug. 4– ,, 17, 1934	,, ..	5,241	707
,, ..	,, 20–Sept. 3, 1934	,, ..	5,241	689
,, ..	Sept, 8– ,, 21, 1934	,, ..	5,241	642

Number of Cruises   54
Mileage   252,040
Passengers carried   31,517

SPECIFICATION

Name of Builders	Swan, Hunter & Wigham Richardson, Ltd., Wallsend-on-Tyne.
Name of Owning Company ..	Cunard.
Construction begun	1905.
Launch	September 20th, 1906.
Trials	November 3rd to 5th, 1907.
Maiden voyage	November 16th, 1907 : Liverpool—Queenstown—New York.
Last Atlantic voyage	September 26th, 1934 : New York York — Plymouth — Cherbourg —Southampton.
Sold for breaking up	April 2nd, 1935, to Metal Industries, Ltd., Rosyth.
Last voyage	July 1st, 1935 : Southampton—Rosyth.
Length over all	790 feet.
Length between perpendiculars ..	760 feet.
Breadth	88 feet.
Depth, moulded	60 feet 6 inches.
Gross tonnage	31,938 tons.
Draught	33 feet 6 inches.
Displacement	38,000 tons.
Number of Passengers (when commissioned)	First, 563 ; second, 464 ; third, 1138.
Machinery makers	Wallsend Slipway & Engineering Co., Ltd.
Type of engine	Parsons turbine.
Number of screws	Four.
Number and type of boilers ..	Cylindrical : 23 double-ended, 2 single-ended.
Number of furnaces	192.
Steam pressure	195 lb. per square inch.
Total heating surface	159,000 square feet.
Total grate area	4,060 square feet.
Draught	Howden's.
Total indicated horse-power ..	68,000.
Designed speed	25 knots.
Revolutions per minute ..	180.

Crew (when commissioned) :

Navigation.		Engineering.		Personal.	
Officers ..	9	Officers ..	33	Doctor ..	1
Quartermasters	8	Refrigerating Engineers ..	3	Purser ..	1

Crew (when commissioned)—*continued.*

Navigation.			Engineering.			Personal.	
Boatswains	..	3	Firemen	..	204	Assisant	
Carpenters	..	3	Trimmers	..	120	Pursers ..	2
Lamp - trimmer			Greasers	..	33	Chief Steward	1
and Yeoman		2				Chief Stewards'	
Masters - at -						Assistants ..	2
Arms	..	2				Chef	1
Marconi tele-						Barbers ..	2
graphists	..	2				Cooks and	
Seamen	..	40				Bakers ..	28
						Matrons ..	2
						Stewardesses..	10
						Mail-sorters ..	7
						Typists ..	2
						Leading Stew-	
						ards, bar-	
						keepers, etc.	50
						Stewards ..	367
		69			393		476

Total .. .. 938.

CAPTAINS

1907–1909 ..	..	..	Captain John Pritchard.
1910–1914 ..	..	..	Captain W. T. Turner.
1914 ..	..	..	Captain Sir James Charles, K.B.E., C.B.
	..	..	Captain Sir James Charles, K.B.E., C.B.
1914–1918 (War period)	..	..	Captain Daniel Dow
	..	..	Captain J. C. Barr, C.B.
	..	..	Captain Sir A. H. Rostron, K.B.E.
1918–1926 ..	..	..	Captain Sir A. H. Rostron, K.B.E.
1926–1927 ..	..	..	Captain E. G. Diggle; R.D., R.N.R.
1928–1931 ..	..	..	Captain S. G. S. McNeil, R.D., R.N.R.
1931–1934 ..	..	..	Captain R. V. Peel, R.D., R.N.R.

CHIEF ENGINEERS

1907 to January, 1910	J. Currie
January, 1910, to July, 1912	J. Kendall
July, 1912, to February, 1916	J. Carruthers
February, 1916, to July, 1918	A. Allan
July, 1918, to September, 1919	J. McDonald, O.B.E.
September, 1919, to December, 1932 ..	A. Cockburn, O.B.E.
December, 1932, to May, 1933	E. Barton
May, 1933, to 1934	W. Sutcliffe

INDEX